THE GIFT OF SEX

A Guide to Sexual Fulfillment

CLIFFORD AND JOYCE PENNER

WORD PUBLISHING

Dallas·London·Vancouver·Melbourne

ISBN 0-8499-2893-1
Library of Congress Catalog Card Number: 80-54552

Printed in the United States of America

4 5 6 7 8 9 LBM 33

Contents

Sexual Enhancement Exercises

Illustrations

Preface

We want to share our pilgrimage from a mutual rural Mennonite heritage to where we are today.

Even though we were raised 2000 miles apart, we could have grown up in the same community. The German Mennonite tradition had its strong impact on us in the unique foods we ate, the yearly church festivals, the speaking of the low German dialect, similar dating patterns, and kindred values. Those values included a hard-work ethic, the expectation of setting and attaining goals, yet a strong pacifistic approach to life, and not just in regard to war. While on the one hand we were taught to push and scramble to get what we could out of life, on the other hand we were guided to gain fulfillment of the capacities within us rather than to trample underfoot those around us. One example of this philosophy occurred when a lawsuit seemed the best business decision, but was not pursued because, "As Christians we don't sue."

This mind set about life has affected our sexual lives together. We came to marriage with the expectation that marital and sexual happiness was a goal we could strive for and attain. Yet neither of us would pursue that happiness at the expense of the other. The pacifistic, Christian-love style mellowed out the aggressive, "go-after-your-goals" approach to life.

Another integral dimension of our Mennonite church and home emphasis was that personal conversion was the necessary beginning of a Christian life. Even though there was a legalistic approach to Christian growth, one did not automatically become a Christian by being born into a Christian home or religiously following the legalisms of the church. As a result of this spirit and the strong biblical teaching we received from childhood on, we both made clear decisions at an early age to commit ourselves to Christ and his teachings. What that means has continued to develop in our understanding and experience. It is a commitment both of us have made as young children and adolescents. The going has not always been smooth. There have been and are struggles, doubts, and our own subtle (pacifistic, probably) kinds of rebellion.

What was probably most beneficial to our Christian and emotional development was that both of our homes were warm, safe, family- and church-centered environments. Growth and achievement were encouraged intellectually, educationally, musically, athletically, socially, biblically and spiritually; yet, as was typical in that era, sexual awareness and understanding received very limited, if any, encouragement. Our families were not unique in their limited sexual communication and expression. Rather, their attitude was typical of the day. So our parents were not remiss by the standards they had been taught or that were common to their culture.

Given this setting, sexual feelings or sexual behaviors were not discussed openly or freely. There was, however, direct positive instruction about growing up to be a man or a woman. Good feelings were communicated about breast development; buying the first bra was a special event; menstruation was well prepared for and was experienced as a positive sign of becoming a woman. Shaving, muscular development, and voice change were all welcome signs of emerging as a man.

The conflict was that specific instruction about sexual interaction between men and women was either absent or limited. Instruction regarding sexual involvement within marriage was lacking; at the same time, the church, the books we read and Christian radio broadcasts clearly warned about keeping oneself pure. Rigid rules were defined for acceptable dating habits. Dating was only permissible with "one of our own kind"—Mennonite—promoting a narrow view of the biblical concept of being "unequally yoked together." Holding hands with a member of the opposite sex was talked about as serious business.

Caressing and making out were obviously unacceptable, and kissing was to occur only with the person you were sure you would marry. In fact, the feeling often came across that if you did weaken and kiss your partner on a date, such action destined your marriage to that person.

The absence of positive sexual teaching, combined with the rigid rules about sexual expression, led us both to believe that sex between a man and woman was seen by our church as very negative, even though we did not feel this way about it ourselves.

We are not exactly sure why we did not assume this negative stance. Probably the natural peer input that occurred in our rural, extended-family type of communities allowed us to be very free-spirited as young children. We had large family gatherings, with cousins of about the same age and of the opposite sex; we had the freedom to roam and explore; and so we played fun games like jumping in the hay in the nude or playing nudist colony in the corn fields. Thus we came to adolescence rather naïve, but with good feelings about ourselves sexually. But then the struggles of adolescence—the awkward sexual feelings along with the rigid controls on behavior—caused some doubt about ourselves sexually; we experienced a reduction of freedom during the growing-up years.

A beneficial factor was that we went through our broadening or stretching experiences simultaneously. We met during our first year at a mainly Mennonite college. From our similar backgrounds, we came together and learned as we moved away from the rigidity of our history. Together we experienced a variety of church and Christian growth experiences that brought us to where we are today.

Probably our most enriching emotional input and sexual education occurred while we were attending, respectively, a Baptist school of nursing and a Baptist liberal arts college. We took a preparation-for-marriage class and talked with professors. There we received accurate sexual data, along with warm, positive feelings about the love-making experience we were anticipating in marriage. It became clear to us, from the people we valued as sound Christian believers and mentors, that the sexual drives we felt so strongly were God-given, normal and natural. While behavioral decisions had to be made about how those urges could be handled before marriage, the feelings were considered to be as positive as we experienced them.

Why the sexual part of our marriage started out as positively as it did, we are not certain. Maybe the determination that sex in marriage could be positive was our way of rebelling against our past. Whatever the case, the sexual dimension has for the most part continued to be very satisfying. This is true even though the level of our knowledge has changed with time and experience. When we look back, we wonder how our initial experiences could have seemed as satisfying as they did, but at the time they were all we knew and they felt right and good. That is not to say that we have been without the times of sexual difficulties typical of any couple wanting enhancement—times of varying interests, a difficult adjustment after a new baby, focusing on performance rather than on enjoyment, or adjusting to interim birth control measures—but underlying all this, we have enjoyed our sexual relationship and have experienced it as being right for us.

As a result of our positive sexual experience and the conflict we thought this created with our Christianity, during our first year of marriage we used our Bible study time to look at what the Bible had to say about sex. We came out convinced that the Bible is a very prosexual book. We had heard our church's message about the "don'ts" of sexual behavior outside marriage, and, lacking a balancing positive input about sex in marriage, had generalized to the point that we thought the church's message was entirely negative. Our conclusions from this study were probably the beginning of our current emphasis on bringing a positive sexual teaching to the Christian community.

After the issue was settled for us personally, we did little with it until long after we completed our formal education. Joyce received her Bachelor of Science and Master's degrees and then taught nursing at the college level. Cliff finished his seminary and doctoral degrees and then began private practice as a clinical psychologist. Our professional energies were focused on areas such as training lay counselors and dealing with grief, death and dying.

One day we were asked to teach a class for seminary wives on sexual adjustment in a Christian marriage. In an initial survey we discovered much the same confusion about sexual feelings and Christian beliefs that we had experienced. For many, this confusion had led to unfulfilled sexual lives. We took this teaching assignment with no expectation that education would produce change in actual sexual behavior and satisfaction. Assuming that such change would have to come through therapy and counseling on a much more intimate level, we saw the class as a way to help the women define their needs (if there were needs present) and find the desired professional assistance. Much to our surprise, some of the women reported dramatic sexual changes in their marriages. Others were able to enrich already good relationships. These reports demonstrated the ability of such a seminar to produce behavioral change in and of itself.

The timing was right: the word of what we had to offer spread, and the churches were ready. As a result, we have continued to work on the seminar and to offer it to couples within church settings around the country. Some couples receive help for specific problems, others revive the spark that has been lost, and still others identify the need for further treatment. Those who identify the need for further help may come to our office or may be referred to a counselor or counseling team more convenient to their location.

Early in the history of our sexual adjustment seminar, we realized the need to prepare ourselves further, so we both took some training from the Masters and Johnson Institute and other experts. This specialized preparation, our personal experience and professional backgrounds, along with the fact that we work as a team, are the assets we believe we bring to the couples we teach and counsel. The leadership presence of both a man and a woman and the representation of both the medical and the social science fields are the ingredients which have led to the helpfulness that couples report.

So with our roots still deeply planted in our Mennonite heritage, we have branched out through our broadening church experiences: first within the Baptist community; then in a large Presbyterian church; and now as members of a growing Congregational church. Our personal life experiences and the variety of educational and professional experiences have also added extensively to our present views.

We trust that where we are and what we have to offer will reach you at your point of interest and need.

Acknowledgments

Our deep gratitude goes to:

Our "small group" for their emotional and spiritual support—for lifting our spirits and adding lightness to our serious moments.

Our colleagues at Associated Psychological Services who not only carried some of our load, but also listened to our "book talk" for two and a half years.

The many professionals in the field of human sexuality whose knowledge and research has been the catalyst for much of what we share.

Those couples who opened up their lives to us in sexual therapy, where the principles we hold continue to be tested, polished and made real.

Wayne Coombs who gave us the initial push to write and Peb Jackson who kept us going. Our artists, Kathy Shoemaker and Erika Oller.

Our typists, Vera Wils, Tammy Weathers and others who typed, retyped and were there to help with the details.

Our editor, Carol Bostrom, whose thorough and painstaking work clarified and corrected when our literary skill was lacking.

And to our parents and children:

Julene, Gregory and Kristine

whose lives most deeply influence our view of God's gift of life and love.

For further information regarding seminars or other speaking engagements please write or call:
Dr. Clifford and Joyce Penner
2 North Lake Avenue, Suite 610
Pasadena, California 91101
818-449-2525

THE GIFT OF SEX

_____ 1

Is This Book for Me?

My husband and I have been married for 15 years. We have two children under the age of 10. There has been very little intimacy in our marriage—either emotional or physical. I have been the initiator and my husband the avoider. We have gone to a Christian marriage counselor and my husband is now going for therapy, but I have lost absolutely all my feeling for him. As a Christian where do I go from here?

As you open this book to read about sex from a Christian perspective, you may be asking, "Is this book for me?" There are many books to help couples improve their life together. One book emphasizes submission, the next stresses communication, another speaks of servanthood; some push for a spiritual approach, while others provide psychological answers. With all these messages coming at you, it's natural to ask, "Is this book for me?"

It is for you, if you are a couple interested in learning all you can about the God-given gift of sexuality, to enhance your own sexual experience. This is true whether you are newly married or "not so newly" married.

Newly Married Couples

Those desiring knowledge and enrichment. When a young man and a young woman are experiencing the full flush of their love during those months just before marriage, they usually don't talk much about their sexual knowledge or experience. Rather, they hope and expect that the excitement, the joy, the delight they now experience with each other will carry over into their sexual relationship after marriage. Yet whenever we speak privately with people who are about to be married, or just beginning a marriage, they have many questions about sex, questions that leave them perplexed. There is no easy, natural place to find the needed information.

For example, a vibrant youth leader's wife came up to us after a meeting. In an embarrassed way she explained that after every sexual experience they had this "mess" to clean up. They were afraid there was something wrong with them.

An older but just married schoolteacher was surprised to discover it does enhance the experience for the woman to be physically active during a sexual experience. Up to that point, she had been completely passive.

Whenever we begin a new activity, it takes time to adapt. We have to get used to the experience. This produces a dilemma in our sexual experience. In our first encounters our knowledge is incomplete. We have not observed anyone else involved in this behavior. Thus we have to learn everything either by reading about it or by trial and error with our partner. If you are newly married, you may be in search of knowledge and enrichment for your sexual life. It is our hope that this book will help to broaden that knowledge so that you can find the freedom to go after your own discoveries.

Those experiencing stress and wanting to avoid serious difficulties. The newly married couple may experience a great deal of stress as they approach their early sexual contacts. This stress does not necessarily diminish after the first experience or two. It may increase if the person is concerned about how he or she is functioning. So you may be looking for help to reduce that stress and help to avoid moving into serious difficulties.

One young woman was raised in the Midwest in a family that was very hesitant about being explicit sexually. She had learned that all sexual response was sinful, and so she would not let herself be responsive in thought or action until she married and was ready for a full sexual experience. She learned along with so many others that the anxiety, the tension about the sexual experience did not go away at the marriage altar. It continued as she and her new husband began their married life together. She was anxious about how to function as a sexual person, concerned about the various sexual activities and about her own responsiveness sexually, and greatly preoccupied with the question of whether or not she was pleasing her partner.

If you find that tension or concern about your sexual experience is greater than you feel it should be, this book can help you find ways to reduce some of that tension.

Those with sexual blocks brought into marriage. Some newly married people have specific sexual blocks or habits that hinder their satisfaction. These blocks can impede sexual activities or interests so much that the couple's life together is jeopardized. One man who was seldom interested in sex was clearly devoted to his wife. He was highly committed to marriage, especially since he intended to become a minister. Deeply in love with his wife, he enjoyed every part of their life together, but had little interest in any kind of sexual activity. He sought help because he believed that eventually his lack of sexual interest was going to damage the marriage, a concern that was certainly justified. Much in his past led him to this position.

A couple with similar problems will benefit from this book in that it may help them to define the problem. It does not have all the answers for those with blocks in their sexual experience, but rather it is a guide to help couples work toward a better understanding.

There are many couples who have been raised in the church and have a Christian commitment. They have heard and read many things about the sanctity of marriage—the beauty of the sexual experience, and the concern that it not be misused. These couples may have questions about the appropriateness of enjoying pleasure—enjoying their own bodies—from a biblical and Christian viewpoint. For a couple with this concern, we will point to the Bible's clear message validating sexual pleasure in marriage (see Chapter 4).

The Not-So-Newly Married

Those looking for enhancement. Couples whose sexual lives are happy and fulfilled are continually looking for ways to add new joy and delight to their sexual experience. We might compare them to people who are wonderful cooks. They have enough recipes and cooking concepts to keep them happy for years to come. Yet they are continually looking for new ways to put meals together, new ways to make sauces or desserts, new ways to please those who eat what they cook. In the same way, couples who are satisfied in their married life, whether they have been married ten years or forty, are often looking for additional input, knowledge, insight, or awareness to add to their already full experience.

Those who want to spark a "ho-hum" relationship. Many couples do not experience much excitement in their sexual relationship. Even though everything is working out well enough from a technical standpoint, their experiences are boring.

For the couple suffering from a "ho-hum" relationship, this book can add a new spark. It can provide suggestions for building an experimental, creative sexual life style into the marriage, so that a couple need not look for outside stimuli.

Those looking for help with technical problems. It is possible to have a stable foundation in a relationship, and yet have a serious technical problem in the sexual dimension of life. There are many such problems. The man may ejaculate too quickly, have difficulty getting interested, or difficulty in responding with or keeping an erection. The woman may have problems with pain, lack of interest, difficulties with arousal or with letting go orgasmically. All such dilemmas get in the way of the sexual experience; and they usually cause people to draw away from each other as time goes on.

For some readers with technical difficulties, this book provides information which will help you work out problems by yourselves; for others, it will help you define the problem so that you can seek outside help.

Those making a last-ditch effort. Some couples will view the reading of this book as their "last-ditch" effort. One couple told us that their attendance at the retreat where we were speaking was their final effort to work things out sexually. They had been married for twelve years, and from their own report had a good marriage, except that the woman had never seen herself as a sexual person. As far as she was concerned, she had never been aware of any sexual feelings in her body. Both hoped that learning new information and talking about this area with each other as part of the seminar would help them to discover what they needed to do to find the fulfillment they so deeply desired.

Summary

This book can provide needed information. It will also guide you through steps that intend to open communication and sharing so that a process of mutual discovery and openness may be initiated in your relationship. We are writing for all those who seek to explore and discover together.

It is true that the technical material in this book is already available—for professionals and for lay people—and from both a Christian and a secular point of view. However, we do feel that there are several approaches to a healthy sexual experience which have not been promoted in the way that we see important.

The following are three distinctive themes that will be found throughout this book:

1. Individual Responsibility—A New Attitude

We want to promote a new attitude or mind set about individual responsibility. As we see it, one of the biggest difficulties that couples experience is this: each one feels responsible for the partner's sexual satisfaction and fulfillment. This concern has grown somewhat naturally out of the correct emphasis on love, care, concern, and submission to one another. And yet, we have discovered that for many people a major barrier blocking their enjoyment of sex is just this: a feeling of obligation to provide one's partner with sexual satisfaction. If there are problems, many people feel it is their responsibility to "fix" those problems—that it is their fault if the other person is having difficulty. For example, if the man is not able to respond with an erection as he would like, the wife may feel it is her responsibility to bring him sexual happiness. If the woman is not satisfied, the man may feel it is his "fault" she is not experiencing full satisfaction. So our emphasis throughout the book will be on each person taking responsibility for his or her own sexual happiness rather than expecting one's partner to assume that responsibility. Obviously each partner does his/her best to pleasure and stimulate in a way that is most pleasing. But we cannot be responsible for each other's emotional barriers, nor can we read each other's minds.

2. Weaving Together Our Biblical, Psychological and Physical Knowledge

Our intention is to combine and integrate what we understand about traditional theology, generally accepted psychology, and recent physiological discoveries. We are confident that theology and biblical truths are not in conflict with current psychological understanding; rather, the latter function as endorsements, confirmations, and amplifications of the scriptural teaching. It is true that many new and contradictory theories emerge in current theology and popular psychology. But when we go back to the basics of the Bible and to the broadly accepted truths about human behavior and feelings, these do not contradict each other. We examine and describe the physical side of sex because it is important for God's people to accept and enjoy everything God has given us.

3. Many Individual Differences with Few Easy Answers

We have become concerned as we have read much of the current material being produced on sexuality, both secular and Christian. The underlying implication is that there are very clear and specific, one-two-three kinds of answers to the various sexual difficulties which people experience. If the reader would only do this one thing, or push this one button, or stroke in this way, then everything will be all right. Now there is a germ of truth in this: there *are* some general principles that can be applied, and all human bodies *do* function similarly. But information left out of so much material is that even though there are many similarities, there are also many ways in which each of us is unique, different from anyone else.

Many of the current books, for example, emphasize that there are certain ways in which a woman will become aroused sexually; if the man learns these methods, the woman will be responsive and everything will be wonderful. What these books fail to recognize is that each person is different: each woman is different from all other women, and each man is different from all other men. This approach also fails to recognize that a person's feelings are different from day to day and even from moment to moment. What is satisfying and pleasurable at this moment may not be satisfying and pleasurable later on. This is why it does not work to list certain steps as if they will work for everyone. Such a simplistic approach makes many people feel like failures because they do not achieve the sexual satisfaction and delights promised to them if they follow the "easy steps."

Christian authors and speakers have had much to say about the marriage relationship. Some have stressed that the woman "makes" the relationship: she must build up the man, praise him, make him feel masculine. If she says and does the right things, the relationship will be good and the man will meet her needs. In essence, this teaching is saying that the woman is more important to the relationship than the man, because she has the ability to build him up or tear him down. It is a manipulative relationship—the implication is that the woman is building up the man to get her own needs met. Furthermore, this sort of relationship fails to take into account factors such as long-term hurt or anger, physical pain, lack of sexual desire, and absence of arousal.

Another approach has been to try to learn all about the physiological aspects of the sexual relationship: If people understood everything that was going on physically, they could perform more skillfully and thus experience a more fulfilling response. We agree that it is vital to be interested in what arouses one's partner. To function in a physically accurate manner is important. But we don't agree that knowing all about the physical aspects of sex is the total answer to a satisfying relationship. Any time we focus on one dimension of the sexual relationship to the exclusion of the others, we lose something. Obviously, for communication purposes we have to deal with one dimension at a time; but until we reach the place where we can integrate our biblical understanding, psychological awareness, and physical skill into one total relationship and experience, we miss the full joy and satisfaction that can be ours.

In general, what we have to offer in this book can be summed up thus: we are attempting to present an integrated picture of our sexual selves, rather than focus on one aspect or another. We hope that you will read these pages with the goal of developing comfort and satisfaction with yourselves as sexual beings. In turn we pray that you will share this comfort and acceptance with those around you.

2

Why All the Confusion?

The sexual part of us is a simple yet complex aspect of our being. It is predictable, yet changeable, diverse, unknowable, mysterious and forever beyond our full understanding. If this sounds confusing and contradictory—it is. We have all come to our present understanding about our sexuality by different routes and through different experiences. The messages we have received have come from many sources: family, school, church, society, friends, college, spouse, experience, and our reading. We gather bits and pieces of information as we go along, often unsure how they fit with what we already know. Sex is a topic that leaves almost everyone uncomfortable. Thus many of its messages are not spoken directly but rather are implied or inferred. This is not to say that society is quiet on the subject. On the contrary—we are bombarded with sex appeal in advertising, sexual assistance in family and women's magazines, "sex education" in the classroom, sexual guidance in the latest marriage manual, and sexual jokes in the barber shop.

Why then all the continued confusion and lack of accurate and helpful information? There seem to be several reasons. There is no organized, systematic way of teaching about sex in any setting—family, church or school. Every other body of knowledge is communicated at various ages in a way that can be understood at each level. At each step more is added to what has already been learned. When we teach a child to read we begin with the ABC's, move to short one-syllable words, and then to brief phrases with only one sentence on a page. We gradually add to this until the educated person can read and understand long words in complicated sentences that express elaborate ideas. In contrast, sexual information is gained mainly by osmosis.

To get the most out of sex, you need to sort through the sexual information and attitudes you have accumulated over the years. You need to determine the accuracy of the information and the appropriateness of your attitudes, and to define your sexual goals.

What You Bring with You from Your Home and Family

You may come from a home in which absolutely no reference was made to anything overtly sexual at any time. As far back as you can remember, even words with a sexual connotation were avoided, disregarded, frowned at, or punished. You may have developed a natural curiosity because the subject was avoided so carefully. Any time you ran across a sexual word in a dictionary it held special interest for you. Or whenever you saw a magazine article or overheard a conversation dealing with sex, it tended to be titillating. At the same time, you may have felt guilty about this response (since at least by implication what you were doing was bad and unacceptable behavior).

On the other hand, the total absence of any reference to sexual material may have had the effect of overprotecting you emotionally, making the sexual part of your life or anyone else's seem unnatural and uncomfortable to you. The restraints on sexual information hindered the normal learning process that would have occurred naturally for you if this had been an open subject. As you grew up, each new step of discovery may have caused a great deal of anxiety, perhaps even avoidance, because of the conditioning you experienced in your home. Eventually you may have learned to accept the "sexual you" as a natural God-created gift in your *mind,* but even at this point, you may still have emotional barriers to that reality. It may still be hard for you to *feel* or *be* sexual.

In contrast to the absence of instruction, you may have come from a home where there was some very positive teaching about the sexual part of you. Yet at the same time you may have found it confusing. That confusion could have risen from several areas:

First, you may have been confused because what you heard did not coincide with what you saw. Your mother and/or father provided a confusing model. They told you that sex was a delightful part of adult married life, and yet also communicated a message that said, "This really isn't all that natural and comfortable for us."

Second, it may be that you received a positive message concerning your own body and your own sexuality—but it became confused with the expressions of legitimate concern about "saving" that sexuality for your marriage partner. The preoccupation with "keeping yourself pure" may have made all sex seem impure.

Third, you may have come from a situation where parents or others gave you good, clear teaching, but the message was clouded by additional input from older brothers and sisters, cousins, or peers. The double message left you in a confused state.

Perhaps your environment was totally negative. You were raised in a home where the sexual messages were very loud and clear, nothing was hidden—but they were all negative. If you are a woman, you may have been taught that sexual experience is always negative for a woman; that it is something to be avoided if at all possible, even in marriage; that there is no enjoyment in it; that the sexual feelings which naturally occur in your body are disgusting; and that the best thing to do with this part of your life is to avoid it as much as possible.

A woman raised in a small rural town in Wisconsin reported that she had received no instruction regarding male-female sexual interaction until two weeks before she was to be married. At that point her mother took her aside and lovingly and caringly communicated three basic warnings: first, the honeymoon would be awful; second, she should expect to feel very tired; and third, "Don't let him use you."

If you are a man raised in an atmosphere hostile toward sexuality, you may have received messages critical of any men who were sexually aggressive. Sexual activity was spoken of with disgust and distaste, communicating the idea that you certainly wouldn't want to behave in this way—and that you should not do so as you grew up. You received the message that sexual behavior is abusive toward women and is not to be engaged in by a gentleman.

Or you may have had the good fortune to be raised with good teaching and positive modeling. If that is so, you are probably reading this book for further understanding and enhancement, rather than seeking to undo the effects of your upbringing.

Mother As a Model

Modern research has confirmed what has been preached for generations: namely, what we do speaks more loudly than what we say. The mother in the home is clearly a model to both her sons and her daughters. The attitudes she communicates about her body, bodily pleasure, or affectionate gestures from her husband will reveal to her children how she feels about herself as a sexual being. How she answers questions about sex will also shape the child's view. If there is embarrassed silence, sputtering attempts and finally obtuse responses, again the message is clear. That message is: "We don't know how to talk about this. It is uncomfortable for us to have you ask us. You shouldn't be interested anyway."

On the other hand, if children are answered simply, openly, without judgment or guilt, they learn the naturalness of this part of our lives. This is one of the easiest times to teach them the moral standards surrounding all sexual activity. At this time we can begin to plant the seeds of moral responsibility that go hand in hand with the enjoyment of sexual pleasure.

Another important part of the mother's modeling has to do with what she communicates about women and sexuality. Her daughter will learn whether sex is fun and satisfying, or a burden to be endured. Is it a male conspiracy to be avoided, a duty to be accepted with grace, an area where the woman has to watch out for herself since the man will automatically want to use her? Or is it a source of great fulfillment as it expresses the love she feels for her husband? Usually these attitudes are transferred without any direct communication.

A son also learns a great deal about women and sexuality by what he observes in his mother. If he senses in her the same excitement and pleasure which he sees in his father, he will not grow up viewing sex as a battleground. Rather, he will learn that sexual interaction is a source of pleasure for both parties.

On the other hand, if mother pulls away even from a kiss on the neck, the son learns that the woman always objects but the man goes after what he wants anyway.

Every one of us has had a mother or some adult woman as a model. Think about yours for a moment: what did she communicate to you directly or subtly about women and sexuality? These were the attitudes instilled in you early in life; so it is not surprising that you may still be living in accordance with them even if you no longer totally accept them on an intellectual level.

Father As a Model

Most of what we learn from our fathers about the sexual aspect of life is based on how we see him interact with our mother. If the only time dad touches mom is when they're going into the bedroom and closing the door, we learn that habit pattern. We don't understand it at the time, but we have learned that men are interested only in overt, genital sex. On the other hand, if dad communicates warmth and interest in mother's whole being—spiritual, intellectual, and vocational—then we learn that a man values a woman highly as a total person, not just as a source of sexual satisfaction.

Father's openness in the expression of his feelings, especially his softer feelings of warmth, care, tenderness, sadness and hurt, will probably be the example we use in our own understanding of "how men are." As he is able to share the full range of his emotions, he is also able to respond to his wife with the total intensity that makes for a fulfilling sexual life. In homes where the father has difficulty with the expression of his emotions, the children often grow up to have difficulty with a satisfying sexual expression of themselves.

A son, particularly, will model himself after his father. How much did your father feel free to touch and stroke you or other family members? How free was he to express his feelings? How willing was he to admit his mistakes? What kind of care and respect did he show for your mother? Was he tentative and unsure in relation to her, or confident and caring? Were you able to sense that he loved her totally, not just as an object of his sexual release? All of these issues are the threads from which your sexual attitudes are woven.

One other area where fathers make a major impact is the influence they have on how their daughters feel about themselves as women. This influence begins at birth but reaches a particularly critical point during the early teen years when the girl is going through puberty. It is during this time that she is becoming a sexual person. If father can be honestly supportive and affirming through this process, without being seductive or sending put-down messages, he will help her build good feelings about herself as a woman and a sexual being.

Whether we are male or female, there are obviously many ways that father affects how we view ourselves and our partners. In trying to understand what has influenced you, review your father's part in it.

Society's Input

You may have come from a community where all of the families were very similar. Thus you and your peers received the same kind of sexual message. If you explored or discovered together, you were doing so outside the limitations of your homes. If your family was less open than the rest of your community, you probably gained a lot of your knowledge about sex from the other children in your world. If your family was more open than most, it would not be surprising if you felt a kind of superiority, and at the same time a kind of isolation, as a result of being different.

Many variables may have helped form your present attitudes and understanding. If there was a big controversy in your community about sex education, this will have left its mark on you. If someone close to your family, either friend or relative, became pregnant out of wedlock, and you sat in on discussions of the situation, you will have picked up some attitudes about sex. If any sensational sexual events happened in your family or community, such as kidnaping, molestation, or rape, these will have affected your view of the whole sexual world. This will be especially true if there was a great deal of excitement and hush-hush conversation about these events.

As you moved into your adolescent years, your dating experiences, reading habits, discussions, and the social customs in your community added more to the already large data base of information and misinformation.

If you became involved in activities that were outside the acceptable standard set by your church or society, or a biblical norm, the consequent emotions interfered with your natural development. Depending on your environment, such forbidden activities could range from "mixed bathing" and holding hands—all the way to premarital intercourse.

The Church As an Influence

If you were raised in a church setting, the church had its effect on your sexual attitudes. For some the message was at least hesitant if not negative. As one pastor at a Christian Workers Conference mentioned, "The church has often dealt with sex by having the pastor make his annual visit to the youth group with the challenge to 'keep thyself pure.'" This is an important message for the youth to hear, but by itself it is incomplete.

Until recently, the church has often failed to address itself to issues regarding sexuality. This may have been due to the influence of the Victorian era. Also, since sex involves intense emotional feelings, and since many of us experience so much discomfort around the subject, there has been a tendency to view sex as a private dimension of our lives. The indirect message has often been that there is something basically sinful about our sexual natures—that this is part of the "lust of the flesh."

Much of this negativism has grown out of the scriptural limits set on sexual behavior. There is no doubt that the Bible has much to say about the misuse of our bodies in unacceptable sexual behavior with partners other than one's spouse. But the church's emphasis has not been balanced by the Bible's loud prosexual message. So we have heard plenty about the sexual rules, but little that builds in us a positive attitude.

Now the church is becoming more and more open about sexuality as it recognizes the severe problems that plague its members. Everyone is exposed to the effects of a rising divorce rate and the unrelenting sexual exposure in the media. New findings by researchers, especially Masters and Johnson, have helped the church (both pastors and people) face the sexual realities.

Whether you were raised in a church setting where sexual issues were dealt with in a rigid, austere manner, or in one with a more contemporary, understanding approach, the church has influenced who you are today. Some of the messages you have heard may not fit with your own experience or knowledge, and hence they have added to the confusion already present.

Early Sexual Experiences

Our adult sexual understanding is greatly shaped not only by our home and social environment, but also by our early sexual experiences. For example, if you had any frightening experience as a child, such as molestation or kidnaping, early introduction into sexual activity by a family member, or sexually arousing play with a person of the same sex, that experience will shape who you are today and will influence not only your sexual knowledge, but also your sexual response. If you were not a Christian when you became involved in early sexual activity, the experience may have been confusing but not very guilt-producing. However, if you came from a home where moral values were clearly taught, any early sexual involvement probably produced a significant amount of guilt, and that guilt will have shaped your early experiences in the sexual realm. We find that a person who engages in sexual activity while feeling a great deal of guilt will usually develop some negative, unhelpful sexual habits. These will stay with him or her for many years to come. Therefore, guilt can greatly influence your present state even though the guilt-producing behavior may have occurred years ago. This happens when the positive feeling of sexual pleasure becomes automatically associated with the conflicting negative guilt feeling.

In some situations, you may be the kind of person who has learned to feel guilty even though there is nothing specific to feel guilty about. This is sometimes referred to as "inauthentic guilt." You have learned a pattern of responding with guilty feelings whenever you experience sexual feelings or arousal. As you read this book you might look for ways to accept the God-given naturalness of your sexual feelings, feelings of pleasure, and bodily responses.

Early Marital Experience

Your early marital experience also affects your sexual attitudes today. As you became involved with your new partner, habit patterns developed which grew out of the accumulation of the experiences you had together. If these were positive, rewarding experiences, your current sexual self-image will probably be a wholesome one. If, on the other hand, these experiences turned out to be negative because of an unfulfilling process and an unsatisfying conclusion, then you may feel somewhat inadequate, incompetent, or unfulfilled.

Remember, where you are today is a result of the cumulation of all the input, all the experiences you have had up to this point. Obviously some of those have spoken to you more loudly than others.

The honeymoon is supposed to be that delightful time when two blissful, innocent young lovers discover all the joys and delights of sexual life together. Unfortunately, it does not always turn out that way. Many couples whom we see in sexual therapy have never recovered from the jarring disappointments of that first experience together. Because so much hope and anticipation had gone into that long-awaited event, a major letdown occurred when the first sexual experiences were not as satisfying as expected.

If your early marital experiences were disappointing, you may still be suffering their effects. This book can help you sort through those memories and begin to overcome the negative way they have influenced you.

The Effect of Children in the Home

Radical changes take place when children come into your life. Your sexual experience is not exempt from those changes. You must give much attention to the new child or children; you have added fatigue and heavier financial responsibilities. It all takes its toll.

It is not uncommon for women to experience sex differently after going through childbirth for the first time. Not only is the vagina altered by the birth experience, it also has a new function (birth) which can bring attitude changes.

Some couples find they never quite recover from the effects of adding children to their family until the last child leaves home. If this is your situation, the chapters ahead offer encouragement and new help.

You have been influenced by many and varied experiences in your life as a child and an adult. Some of the input you have received may have had lasting effects on your present-day sexual experience. You may be very aware of your past and how it is affecting you now, or you may tend to disconnect past family or outside influences from your present struggle. If you are in the latter category, we encourage you to work actively at reviewing your past and trying to remember what feelings you had in various situations. You might do so by talking about it with your spouse or writing a sexual autobiography. As you continue in the struggle, it is our hope that this book will further help in unraveling your confusion.

3

Sexuality Is a Gift from God

Our Sexuality Is Part of Our Creation

The worlds of theology and sexuality are commonly viewed as being miles apart. People tend to think of themselves as being divided into two parts, body and soul, with the soul being the good part and the body the evil or bad part. We do not agree with this view and hope to present what we see as a more holistic, biblical view.

We are convinced that Christians can affirm the body, including its sexuality, as a God-given gift to be enjoyed as it is used responsibly. Our sexuality is part of our total being—not merely a physical, fleshly, or "evil" part of us. It is a combination of our spiritual, physical, and emotional being.

Many of the Christian assumptions found in this book come from Genesis, particularly the creation account: "So God created man in his own image, in the image of God he created him; male and female he created them" (Gen. 1:27).

We are sexual beings by creation. Sexuality is part of God's plan of creation. Our maleness and femaleness, our sexuality, is not something added on, or part of our sinful natures; it is part of the original perfect creation of mankind. It's "in our bones." By implication, then, our sexuality is nothing to be ashamed of, but rather something to enjoy.

Our maleness and femaleness are in God's image. As we see in Genesis 1:27, not only were we made as male and female, but that maleness and femaleness are representative of God's image. We don't know exactly how, but in some way our sexuality reflects the image of God.

Genesis 1:26, 27 tells us:

Then God said, "Let *us* make man in *our* image, in our likeness, and let them rule over the fish of the sea and the birds of the air, over the livestock, over all the earth, and over all creatures that move along the ground." So God created man in his own image, in the image of God he created him; male and female he created them.

It is clear from this passage that man was created by God in accordance with a particular model or design. That design is described as the "image of God."

We should point out that it is not the male alone whom God made in his own image, because the passage says, "God created man in his own image, in the image of God he created him, male and female he created them." Man and woman, male and female, are created in God's image, not the male only. This is an important distinction, because what you do with this passage in Genesis affects your view of the human race from that point on. Any view of marriage starts in Genesis too. Whether you develop a strong equality emphasis, a strong submission emphasis, or an in-between view, it begins with your understanding of this passage.

What else can we learn about the meaning of our creation in the image of God as we study Genesis 1? We see that the man and woman were created after the animals, and that they were the only part of creation identified as being in God's image. Thus it becomes clear that we are separate from the animals; we are in a different category. God's image is something we have and they don't. So it cannot be anything we have in common with the animal world. We have physical bodies, and so do animals, so the body can't be a distinguishing factor. The meaning of God's image is that we are created to be in relationship. That means we have the capacity to have a relationship with God, which the animals do not have. It means also that we have the capacity to have relationships with each other.

Having defined the image of God as a capacity for relationship, we are ready to examine the way in which our sexuality fits into our understanding of his image in us.

Our image, as it reflects God and as it relates to sexuality, includes two dimensions: our sexual functioning and our functioning in relationship as a couple. Both of these functions grow out of our becoming "one" physically, spiritually, and emotionally. Genesis 1:28 reads: "God blessed them and said to them, 'Be fruitful and increase in number; fill the earth and subdue it. Rule over the fish of the sea and the birds of the air and over every living creature that moves on the ground.'" Then it goes on in verse 29 to talk about the plants on the earth being food for mankind. The first command given to mankind was to reproduce. This is a sexual function. The second command involved dominion and choice. These are relationship functions. As we move further in this passage, the freedom of choice includes the choice of obeying or disobeying God's commands. Therefore, being in the image of God includes a higher level of function than just animalistic sexuality. Ideally the sexual expression demonstrates more than just a rapid, physical, sexual release. Sexual interaction must include love, care, pleasure, and total expression of ourselves if we are fulfilling our sexuality as God intended.

God-given sexuality includes sexual intercourse. The perfect, sinless state of man and woman included sexual union, and this too was a perfect and beautiful part of God's creation plan—part of our being reflections of him, here on earth.

The two of us grew up with the implicit view that sexual union occurred after man's fall into sin. Given our view of sexuality, there was no way God would be with Adam and Eve if they had been involved sexually. After all, we thought, sex is at least somewhat sinful, and thus God would absent himself if Adam and Eve were acting "like that!"

On the contrary, Genesis 2:24 occurs in the account before sin is reported to have entered the scene. It says, "For this reason a man will leave his father and mother and be united to his wife, and they will become one flesh." The phrase, "becoming one flesh," refers to sexual intercourse. This becoming one also reflects our being created in his perfect image. Furthermore, "the man and his wife were both naked, and they felt no shame" (v. 25). Apparently there was a completely open relationship between male and female and there was completely open relationship between God and man. This honest fellowship continued until they disobeyed God; then sin interrupted the relationship.

Human Sexuality Symbolizes the God-Man Relationship

Our second assumption is that the husband-wife sexual relationship is used throughout Scripture to symbolize the God-man relationship. This imagery begins in Genesis.

Read Genesis 3:7–22. When sin interrupted the communication between man and God, interestingly enough, it also interrupted the communication between man and woman. Notice verse 7 of chapter 3: "Then the eyes of both of them were opened, and they realized they were naked." Apparently they became ashamed. "They sewed fig leaves together and made coverings for themselves." One result of the fall was that mankind lost some of that image of God which had been given them. They no longer had that unashamed, open, perfect relationship with their human partner. And then an even more interesting thing happened: Adam and Eve hid from God. They no longer experienced openness with God. They felt the same kind of embarrassment with God that they had demonstrated toward each other.

Now God enters the scene. He comes to deal with Adam and Eve in their disobedience. The first action he takes is to make permanent coverings for their genitals. Have you ever thought about what a strange sequence of events this is? Why, after these two people disobeyed God, would God enter the scene and make them loincloths to cover up their genitals? Why would those two events be connected? We believe that somehow human sexual organs and the potential they represent are symbolic of the human potential to have a relationship to God. Why else, when the relationship was broken, would God come and cover his creatures up?

It would seem that the *total* way in which two people get involved with each other in a sexual experience—the ecstatic, frantic, intense union that can occur—is a symbol of the way in which we can be intensely involved with God.

The concept that sexual union is an example of the way God would like to relate to mankind is further developed throughout the Old Testament.

The Old Testament frequently refers to Israel as God's bride. In Jeremiah 7:9 and 23:10, the term "adultery" is used to describe Israel's sin of worshiping other gods. Ezekiel 16 talks in great detail of how God's grace was demonstrated to unfaithful Jerusalem. It talks in symbolic terms of a lover preparing his bride. The passage refers to bathing, oiling, clothing, adorning her; and yet she becomes an adulterous wife, who takes strangers instead of her husband (v. 32).

The entire Book of Hosea is an account of God's relationship with Israel, his bride. This symbolism is used regularly when God is trying to establish his relationship with his chosen people. When God began to make his covenant with his people, he said, "This is how I'm going to relate to you," and then he laid out the conditions. And the conditions included his steadfast love and mercy. God wants to have a loving relationship with his people. This is symbolized in the sexual relationship. Isaiah 62:5 reads: "As a young man marries a maiden, so will your sons marry you; as the bridegroom rejoices over his bride, so will your God rejoice over you."

Here is another interesting bit of light on the subject: throughout the Old Testament the Hebrew word meaning "to know," referring to sexual intercourse, is the same Hebrew word used when the Bible refers to man's "knowing" God. For example, Genesis 4:1 says, "And Adam knew Eve and she bore a son." Jeremiah 16:21 speaks of "knowing" God.

The sexual symbolism in the New Testament describes the church (the body of believers) as Christ's bride. We find the most explicit passage for this symbolism in Ephesians 5. It says, "Submit to one another out of reverence to Christ. Wives, submit to your husbands. . . . For the husband is the head of the wife as Christ is the head of the church. . . . As the church submits to Christ, so also wives should submit to their husbands in everything. Husbands, love your wives, just as Christ loved the church and gave himself up for her" (vv. 21–25). The writer, Paul, keeps interweaving the relationship of husband and wife with the relationship of Christ and the church. Then Ephesians 5:31 quotes Genesis 2:24 where it summarizes leaving mother and father, cleaving and becoming one flesh.

The whole passage is basically saying that the sexual relationship is what best symbolizes the relationship between Christ and the church. This is not only true in Ephesians but in other places, including the Book of Revelation. The Bible, particularly in Revelation 19:6, 7, talks about Christ's bride, the church, coming for the celebration, the wedding supper. This is a constant theme throughout Scripture. We have to assume that this symbolism is telling us that there is something more to sex than physical release, since our sexual relationship is a model of how we can best understand God's desire to have an intense relationship with us.

Furthermore, it seems clear that if God, in communicating through the Scripture, chooses to use sexual terms to describe his relationship with us, then we may assume that this is a hearty endorsement of the sexual part of ourselves.

The full meaning of this symbolism is a "mystery." "This is a profound mystery . . ." (Eph. 5:32). When the word *mystery* is used in the New Testament, we understand it to mean that the purpose of the event or teaching is in the process of being revealed to us. What we did not understand at all before, we can, through Christ, grasp with some degree of enlightenment. And some day the same concept will be clearly understood by all believers.

One thing most of us can be fairly sure of is that we do not experience the impact of this symbolism in the process of love-making. It's not likely that a sexual experience is going to trigger great thoughts about our relationship with God. We are much more apt to be intensely aware of our own physical and emotional expressions and sensations.

We *do* believe that it is in this mystical union of two bodies that body and spirit come closest to a merger. Most of the time we let our minds control us. But in the moment of orgasm we are released from that control; climax is something that we experience as a totality. Everything about us enters into it. Perhaps this is how the sexual experience represents our relationship to God. In this total, intense fusion of body, emotion and spirit we are connecting with what it can be like to be totally one with God. This is, indeed, a mystery. One day we will understand it fully. Meanwhile, we can simply accept and enjoy the truth of it.

4

What the Bible Says about
Our Sexuality

Key Old Testament Teachings about Sex

Our third set of assumptions regarding a scriptural view of human sexuality has to do with *the Old Testament input regarding sexuality.*

To understand the Old Testament input regarding human sexuality, we must understand the *Hebrew view of the human person as an integrated whole.* The Hebrews never divided people into body and soul, as did the Greek dualists, or into body, soul and spirit, as some of us tend to do today. Rather, the Hebrews thought of a person as a unity. The physical, emotional, and spiritual were various dimensions of a person, but they were closely related and were often used synonymously or interchangeably.

Now we come to the Old Testament's description of the human sexual experience in Genesis 2:24: ". . . they will become one flesh." This means far more than a mere physical meeting of bodies. In fact, the New Testament quotations of Genesis 2:24 omit the word *'flesh'* and talk only about "becoming one" (see Matt. 19:5; Mark 10:7; Eph. 5:28–31). The scripture is talking about that mystical union between husband and wife that includes the emotional, physical, and spiritual— *the total person.*

For the Christian, love-making cannot be just physical. It has to be more than that if there is to be anything happening between two people. That does not mean that there is never a time when you only need the physical release, and you provide that for each other. But if there is to be a fulfilled relationship, there must be more to it than meeting physical needs. The total person—intellect, emotions, body, spirit and will—becomes involved in the process of giving ourselves to each other. In his book *Sexuality, the Bible and Science,* Sapp summarizes this concept most explicitly:

> Once and for all, any dualistic view of the body as evil and less valuable than the soul has been laid to rest, and the Christian can affirm the body and therefore human sexuality, neither solely as a "natural" phenomenon nor as a regrettable necessity, but as a God-given gift to be used responsibly and to be enjoyed.*

A second perspective comes from looking at men and women of faith in the Old Testament. The assumption we arrive at when we look at a number of these "greats" is that human sexuality not only is representative of our relationship with God (which is a high and lofty concept), but is accepted as being an internal part of human nature. One can be a great hero of the faith and still be an intensely passionate person, i.e., people like Abraham, Jacob, David and others (see Gen. 26:7, 8; 30:6, 7; Heb. 11:31).

We learn from this that human beings are accepted by God as beings with a sexual nature. God does not condone disobedience to his standards in the expression of our sexuality; but he does not condemn our sexuality itself, nor does he condemn us for being intensely sexual beings. He recognizes that the sexual part of us is a very powerful element of our being—a forceful drive. We can see the power of sexuality in the men and women who were chosen as models of faith (see Heb. 11). Our human sexuality is not something to be diminished as we become more "spiritual." It is part of us as spiritual, godly persons, and it is good. However, we do need to follow our Lord's instructions for the responsible use of this important part of ourselves. Evil comes from the misuse of sex, not from its mere existence.

---

* Stephen Sapp, *Sexuality, the Bible, and Science* (Philadelphia: Fortress Press, 1977), p. 132.

Key New Testament Teachings about Sex

To have a complete Christian view of our sexuality we must look at the New Testament contribution to our understanding of the husband-wife sexual relationship.

One clear difference between the Old and the New Testaments is this: the New Testament teaches that *the barriers between men and women have been broken down because of Christ.* No longer do women and men live by different standards. This teaching is a radical departure from the culture that surrounded the church in New Testament times. The main view of that day was that women were clearly beneath men.

The basic concept the New Testament teaches about men and women is that they are equal—not identical, not necessarily the same in roles—but equal in terms of value, ability, and position before God. (See Col. 3:10; Eph. 5:21 and passages mentioned below.) This concept of equality is important because a myth has been perpetuated within the church, the community and society. This myth assumes that a man has some sexual rights that a woman does not have. We see that mentality as completely contrary to Christian teaching. The woman has as many rights as the man has, or the man has as few rights as the woman. This is particularly clear in Galatians 3:28: "There is neither Jew nor Greek, slave nor free, male nor female, for you are all one in Christ Jesus." There are many similar passages.

Ephesians 2:13–22 is extremely important. It talks about Christ breaking down the human barriers, making people into the one household of God when they were formerly divided and at war with one another. This has a great deal of meaning at many levels of our Christian experience. What we take it to mean for our sexual experience is that men and women are equal before God in their right to sexual pleasure.

We are all expected to give ourselves to each other in marriage, but that is a mutual command, not one for wives only. "Let the husband fulfill his duty to his wife, and likewise also the wife to her husband" (1 Cor. 7:3, NASB). Each passage in the New Testament that teaches about the husband-wife sexual relationship either begins or ends with a command for mutuality. Not only are husband and wife equal in God's sight, but they have mutual rights and responsibilities.

Even in Ephesians 5, which deals with submission, the section starts with a command for *mutual* submission (v. 21). Mutuality in sexual rights and responsibilities is a Christian principle that has made a significant positive impact on many a couple's sexual relationship. As a woman accepts the fact that she has the right to have her own needs met, she may begin initiating or become more expressive as to what brings her pleasure.

The New Testament introduces the concept of "love" between husband and wife as an expected part of the marriage relationship. Love is the new guiding principle for sexual behavior in marriage. This is not to say that love was never a part of the Old Testament marriage relationships. Certainly Isaac and Rebekah and many others demonstrated loving, caring relationships. There was concern when a wife was unloved: "When the Lord saw that Leah was not loved, he opened her womb, but Rachel was barren" (Gen. 29:31). However, love was not commanded or expected, because marriage was more of a business deal.

In the New Testament, however, the husband-wife relationship is to depict the kind of love we see Christ lavishing on the church. "Husbands, love your wives, just as Christ loved the church and gave himself up for her. . . . In this same way, husbands ought to love their wives as their own bodies. He who loves his wife loves himself" (Eph. 5:25, 28). This was news to the people in New Testament times; love in marriage was not a part of their culture. It is a specifically Christian concept—another one of God's good gifts to his people, along with sex.

Love has to be the guiding principle for deciding what sexual behaviors are right and wrong for a husband and wife. We look to love as our criterion because the New Testament gives us no teaching on how to enjoy each other sexually. There are no "do's" and "don'ts." Though there are many restrictions regarding the person with whom one may be involved sexually, there are no obvious limitations on "how" one may enjoy oneself within marriage. Later we will talk about how love affects what a couple will do in their sexual relationship.

Sexual Pleasure—a Christian Concept

The final Christian assumption that we would like to discuss is this: *sexual pleasure within marriage is encouraged and expected.* While there is an emphasis in the Old Testament on being fruitful and filling the earth, especially with the emphasis on propagating the messianic line, the other consistent expectation throughout Scripture is that the sexual experience is for the pleasure of the relationship, not just for procreation. This, again, is how we reflect God's image and are different from animals. Animals respond according to the time of their hormonal cycle only. They mate in order to reproduce; they don't make love for the fun of it. Humans, on the other hand, do make love for pleasure. In fact, Scripture instructs believers always to be available to their spouses (1 Cor. 7:3–5), not just for making babies at the time of the month when that is possible. Therefore, we see sexual pleasure as superseding procreation.

The Bible endorses the concept of sexual pleasure and assumes a healthy passion. Read the Song of Solomon; it contains some of the most beautiful and erotic poetry ever written. This Scripture is here for our benefit. Here are some segments: "On my bed night after night I sought him whom my soul loves" (3:1, NASB). "My beloved is dazzling and ruddy. . . . His hand is like gold. . . . His eyes are like doves. . . . His lips are lilies, dripping with liquid myrrh. . . . His legs are pillars of alabaster set on pedestals of pure gold. . . . and he is wholly desirable . . ." (5:10–16, NASB). "How beautiful are your feet in sandals. . . . the curves of your hips are like jewels. . . . your belly is like a heap of wheat fenced about with lilies. Your two breasts are like two fawns. . . . Your stature is like a palm tree. . . . 'I will climb the palm tree, I will take hold of its fruit stalks.' Oh, may your breasts be like clusters of the vine. . . . Come my beloved, let us go out into the country . . ." (7:1–11, NASB).

Obviously, these passages don't encourage us to hold back our passionate feelings! Yet many people come to the sexual experience with the feeling, "I can't really let go." "It's not right for me to feel that strongly." "I couldn't face God again." "Nice girls don't behave that way." Yet as we understand God's message, it is his intention for us to enjoy the sexual experience and to let our feelings flow freely. The Song of Solomon is loaded with erotic messages of two lovers enjoying each other's bodies fully. Nothing seems to be restricted.

Proverbs 5:18, 19 is also interesting: "Let your fountain be blessed, and rejoice in the wife of her youth. As a loving hind and a graceful doe, let her breasts satisfy you at all times; be exhilarated always with her love" (NASB). The teaching is that our feelings of sexual pleasure are permissible, and that we are encouraged to enjoy them. If we are holding back on our sexual experience for "religious reasons," that is a cop-out. From a biblical point of view, there is no reason to hold back.

In conclusion, we cannot overemphasize how important it is for Christian couples to understand the Bible's prosexual message. To the degree that the church has been antisexual and antipleasure, it has failed to be consistent with our understanding of what the Bible has to say about sex within marriage.

___5

Bodies

"He never lets me see him. He just quickly slips into the shower after he gets his clothes off." This was Mary Jo's tip-off about how Gary felt about his body. He had grown up in a home where there was little openness. Now, even after fifteen years of marriage and two children, he still could not let himself be open with her. He was too fat, his penis was too short and it was simply too embarrassing. He knew *she* enjoyed his body, but *he* couldn't. This attitude affected his freedom and security with Mary Jo and had led to problems in their relationship.

How we feel about ourselves affects how we relate to another person, particularly sexually. It has been found that preorgasmic women (those who have not yet experienced orgasm) who feel unworthy and who have difficulty accepting themselves as persons cannot be helped to become orgasmic until they deal with these feelings of low self-worth. When Christ gave the commandment to love your neighbor as yourself, he was spelling out the principle that your feelings about yourself affect your ability to love someone else. His command assumes that we love ourselves—and to the degree that we love ourselves we are able to love our neighbors. We have a hard time giving to or caring for someone else if we feel we are not worthy persons and do not have anything to give.

Body image is the part of our self-image that deals with our attitudes about our bodies, especially our bodily appearance. There is a tendency in our culture to be dissatisfied with one's body shape. We are all striving for that perfect figure or physique. Women are often concerned that their breasts are too big, too small, too flabby, or too whatever. A man may be concerned with the size of his penis, fearing that a smaller penis is indicative of being less of a man and less likely to be able to satisfy a woman. There are a number of myths to be dispelled to counteract this concern with penis size. One is that it is the duty of the man to satisfy the woman. The second is that this satisfaction is dependent on the size of the man's penis. The truth is that the woman has the organ of accommodation; that is, the vagina changes to accommodate any size penis. Therefore penis size has little to do with sexual pleasure or satisfaction. We will deal with this more technically in the next chapter.

Another focus of body dissatisfaction for both men and women is one's weight. We are either trying to lose weight or gain weight—or get our weight properly proportioned. Whatever the specific focus, often our feelings about ourselves, good or bad, are related to how we feel about our bodies.

We have talked about the dissatisfaction we frequently have with our bodies. What about the opposite dilemma? Can you place too much value on positive feelings about your body? If you see yourself as having the perfect figure, you may be in danger of depending on your good feelings about your body for your good feelings about yourself in general. In this case, your self-esteem is totally dependent on your appearance. But what happens when illness or injury damages that beautiful body? You will have a hard time continuing to feel good about yourself.

Whether we devalue ourselves because of our appearance or feel worthwhile only because of our appearance, this kind of preoccupation with our bodies distorts our position as God's creation. We must look inside ourselves for other positive assets. What qualities do you have as a person that make you unique and special? What is your real value as a person, aside from your physical attributes? These are the important questions.

Getting back to the physical, how does a person develop his or her body image? There are three factors that affect how we perceive and accept our bodies. These are the sensory experiences we had as children, the feedback we received from significant others as we were growing up, and the models with which we compare ourselves.

First of all, the development of our body image started with the sensory experiences we had as children. This included both internal feelings and external input. Internally, you may have experienced hunger or pain. You did not develop positive feelings about your body because it gave you so much pain or discomfort. Another person was constantly stuffed with food, and grew up with that form of discomfort. It is difficult to do much about reversing the effects of these internal negative experiences, except to understand them.

External sensory experiences are those received from the world outside us. The first external stimulus that affected us was the kind of touch we received—the tactile input. Was it gentle, warm, comforting and loving? Were we given caring input as babies and growing children? Did we get a positive feeling about touching? The second external sensory input that affects how we value our bodies has to do with the "kinesthetic sense"—the kind of movement we experienced. This includes how we were rocked, picked up, and played with, whether or not we were jerked around, and whether the primary caretakers (usually parents) in our world were secure or insecure in the way they held us.

Another important area of input that affects our body image is the verbal feedback we received about our appearance from significant persons in our lives when we were forming our opinions about ourselves. Such persons include parents, relatives, and children at school. Sometimes children are teased and thus become self-conscious about aspects of their appearance that adults view as attractive. For example, our son tried to cut the curls out of his hair when he was in kindergarten because he was being called "curly head." Freckles can be a similarly disdained feature. "Fatty" or "skinny" are labels that may leave a person with a negative feeling about himself for the rest of his life. Even after "fatties" lose their excess weight, they may still view themselves as fat.

Negative labels can inadvertently be given to children by parents as well. Often we do not give little children credit for their ability to understand what adults are saying. We have heard parents openly discuss the fact that their daughter "just doesn't have it as far as looks are concerned, so we'll really have to work on developing her personality."

Other adults in the child's world may also give feedback that labels the child. More often these will be positive rather than negative, but not always. It is disappointing and amazing to find how easily teachers will label a child.

The daughter of some close family friends, who is a gifted child and an excellent student, was identified as "slow" in front of the rest of her class when she was in first grade. She was a perfectionist and had much creative imagination. This often kept her from completing her work as quickly as the teacher expected her to, for her level of ability. Five years later she is still extremely sensitive to any suggestion that she is doing a task slowly. Recently, as she was being tucked into bed, she said, "You know, Mom, whenever anyone tells me to hurry or says anything that might mean I'm doing something too slowly, I get this terrible feeling all over me and I see the whole picture of what happened in first grade. It's just as clear as if it were happening right then. Miss Harris had reminded me several times to hurry with my work. She was helping the person in front of me. She looked back at me and instead of writing I was thinking about what I was going to write next. In front of the whole class she said, 'I know what's the matter with you. You're a daydreamer and you're much too slow.' "

That example does not have to do with body appearance, but its effect on self-worth is the same.

Our daughter has received a more positive kind of labeling. From infancy on, she has received a considerable amount of feedback about her physical attractiveness. She is also aware that she was born breech—feet first instead of head first. One day, when she was about seven, we were driving along in the car and she said, "Mommy, I have figured out why I am prettier than most other people. It's because my face came out last. Now, my feet might not look as good as others because they came out first, and they had all the pressure on them, but my face looks better than others." She had developed her own rationale for feeling set apart from the rest of her world because of excessive positive input about her appearance.

The third major influence on our self-image is the comparison of ourselves to others. The models we choose to compare ourselves with are critical. In our Western world of TV ads, glamor magazines, and billboard ideals, we may be trying to measure up to a rather unrealistic and unimportant ideal. Stop to think, are these "stars" valuable to you as *people?* What is the physical appearance of the people whom you value? How much is your choice of friends affected by a person's natural physical features? In some of our subcultures, the "beautiful people" have become more likely to be chosen as friends, which certainly represents a warped value system. Nevertheless, even in these situations, the treasured attributes usually have more to do with self-confidence and how one is put together—the external additions—rather than natural body characteristics. Cultures vary considerably as to what is defined as attractive. Most cultures have ideal male and female body images. What is your ideal? What has influenced the development of this ideal? Whom have you chosen as models? How do you see yourself in view of this ideal?

Body image problems occur when there is a large gap between how we view our bodies and what we define as the ideal body. When the way we would like to look is different from the way we think we do look, we will have difficulty accepting ourselves and will probably have difficulty being free with our bodies sexually.

How do we bridge the gap? How can we bring our view of ourselves closer to our ideal?

The first step toward body image enhancement is to examine your view of yourself. Is how you see yourself fairly consistent with how others see you? Get some honest feedback from your spouse and others close to you. Maybe you are stuck with a childhood label that does not reflect who you really are.

This issue entered into one of the funniest events we as a couple experienced when we were dating. Cliff tells the story best: "I had selected Joyce as one of the prettiest girls in the freshman class, and so pursued dating her. She had a poor image of her physical appearance. She saw herself as skinny, with a long nose and puffy eyes. The rest of her family had lighter complexions than she. So she had the fantasy that she must have been adopted from a partly Oriental or Indian family.

"After we had been dating rather regularly for several months, we ended up in an argument about my feedback regarding what I saw as her beauty. I argued that I could not believe she did not really think she was pretty. I thought she was just fishing for compliments. The evening ended with my telling Joyce that she should go up to her room and look in the mirror—because all people, when they are by themselves looking in the mirror, really believe they are good-looking. At that time we did not realize what a wide range of views people have of themselves."

We have a mirror assignment for you that we recommend for married couples in seminars or in therapy. This assignment gives you a structured plan for looking at yourself realistically and getting some honest feedback from your spouse.

Exercise 1
Body Image Assignment

Partner #1: Stand in front of full length mirror in the nude. Describe your body as honestly as you can to your partner. Start with general feelings about your body as you see it. Then talk about each specific body part starting with hair and working down. Talk about how your body feels and looks, ways you wish you were different, what you feel particularly good about.

Partner #2: Only listen and observe. Listen to both the words and feelings of your partner as he/she talks. *Do not interrupt!* When your partner is finished, feedback to him/her what you have sensed and heard.

Partner #1: Clarify or expand on what your partner has heard from you.

Partner #2: Fill in any positive messages that you can give that will be constructive.

Partner #1: When you feel you have been understood accurately, reverse this procedure and you be the quiet observer and listen while your partner describes his/her body.

Another area in which you may need feedback to enhance a realistic acceptance of your body may be the sensory dimension. If the touch and movement you received as a child left you feeling uncared for and unaccepted, you are likely to need much more affirmation of your body through touch and holding—even though you may resist it. We hope you have a spouse who is willing and able to fill that need for you. If you are aware of a need for more touching, talk about this with your partner. Talk about what feels good to you and what would be a comfortable way for your spouse to respond to your feelings.

The second step in bringing your own body view closer to that of your ideal is to determine ways it is possible to change your body. There are many different ways this might be done. Joyce has become very positive about her eyes since she has learned to use eye makeup that distracts from her puffy eyelids and makes her eyes appear more open. There are other ways in which women can learn to use makeup to hide the features they do not like and to accent those they do. Men might grow a mustache or beard or shave these off to vary some aspect of their facial features. Straightening or correcting faulty teeth is important for some people, whereas others accept such defects as part of who they are, something that they would not want to change.

Additional ways a person may plan to change his or her body include losing or gaining weight, an exercise program, posture correction or other body enhancement processes. Plastic surgery is an option when there is serious dissatisfaction with one's body or when there has been a traumatic disfigurement. There are successful surgical procedures for noses, eyelids, breasts, and other features. We would recommend that you get some professional assistance in evaluating cosmetic surgery as an option before you pursue it as the solution to a body image problem. It is usually a big investment financially—and a rather permanent change that may or may not be the answer for your particular dissatisfaction. There may be other emotional barriers that hinder your acceptance of yourself. In such cases, the correction of one body part would probably only lead to finding dissatisfaction with yourself in other ways.

The third and final suggestion for bringing your ideal closer to your real view is to reevaluate what you're measuring yourself against. What kind of models have you chosen? Are you looking at the extremes held up by the media? How do these "ideal" images compare with the significant and valued people in your life? In other words, are your expectations so far out of reach that you will always feel dissatisfied? If that is the case, we recommend the following procedure: commit yourself to one other person who will hold you accountable to get rid of the current ideals and to start selecting more realistic body models acceptable and attainable for you. If your new models are people with whom you can talk freely, ask them how they achieved their physical condition.

The struggle to feel good about your body is a process of becoming open with yourself and your spouse. It also includes honesty concerning your feelings about yourself, feeling comfortable being in the nude, caring for your body, and allowing yourself to receive affirmation through touch and verbal feedback from others in your world. A new sense of comfort with and acceptance of your body can bring increased freedom and pleasure to your sexual experience.

In all this, it is crucial to maintain a healthy perspective on where your value as a person is centered. Christ's message is loud and clear— man looks on the outside but God looks on the heart. We cannot disregard either part: the part that man looks at—the outside, nor the part God looks at—the heart.

6

Discovering and Sharing Our Bodies

"*And God created man* in His own image, in the image of God He created him; male and female He created them" (Gen. 1:27, NASB).

Our bodies—including our sexual anatomy—are God's work. He created us with all of our internal and external body parts; all of our sexual organs were made by him. "And God saw all that He had made, and behold, it was very good" (Gen. 1:31, NASB).

Even our sexual *parts* are good. They were not added as a result of sin. They were there from the moment of creation, and are to be enjoyed and discovered. The entire sexual anatomy is present in a newborn baby. This was affirmed for us when each of our children was born. It was amazing to us that each body part was there. They were like miniature adults in their newborn bodies.

It is natural for children to discover their genitals. Even in infancy, during the first year of life, a girl may find her clitoris and enjoy touching it because it *feels* good. In the same way, the boy finds his penis. These good *feelings* are God-given. They are natural and normal; they have not been conditioned by a sinful society. Rather, sexual feelings are God's gift to us, just as intellect is or other abilities are.

If we accept this premise—that our sexual *parts* and *feelings* are of God—then it would follow that, as with any other gift from God, we should become familiar with them and develop them. A child will naturally become familiar with sexual anatomy and feelings if allowed the freedom to do so. Unfortunately, too often this is not the case. Most of us have been brought up to believe that sexual exploration is "bad" or sinful. Without really stopping to think about the biblical teaching regarding our bodies, we automatically impose on our children the negative standards we learned. The constant repetition of the warning to keep yourself pure from sexual play outside of marriage tends to affect both childhood and marriage. That is, we do not allow children an innocent touching of their bodies; and we do not allow ourselves the full freedom of sexual pleasure in marriage.

Most children between three and six years of age will engage in self-exploration and discovery activities, as well as "playing doctor," or peer exploration, with children of the same and/or opposite sex. When our daughter was four years old, Joyce walked into her bedroom after her bath. She found Julene sitting on the floor with her legs spread apart, her head down as she tried to examine her genitals. When she heard Joyce enter the room, she remained in the same position and casually asked, "Mom, what is that hole in my bottom?" Joyce's first tendency was to respond with shock, but Julene's comfortableness made her stop and think. She remembered that just the day before Julene had spent a long time in front of the bathroom mirror looking down her throat, trying to examine and watch her uvula at the back of her throat. There was no difference in the child's intent in discovering her body. She did not think that looking at her throat was fine, but looking at her genitals was "sinful."

Joyce withheld the negative response that would have been an outgrowth of her own experience. Instead of making Julene feel badly about her self-exploration, Joyce got a hand mirror so Julene could see her own genitals better. She sat down with Julene and pointed to the various openings, the lips and the clitoris, and indicated their technical names. Julene's curosity seemed satisfied and she was never found exploring herself again until she began experiencing the changes of puberty and asking questions about what was happening to her body.

You may be a woman who never felt free to sit down with a mirror and really find out what your genitals look or feel like. For men, this lack of exploration is unlikely, since a man's sexual anatomy is so externally evident. As a woman you may think of your genitals as the "doctor's area"—he's the one who examines you regularly—or maybe as your husband's territory to fondle; but you have never really thought of becoming familiar with your own genitals. Joseph and Lois Bird write: "Many women interviewed showed a greater familiarity with the map of Europe than their own sexual anatomy. This is understandable. They were never punished for studying geography."*

We encourage you to engage freely in a natural discovery of your sexual anatomy. You probably will not have the spontaneous feeling that a young girl would have, but you can think of it as something you missed in your development and understanding of yourself. It is something you need to do to have complete sexual freedom with your body. The more familiar you are with your own and your partner's sexual anatomy and feelings, the less guessing will be involved in the sexual act. This obviously leads to greater confidence and freedom.

Exercise 2
Women: Discovering and Knowing Your Own Genitals

Begin with clean hands and body. Using a hand mirror, examine your external genitalia. Become familiar with what is "normal" for you. There can be medical benefits from this also. Once you are familiar with yourself, you will be able to notice changes that may need medical attention. You can bring these to your physician for attention long before your next gynecological examination.

When you use the hand mirror to examine your genitals, what you see will look something like Figure 1.

The female's external genitals include the labia majora (the outer lips), the labia minora (the inner lips), and the clitoris. What you see when you look at your genitals before you open the outer lips (the labia majora) are the mons pubis, the soft part above the clitoris that is covered with pubic hair, and the thick outer lips, the labia majora, which are also partially covered by hair. If you have never given birth to a child, your outer lips probably meet in a closed fashion at the center or midline of your genitals, providing protection for the inner lips, the urinary opening and the vagina. In women who have borne children, it is common to find that the trauma of childbirth has interrupted the neat fit of the outer lips at the midline. This change in the midline makes a difference in the changes that occur when the

---

* Joseph and Lois Bird, *Sexual Loving* (New York, Doubleday, 1976), p. 93.

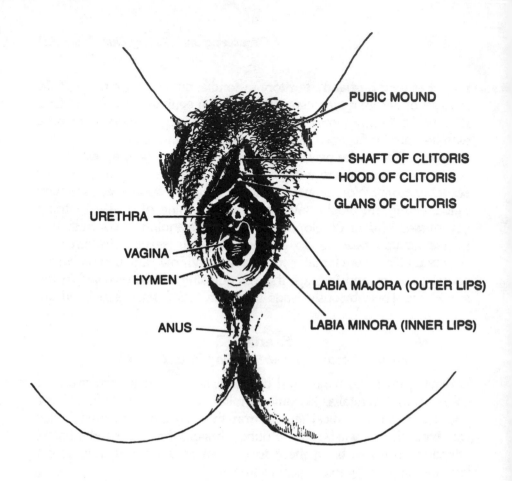

PUBIC MOUND

SHAFT OF CLITORIS

HOOD OF CLITORIS

GLANS OF CLITORIS

URETHRA

VAGINA

HYMEN

LABIA MAJORA (OUTER LIPS)

ANUS

LABIA MINORA (INNER LIPS)

Figure 1

EXTERNAL FEMALE GENITALS (FRONT VIEW)

outer lips spread apart during sexual arousal (refer to the following chapter, excitement phase).

With a hand mirror in one hand, use your other hand to spread the outer lips apart to examine the rest of the external genitalia. Look for the clitoris (refer to the above diagram). Even though the diagram points out the three parts of the clitoris, the glans, the hood, and the shaft, these may be difficult to identify specifically on yourself. The hood which covers the shaft flows down to form the inner lips.

The shaft is a miniature penis-like cylinder located under the hood with the glans or head being the only part exposed. Even the glans may not be easy to locate. For some women the glans, or tip, of the clitoris may tend to hide under the hood and the hood may seem like the point at which the inner lips join.

If you have difficulty visually identifying the clitoris, you may be able to find it by touching the place where you expect it to be. The tip of the clitoris is particularly sensitive to any touch. In fact, rubbing the glans may actually be painful to you. Many women report that the most pleasurable place to receive stimulation is around the clitoris, not directly on it. You may want to touch various points around and on the clitoris, not necessarily for the purpose of stimulation, but to learn where the best feelings occur for you. This would be helpful to communicate to your partner to enhance your love-making experience. We will talk more about this when we get into the enhancement of love-making. The discovery of where pleasure points are for you and where you tend to experience pain is crucial to communicate to your partner for the enhancement of your love-making.

Intense pleasure and pain are closely related in our bodies. Those areas like the clitoris which are loaded with nerve endings are most receptive to pleasure and for the same reason, most receptive to pain. It is difficult for your husband to be able to differentiate where, how much and what type of pressure feels good. He does not know this by instinct. If you learn this for yourself, you can show him and even guide his hand to demonstrate the most pleasurable pressure and touch (refer to Exercise 10 in Chapter 13). This can do away with much of his guesswork and add to your pleasure. Self-discovery comes first, before you try to show or demonstrate. Adding another person introduces some level of tension and/or excitement which may hinder the initial learning that needs to take place.

Before we move on to further self-exploration, we want to say more about the clitoris. This physiological data will be particularly important if you think that men are by nature more sexual than women, or that God created men to have deeper sexual feelings than women. Maybe you have underlying feelings that a woman is to be the passive recipient of the man's sexual desire. Women were created with vaginas as a receptacle for the sperm and seminal fluid of the man, you may reason; should this not make the woman a passive receiver of the man's aggression, rather than an active participant and giver?

The presence of the clitoris counters this attitude. The clitoris is the only organ in the human anatomy designed solely for receiving and transmitting sexual stimuli. Physiologically, that is its *only* function. The woman, not the man was created with the clitoris. The penis is the equivalent organ for the man, in that it is composed of similar erectile tissue—tissue with spaces that fill with blood and become engorged when stimulated, making the organ larger and firmer. However, the penis serves many other functions. The fact that the clitoris in the woman is unique in its function of receiving and transmitting sexual stimuli is confirmation that God intended women to be intensely sexual beings not just "vaginas" as recipients of the man's sexual expression.

This is an important concept to consider. It often affects how couples make love, how a woman feels about herself as a sexual being, and how the man relates to the woman sexually. We feel that the Christian community has assimilated society's "passive woman *vs.* aggressive man" mentality which is sometimes translated into the wife's being submissive and passive in the sexual act. If you hold that view, we challenge you to study the New Testament teachings on sex in marriage (refer to Chap. 3).

Moving on with your hand-mirror exploration, let's talk about the location of the urinary meatus (opening). The urinary meatus is not part of the sexual anatomy, *per se,* but its proximity makes it important to locate. It is found right above the vagina, or, for some women, it may actually be in the opening of the vagina. It may look like a little pimple. It is the opening to the urinary tract that leads to the urinary bladder and on to the kidneys. That entire system is sterile. When there is no infection present, it is free of any microorganisms. It does not carry germs or transmit diseases.

The other two openings the woman has in the genital and perineal area are the vagina and rectum. The vagina is the largest opening you see. In contrast to the urinary system, the vagina does have microorganisms present. The microorganisms present in the vagina are not disease-producing microorganisms (germs). Rather, their function is to ward off infection and to keep the vagina in a healthy state. Therefore, the vagina is considered a clean passageway, when there is no infection present.

Some of us have tended to think of our genitals as dirty. That was also probably what we read into the message, "Don't touch." It might also be a response to the important and necessary sanitary practice of washing after toileting. It is important for us to note that the need for washing after going to the bathroom is not because of the possibility of the *genitals* contaminating our hands, but rather because of the rectum. The rectum is highly contaminated. It is loaded with potentially disease-producing microorganisms. When you wipe after toileting, it is important to wipe from front to back, from the urinary meatus to the rectum, to avoid contaminating the vagina and the urinary system. If you are a woman who tends to suffer from frequent vaginal or bladder infections, begin to note your wiping habits. You may be carrying disease-producing microorganisms from the rectum to the urinary bladder and vagina.

There are other facts about the vagina that may affect sexual attitudes and habits. In a healthy state, the vagina maintains its own acid-base balance. This is another mechanism which helps fight off infections and enhances the process of impregnation. Because of these functions of the normal balance within the vagina, douching is not recommended unless so directed by a physician for a specific health problem.

Exercise 3
PC Muscle Conditioning (Kegel Exercise)

The vagina is the most important anatomical structure for intercourse. It is often referred to as the "organ of accommodation"; that is, the vagina is a muscular passageway very changeable in size. It can tighten or expand to receive any size penis during intercourse. It can even expand to deliver a baby. This ability of the vagina to tighten or expand can be enhanced by exercise, and the same exercise will also increase the vagina's sensitivity to sexual stimulation and its responsiveness. The muscle to be exercised is the pubococcygeus (PC) muscle. It is the same muscle used to start and stop urination. You can identify the correct muscle by sitting on the toilet with your legs spread apart. Start urinating, then stop urination for about 3 seconds, then start again. Do this several times before you are finished emptying your bladder. If you can do it easily, you probably need to tighten and relax this muscle only about 25 times a day to keep it in good condition.

If this process is very difficult for you, however, it means that the muscle is sloppy and needs a great deal of work. We would recommend that you start with tightening it 25 times a day and work up to 200 times a day. When the muscle is sloppy, it may take a great deal of concentration to tighten and hold for 3 seconds before relaxing. As it develops better tone, you can do the exercise anywhere at any time and no one will even know (as long as you don't smile!). It's often helpful to associate tightening the PC muscle with some other daily activity, such as waiting at the grocery checkout counter, stopping at red lights, ironing, washing dishes, taking notes at the board meeting, typing, passing medicines, watching your son's little league game or whatever happens to fit your life style.

Experiment with tightening and releasing the PC muscle during an actual intercourse experience as well. This will be particularly helpful if you are not aware of feelings in the vagina after entry. We will give more explicit instruction regarding this particular enhancement exercise when we talk about increasing the responsiveness of the preorgasmic woman (see Exercise 13, Chap. 20).

One more characteristic of the vagina is that it lubricates during arousal as well as at other times. This lubrication is a normal response that occurs shortly after birth and continues throughout life. It may lessen after menopause, in which case a woman may need to use a water-based lubricant before entry can comfortably occur. Lubrication is an involuntary response of the body. By that we mean it is something over which you have no control. Lubrication can best be described as beads of perspiration along the walls of the vagina. It may occur when you are in a relaxed state, with or without any obvious sexual stimulation. For example, the Masters and Johnson research shows that normal adult women lubricate every 80 to 90 minutes while asleep.

Now back to the self-examination of your genitals. To examine the vagina, we would encourage you to use a lubricant such as K-Y Jelly, Lubrifax or nonlanolin Allercreme lotion. After lubricating your forefinger, insert it into the vagina as far as the second knuckle and slowly follow the wall of the vagina all the way around.

You might think of the opening of the vagina as a clock, with the top of the vagina, the point nearest the clitoris, as the twelve o'clock location. When you follow the wall of the vagina, start at some point on the clock and put varying degrees of pressure on the wall of the vagina with your finger at each point of the clock. As you do this, notice the sensation.

Identify any differences in feeling at the various places within the vagina. For example, identify any areas that are particularly sensitive to touch and seem to trigger either a painful feeling or a pleasurable feeling. In this process, some women for whom intercourse has always been painful locate a specific tear or irritation of the wall of the vagina that needs medical attention to promote healing. Alleviating the pain will enhance the intercourse experience.

Other women have found that a certain area of the vagina is much more responsive to sexual stimulation. If a position is assumed that tends to place the penis in more direct contact with that area of the vaginal wall, this discovery can enhance sexual feelings during sexual intercourse. For example, some women find that stimulation at the four o'clock and eight o'clock locations provide the most pleasurable vaginal sensations. Assuming the lateral position during intercourse (Figure 9 in Chap. 24) will allow the penis to provide more intense friction of the four o'clock and eight o'clock areas of the vaginal wall (see diagram p. 73).

This concludes the self-discovery exercise for women. If this has been difficult or uncomfortable for you, we would encourage you to repeat the process several times in the future until you have a sense of ease with your genitals. If you find that your genitals are distasteful or ugly to you, or that this whole exercise seems like something wrong that would be condemned or frowned upon by God, we suggest that before you enter into this self-discovery experience you read the Song of Solomon in a modern version. Then as you explore your genitals, thank God for creating each part and for its function in your body. If you found the self-discovery exercise to be comfortable, we would still encourage you to take time to thank God for your genitals, for what you have learned about yourself, and for the good feelings this part of your body brings you.

Women: Knowing What's Inside

Now that you're familiar with your external genitalia, let's look at your internal sexual organs. Looking at the diagram of the front view cross-section of the internal female reproductive organs (Figure 2), you will see the ovaries, uterus, fallopian tubes and vagina. The ovaries look like large almonds and are located one on either side of the uterus, below and behind the fallopian tubes. They produce some of the sex hormones that affect the whole menstrual cycle. Primarily, however, they produce the ova or eggs for reproduction. The egg is usually released fourteen days before a woman's menstrual period. It

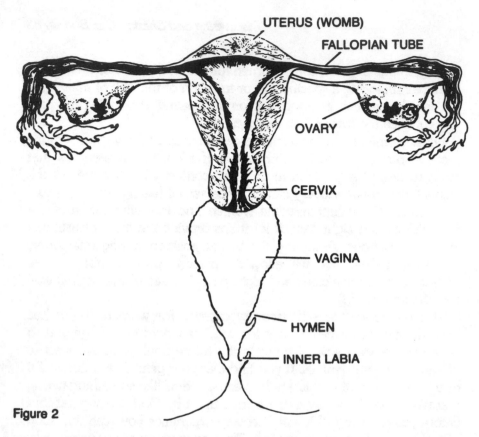

UTERUS (WOMB)

FALLOPIAN TUBE

OVARY

CERVIX

VAGINA

HYMEN

INNER LABIA

Figure 2

INTERNAL FEMALE GENITALIA (FRONT VIEW)

is carried by the fallopian tubes to the uterus where it is implanted if it becomes fertilized. Or it is discharged from the body with the menstrual flow if it does not become fertilized. This process begins in puberty and ceases during menopause.

The uterus, or womb, is a pear-shaped organ located between the urinary bladder and the rectum, as you can see in Figure 3. In its normal position, the uterus is flexed toward the front of the body, pointing forward and slightly upward. If you have been told you have a tipped uterus, this probably referred to a uterus which is retroflexed or flipped back toward the backbone. Less frequently, a tipped uterus may be anteflexed or tipped too much toward the front of the body, putting pressure on the urinary bladder and thus causing the feeling of needing to urinate frequently. A retroflexed uterus is likely to cause

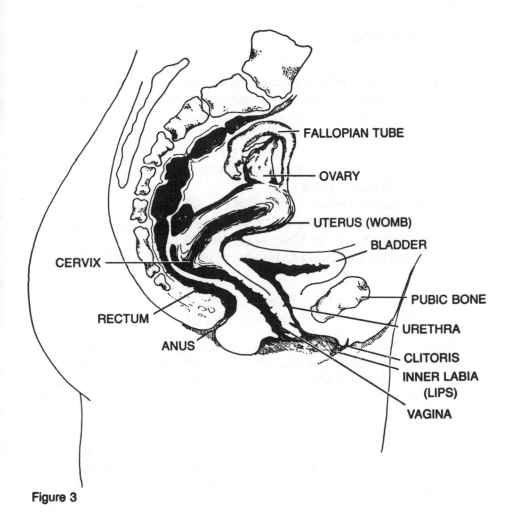

Figure 3

UNAROUSED INTERNAL FEMALE GENITALIA
(SIDE VIEW)

momentary, intense pain upon deep thrusting during intercourse. When a woman comes to us complaining of pain during intercourse, we immediately want to know just where she feels this pain and when in the process of intercourse it is felt.

A woman complained that she was not enjoying the sexual experience. She did as many different things as she could to avoid her husband's approaches. Though she used to become very aroused, as time passed she was less and less responsive. From further questioning we learned that she was almost completely inactive after entry—because "It hurts!" The pain she was trying to avoid occurred when her husband was highly aroused and thrusting deeply. She confirmed that her physician had told her she had a tipped uterus. By some shifts in positioning and exercising, she learned that this pain can be avoided. She was freed to begin to enjoy the sexual experience without pain (see Chap. 32 for more detail on pain).

We have already talked in detail about the vagina, so this about finishes what we have to say about the woman's sexual anatomy and its general functioning. In Chapter 8, we will talk more about how each of these parts respond during an actual sexual experience.

Exercise 4
Men: Knowing Yourself

Now, if you are a man, knowing yourself genitally probably will not be a new or difficult task. Somehow, little boys growing up automatically become familiar with their genitals—maybe because the male's genitals are so obvious. It is not uncommon for a mother to hear her little two- or three-year-old giggling because he has just discovered it feels good to touch his penis. This type of self-discovery is typical for most boys sometime during their growing up period. This tends to be true whether or not the home environment has been open to allowing genital exploration. If your home environment condemned touching yourself genitally you would probably have guilt associated with the good feelings. This guilt associated with good feelings in your body may play havoc with your sexual experiences in marriage. You may find yourself having difficulty really enjoying the pleasure of your body even when this is a condoned, expected part of being a husband. Since you learned to associate bodily pleasure with something not a condoned and expected behavior, you did not automatically unlearn it at the wedding ceremony.

Whether your self-discovery as a child was positive or guilt-related, you probably are familiar with what it feels like to touch or stimulate your penis and scrotum. You may not, however, be familiar with all the various parts of your genitals and what they are called. You will need this information when you learn, in Chapter 8, how your body responds during a full sexual experience.

The scrotum is like a pouch which holds two small glands called the testes (see Figure 4). The testes, or two small balls, which you can feel moving around when you press on the scrotum, are the primary sex organs in the male. They are similar in function to the ovaries in the female. The testes produce the sperm which unite with the female egg to begin a new life. In addition to producing the sperm, the testes also produce a portion of the semen or seminal fluid which carries

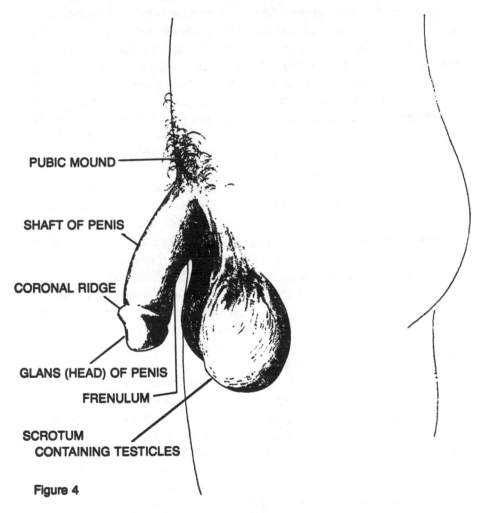

PUBIC MOUND

SHAFT OF PENIS

CORONAL RIDGE

GLANS (HEAD) OF PENIS

FRENULUM

SCROTUM
CONTAINING TESTICLES

Figure 4

CIRCUMCISED EXTERNAL MALE GENITALS (SIDE VIEW)

the sperm from the testes through a series of ducts and out through the penis. The seminal fluid containing the sperm is called the ejaculate. The third function of the testes is totally unrelated to the duct system; it is the production of the male hormone, testosterone, which is secreted directly into the bloodstream.

Testosterone is what causes the changes in puberty that transform a boy into a man. These changes begin to evidence themselves about three years after testosterone has started to be produced in the boy's body. The production of testosterone gradually increases from that time until it reaches its peak around 20 years of age. It maintains that peak level of production until 40 years of age, and then gradually declines until testosterone production is almost down to zero by age 80. The decrease in testosterone after 40 does not need to affect a man's sexual pleasure or sexual functioning (see the section on aging and impotence in Chap. 30). This hormonal function of the testes is something to know, not something you can examine on your body or identify on a diagram.

We would like to guide you into becoming more familiar with the first two functions of the testes, the production and secretion of sperm and seminal fluid. Once these leave the testes, there is a series of ducts through which the sperm and seminal fluid travel. This can be followed on Figure 5. The epididymus begins this duct system. The epididymus is housed within the scrotum and then connects to the seminal ducts, which carry the seminal fluid and sperm to the inside of the body; there they connect with the ejaculatory ducts and pass through the prostate gland, which is doughnut-shaped. The prostate gland at this point supplies additional seminal fluid to the ejaculate. The ducts which carry the ejaculate from this point are short tubes that end almost immediately and join the urethra. The urethra is the tube that carries the urine from the urinary bladder out through the penis. Given this whole setup you can see why swelling of the prostate gland, which can occur in older men, would cause difficulties. This swelling is usually detected when the man begins to have difficulty urinating. However, removal of the prostate gland need not interfere with sexual functioning, since seminal fluid is supplied by other parts of the ejaculatory system as well as by the prostate gland.

The ejaculatory system, as you can see in the diagram, joins the urinary system and leads into the penis. The penis is the obvious essential organ for sexual intercourse in that it is the means by which

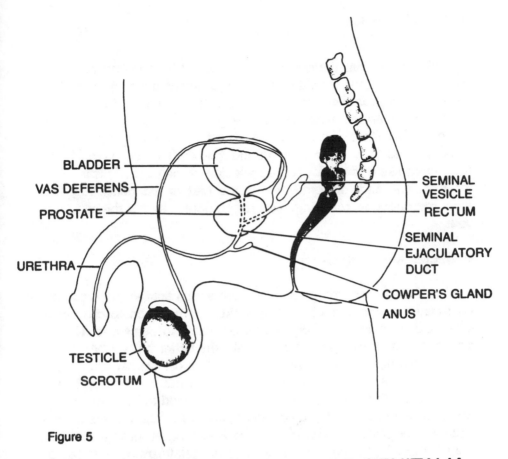

BLADDER

VAS DEFERENS

PROSTATE

URETHRA

TESTICLE

SCROTUM

SEMINAL VESICLE

RECTUM

SEMINAL EJACULATORY DUCT

COWPER'S GLAND

ANUS

Figure 5

UNAROUSED INTERNAL MALE GENITALIA (SIDE VIEW)

the ejaculate can be introduced into the female vagina. The penis is composed of erectile tissue. This tissue has a lot of spaces called venous sinuses. These rush full of blood when there is sexual arousal, causing the penis to become enlarged, firm and erect. This makes possible the penis's entry into the vagina.

The penis has various parts. There is the glans or bulging tip of the penis with the coronal ridge. If a man has not been circumcised the glans is covered with a loose skin called the foreskin. This can be pulled back from the glans; it is important for the uncircumcised man to pull back the foreskin and wash underneath it during his daily showering to promote cleanliness and to prevent infection. For the circumcised man the head (glans) is exposed. The shaft of the penis is the whole cylindrical structure which responds most pleasurably to being stroked. The loose skin around the shaft of the penis forms what looks like a seam down the back side of the penis. This is called the frenulum, and for some men is the part of the penis they find most responsive to caressing. You might note if that is the case with you.

Fallacies about Men

Many fallacies regarding men and their sexual anatomy and responsiveness have been perpetuated by locker room or construction crew jokes and comparisons. Frequently these relate to penis size. The assumption that the larger a man's penis, the better he will be able to satisfy a woman just isn't true. First of all, most women don't gain the majority of their sexual satisfaction from the penis being in the vagina, no matter what size the penis. Women tend to be most responsive to general sensuous body caressing and stimulation of the breasts and external genitalia. Second, Masters and Johnson have found that the unaroused (flaccid) penis size does not relate proportionately to erect penis size. A small flaccid penis, upon sexual stimulation, enlarges to a greater extent than does a larger flaccid penis. In their erect state there is not much difference in size between one penis and another, even though they may differ significantly in size when they are not aroused.

Third, as we will describe in more detail in Chapter 7, the primary contact the penis has with the walls of the vagina during intercourse occurs in the lower one and a half to two inches. During sexual arousal the vagina changes from a collapsed, cylindrical passageway. The inner or upper two-thirds of the vagina expands and the lower third thickens and tightens up due to vasocongestion (blood rushing in to fill up the tissues, similar to a man's erection). This lower third, which is one and a half to two inches into the vagina, becomes highly responsive to sexual stimulation and is the only area of contact the vagina has with the penis. In our seminars we often teasingly tell the men that if they have two inches that's all they need to please a woman!

Fourth, just as the length of a man's penis has little or nothing to do with his effectiveness during sexual intercourse, neither does the circumference or thickness of his penis have any importance for sexual performance. The woman's PC muscle can tighten so as to completely close the opening of the vagina; therefore, a thin penis can still have firm sensation and pressure from the vagina.

If a woman's PC muscle is sloppy, she may need to keep her legs together to help with the pressure until her exercises have enhanced the quality of that muscle. The muscular nature of the vagina is also such that it can expand to allow the passage of a newborn baby, so there is no need to worry about a penis being too large, either in length or in circumference. This fear of the penis being too large is usually experienced by women rather than men.

If you have had concerns about penis size, we trust that these facts will reassure you and allay your self-consciousness in the sexual experience. We would encourage the two of you to talk about the facts just presented regarding penis size and sexual functioning. What feelings have each of you had? How have these affected your sexual experience or feelings about yourselves? Affirm each other when you can honestly do that. For example, if you as the woman are hearing for the first time that your husband has had feelings of inadequacy because of his penis, but his penis size has never been a problem for you, reassure him of this fact. Continue to explore these areas of concern with each other.

Sharing Your Discoveries with Each Other

Many couples have had full sexual experiences with each other for years, but these may have been "quickies" which have occurred at bedtime, in the dark, under the covers and possibly with night clothes on. Or even if the sexual experience hasn't been that "covered" an experience, there may not be a sense of freedom with each other's bodies. For certain, most couples are not very familiar with each other's genitals. Many have the feeling that they would not want such familiarity—that it would take away the romanticism by removing the mystery. We cast our vote for the removal of that kind of "mystery." "Mystery" or unfamiliarity does not enhance the sexual experience. In fact, most couples who have been functioning within a "closed" sexual relationship soon lose the romantic enjoyment of each other and fall into the humdrum of a routine life.

We have found that the process of becoming familiar with each other's genitals may be an incredibly difficult task for some couples. Yet when this hurdle is conquered, the communication may open up a whole new dimension of freedom and enjoyment with each other that they never have had, or at least have not had for years.

What we would like to guide you through is an "I'll show you mine, If you'll show me yours" kind of sharing time. You might think of it as very similar to children playing doctor. It is pretty much a repeat of your self-discovery experiences except that you are now in it together. This may feel awkward. Talk about any uncomfortable feelings before you begin. What fears, concerns or embarrassments do each of you feel? What could make the experience more comfortable without taking away from the openness? Often sharing our hesitant feelings with each other makes moving into the exercise less difficult. Once you both have communicated your feelings, read the assignment together. After gathering the necessary equipment (a light, a hand mirror, lubricant, and tissues), you may proceed as outlined below:

Exercise 5
Genital Examination

Step 1: Shower or bathe together; suds each other's bodies and enjoy the pleasure of relaxation and of touching each other in that process, not for purposes of arousal.

Step 2: In a private, well-lit room, with diagram of male genitalia, identify all the specific parts of the penis and testes. Partner join in the exploration by touching various parts as they are identified. Particularly note the coronal ridge and the frenulum or "seam" on the back side of the penis. After exploring the various parts of the genitals, talk about what kind of touch feels good. Note any stimulation of the genitals your partner has given you in the past that you would like more of and any stimulation and handling of the genitals which has been unpleasant for you. Partner talk about ways you enjoy pleasuring his genitals and/or feelings of discomfort you have with male genitals.

Step 3: Female assume comfortable position with legs spread apart, light focused on genitals, diagram within view, and hand mirror between legs so you can see genitals clearly. Look at how your outer labia come together. Then spread the outer labia and identify the inner labia. Find the clitoris and note how the labia form a hood over the clitoris. See if you can feel the shaft of the clitoris, almost like a hidden, small penis up behind the tip of the clitoris. Touch the tip or glans of the clitoris and then the areas around it, and talk with your partner about what kind of touch feels good and where it feels good. Partner join in exploration and touching as is comfortable. Identify urinary meatus, vaginal opening and any other points of interest. Talk about what genital stimulation your partner has given you in the past that has felt good, what you would like more of, what touching has been negative, how stimulation of genitals might be enhanced.

Step 4: With closely trimmed nails, male gently insert finger into female's vagina to the second knuckle. Then gently press on the wall of the vagina. If you think of the opening of the vagina as a clock, start at the twelve o'clock position and then slowly move around the wall of the vagina, pressing or stroking at every hour. Try varying degrees of pressure and types of touch. Female feedback what sensations you note. Particularly be aware of any points of pain or pleasure. After completing this exploration, female tighten PC muscle when male's finger is in vagina.

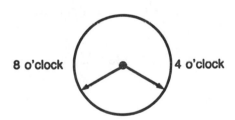

Opening of vagina with four and eight o'clock positions identified. These are often more highly sensitive areas in the vagina.

Step 5: Talk about the experience: What felt good, what you learned, what was uncomfortable about it. You may want to spend some time just holding and affirming each other.

This is a clinical, learning experience, not for the purpose of arousal. If arousal should occur, it is okay. Enjoy the feelings but do not focus on the arousal.

_____7

How Our Bodies Work

Now that you have discovered how you have been made and have shared your discoveries with your spouse, let us take a look at how you function: the physiology of human sexual organs.

Even though all of the sexual parts are present at birth, much of the development and functioning of these parts does not occur until puberty. About three years before any obvious changes take place, the sex glands begin to secrete small amounts of sex hormones. This hormonal activity may be signaled by increased emotionalism in the seven-, eight-, nine- or ten-year-old child long before any actual sexual development becomes visible.

In the young girl, the hormones (primarily estrogen) gradually increase, promoting development of breast tissue, broadening of hips, hair growth on the genital area and other changes that are indications of womanhood. Within several years after these signs of development begin, the girl's sexual cycle starts with the first menstruation. From then on there are rhythmic monthly changes in the level of hormonal production. The effects of these changes on the woman's emotional state and/or sexual responsiveness varies from one woman to another and in the same woman from time to time.

Sometimes early developmental changes in our little girls may surprise or even panic us. It is not unusual for a mother of an eight- or nine-year-old girl, especially if it's her first daughter, to bring her to the doctor with concern that the girl might have a growth under one nipple. A nipple popping out early in the process is one more sign that hormones are being secreted. It is comforting to know that this early sign does *not* mean she is going to be a fully developed, physically mature "woman" too quickly.

Most girls' breast development occurs very slowly. If the girl's nipples have budded around eight or nine, she may not have enough breast tissue to warrant wearing a bra until she is twelve or more. Some girls become self-conscious about their nipples showing through their clothes and others seem to be unaware that anything has changed. Either reaction is normal. Ideally, parents can help most by accepting the child's feelings either way; that is, parents should *not* require the child to become self-conscious and cover up nor should they put the child down for being self-conscious. Allow her to wear vests, full blouses, or whatever happens to be acceptable attire at the time.

In response to the self-consciousness, it is helpful to recognize the feelings of the child verbally, participate actively in providing the clothing necessary to provide comfort, yet give our genuine reaction that the developing body is attractive. Communicate that it wouldn't make us uncomfortable for the child to wear clothing through which the curvature could be seen. Sometimes it's also helpful to talk with the girl about how other girls at her stage of development are dressing and how she feels about their way of dressing. The child may have become so focused on herself that she thinks she is alone in this new adventure. When she looks around and sees that Mary, Jenny, and Tammy also have little bulges under their T-shirts, she relaxes.

It is most important for children this age to sense that they are a part of the norm, that they are not unique. When they begin to develop earlier or later than their friends, they begin to ask the question, "Am I normal?" They need accurate facts and reassurance from their parents.

The woman's cyclic hormonal process continues about thirty years until the function of the ovaries ceases during menopause. This does not affect sexual functioning, except that there may be less vaginal lubrication and possibly a thinning of the walls of the vagina. Both of these changes are best handled by using a lubricant during sexual intercourse.

What about the increasing production of hormones in the young boy? Just as estrogen increases in girls, testosterone in boys increases gradually for about three years before puberty, and then takes some big jumps, causing the commonly recognized changes of deepening voice, growing beard, broadening shoulders, and so on. The genitals also become larger and are surrounded by hair growth. Some boys may have an occasional nocturnal emission of seminal fluid, or what is more commonly referred to as a "wet dream." The boy should be made aware that this is a normal happening, but it is not necessary as a sign that he is developing. It occurs for some, not for others. Just as there is nothing wrong if a wet dream does occur, there is also nothing wrong if it doesn't.

The secretion of testosterone in the male reaches its peak in the early twenties and begins to dwindle after age 40. The testosterone level is almost zero by 80. Many men vaguely sense these changes in their bodies and become concerned that their sexual functioning will be affected. There are several effects of decreased testosterone level on sexual functioning: there may be some decrease in frequency of desire for sexual involvement; it may take longer to get an erection and the erection may not be as firm: and there may not be a need to ejaculate with each sexual experience. None of these need affect sexual enjoyment—nor are they causes for lack of response, unless, of course, anxiety about these changes sets in. Aging slows down all body processes. A sixty-year-old man cannot run around the block as fast as a twenty-year-old. When it comes to sexual functioning for men, "fast isn't equivalent to better." In fact many women are pleased with the man's "after-40 changes." These may be the couple's best years together.

Sex and the Brain

Now we come to another dimension of the sexual process that could involve a detailed technical discussion: the interrelationship of the brain, the nerves (neuromuscular system) and the glands (endocrine system) as they affect the sexual response. The miracle of God's creation is clearly evidenced by the intricate interaction of these systems in the human body, which is quite different from the instinctual sexual drives of animals. In contrast to animals, humans show great variation in response to the same sexual stimuli or input. Depending on the emotional and, possibly, physical condition of our bodies, a kiss may cause sexual arousal or it may not. This will vary from time to time.

In contrast to human variability, animals only mate at the time of the female's cycle when she can conceive. There is no selectivity, there is no difference in drive, there are no influencing factors. The system is simple in contrast to the complex interaction of the human body systems.

We would like to give a general picture of how our total bodies are involved in the sexual process. Many changes occur to prepare an unaroused person for the act of intercourse. These changes are not limited to the genitals. Our nervous system, hormones, blood vessels and muscular responses all affect our sexual functioning. The details of these changes during a total sexual experience will be described for both male and female in the next chapter. We will take you through the four phases of a sexual responses as described by Masters and Johnson.

Right now, however, we will look at the overall effects of our body systems as they interact with each other. There is much about us still not understood. Why do some men and women become aroused more frequently than others? Why do some of us experience our sexual response more intensely than others? Why do we vary from time to time in our responsiveness? We do not have specific answers to these questions, but we do know that the hormones secreted by our endocrine glands affect our bodies and emotions in many ways. One way of picturing this effect is as follows.

The endocrine glands produce hormones (including sex hormones) which stimulate the nerves to carry messages to the brain. The brain then sends messages back via the nervous system to our muscular and vascular (blood vessel) systems. This process produces sexual arousal and response. In turn, this response stimulates the glands to produce more hormones, which again send messages to the brain via the nerves, and thus the cycle tends to be self-perpetuating. Because of the building nature of our body's interaction, the more sexual arousal and satisfaction, the more drive. On the contrary, when one of the body systems interferes with or inhibits this naturally building cycle, arousal and/or response may be difficult. As a rule, emotional barriers are what get in the way of the sexual response cycle.

Because of the building nature of the sexual process in our bodies, the most effective way to break down emotional inhibitors or barriers is to work intensely with couples. When we counsel couples with sexual difficulties we often encourage a ten-day to two-week intensive sexual therapy process. In this process, we see them in the office daily. Each day we give them three assignments for touching and communicating that they are to complete before the next day's appointment. This permits the cycle to begin building and allows us to identify and assist the couple in breaking down the barriers as soon as they occur.

Within this arousal cycle we need to differentiate between the two branches of our nervous system and their effects during the sexual process.

The autonomic or involuntary nervous system has two branches: the sympathetic nervous system (S.N.S.) and the parasympathetic nervous system (P.N.S.). These function without our willing them or even being conscious of them. They affect our bodies' responses in exactly opposite ways. Thus, together they can either increase or decrease the activity of our body organs. The P.N.S. has an upbuilding effect on the body. It is in action when we are relaxed and more passive. The S.N.S is our "fight or flight," that is, our energy system. It goes into action when we are anxious or intensely aroused emotionally.

According to Helen Singer Kaplan,* sexual excitement or arousal is controlled by the P.N.S. When we are aroused, the genitals rush full of blood and fluid producing the erection in the male and vaginal lubrication and swelling in the female. This is an involuntary response.

We cannot decide or try to be aroused. Arousal is a response our bodies make that can occur only as we are relaxed and allow our bodies to receive pleasurable sexual stimuli. Soaking in the positive stimulation will trigger the P.N.S. and set our complicated brain-nervous system and vascular system in motion.

In contrast, anxiety or effort will act as an inhibitor by triggering the S.N.S., shutting off the parasympathetic and, thus, blocking the natural, building sexual cycle we previously described. Thus, when we allow ourselves to "soak in" sexual pleasure through what we touch or hear or see, our P.N.S. will automatically cause us to become sexually aroused. This involuntary arousal will cause a man's penis to become erect and a woman's vagina to swell and lubricate.

Neither of these responses will occur if a man or woman is *trying* to get aroused or watching themselves to see if arousal is occurring. When we are trying, our brain or head is in control, and, again, interferes

---

* Helen Singer Kaplan, *The New Sex Therapy* (New York: Brunner/Mazel, 1974), pp. 13–15.

with the involuntary control of the P.N.S. We have found it helpful for some men and women with arousal problems to think of "getting with" their parasympathetic or getting out of their heads and into their penises or vaginas—going with the sensation of the moment. Or another way of saying this is that we have to let our bodies respond without letting our brains get in the way.

Several days after leading a seminar in a church, we received a call from Sylvia, who had been in attendance. She was calling to thank us for helping her respond sexually. When we inquired what had been so helpful, she reported that in her first four years of marriage she had not been able to allow herself to let go and have an orgasm. After hearing us talk about the nervous system she had gone into her next sexual experience telling herself to let her body respond— or, as she put it, "to get with her parasympathetic." In this experience her arousal became intense enough to trigger her first orgasmic response. We don't tell this story to suggest it as the easy answer for women who have orgasmic difficulties, but rather to illustrate the importance of letting our bodies follow their God-given patterns in response to physical arousal.

Just as Helen Singer Kaplan associates arousal with the P.N.S., she believes the muscular contractions of the orgasmic response for both the man and the woman are primarily a S.N.S. function. The S.N.S. is the involuntary system that is dominant when we are active, rather than passive. Therefore, the orgasmic response can be actively enhanced or inhibited by our behaviors. Our complicated brain centers trigger the sympathetic nerve system to produce the orgasmic reflex. What we do with our bodies, not our thoughts or brain efforts, can enhance this response. Thus, men can learn ejaculatory control and women can learn to actively go after an orgasm, not by tensing up and trying to make it happen (brain action) but rather by engaging in behaviors (S.N.S. action) that will trigger this normal body reflex.

In summary, since arousal is controlled by the passive, receiving function of the parasympathetic nervous system, we enhance arousal most by learning to "take in" sexual pleasure and to distract ourselves from anxieties or demands that hinder the normal response of our bodies to sexual stimulation. In contrast to arousal, the orgasmic response can be actively pursued by the woman who has difficulty letting go, or can be retarded by the man who ejaculates prematurely. This is true because, even though these are reflex responses, they are triggered by messages that come through the sympathetic nervous system, the intense, energy branch of our involuntary nervous system.

An analogy might help us understand this process. When the doctor is performing a physical examination, he taps the patient's knee to check his/her reflexes. The tap on the knee is a voluntary action that produces the reflex of the lower leg jerking. In the same way, when we engage in certain sexual behaviors (breathing, moving, stimulating clitoris), and we don't stop the natural body responses, the muscular contractions of the orgasm will occur as a reflex response. One can stop his leg from jerking even if the knee is tapped. Even so, we can stop an orgasm from occurring when the necessary stimulation has taken place. But, we cannot cause or "will" a leg jerk or an orgasm.

8

Sexual Response—Four Phases

To help us understand the physical aspect of sexual response, Masters and Johnson have broken down the sexual response pattern into four specific dimensions, or phases. These are the excitement, plateau, orgasm, and resolution phases.

Before the excitement phase begins, it is usually necessary to have some level of sexual desire. This is mainly an emotional response, and hence will be dealt with in the chapter on "Getting Interested." It is also important to be aware that the phases are not distinct in terms of how we experience them. There is no "click" as we move from one phase to the next. This way of outlining our sexual response in phases is merely designed to describe the sexual cycle in an understandable way (see graph on next page).

The excitement phase has to do with our initial arousal. It is most clearly evidenced by an erection in the man, and by vaginal lubrication in the woman. The plateau phase, which is ideally the longest phase of the love-making process, is the phase of love play during which arousal intensifies in preparation for the sexual release. The orgasmic phase, the briefest, most intense and most internal phase, is the release. Finally, there is the resolution phase, during which all the physical changes in the body return to their unaroused state. Notice the diagram of the sex response cycle. This graph represents an average or general-ized picture of the total population. The specific physical changes that occur are basically the same from one woman to another and from one man to another. However, every person differs from one experience to the other, and there are certainly differences from one person to another. These differences primarily occur in timing, intensity, and feeling.

In describing the four phases as they have been measured by Masters and Johnson, we will primarily be talking about the physical changes that are the same for all women and for all men. The degree to which the changes occur may vary slightly from younger to older men and women, from sexually active people to those who have been inactive, and from a woman who has never been pregnant to those who have borne children.

Sexual Response Pattern*

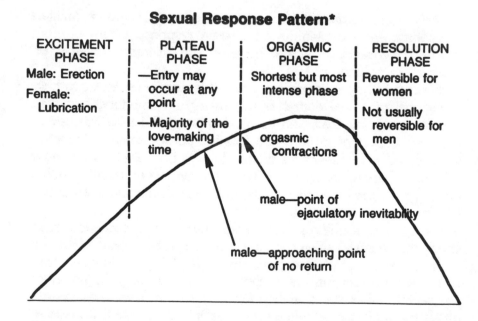

EXCITEMENT PHASE	PLATEAU PHASE	ORGASMIC PHASE	RESOLUTION PHASE
Male: Erection	—Entry may occur at any point	Shortest but most intense phase	Reversible for women
Female: Lubrication	—Majority of the love-making time	orgasmic contractions	Not usually reversible for men

male—point of ejaculatory inevitability

male—approaching point of no return

---

* Adapted from Masters and Johnson, *Human Sexual Response* (Boston: Little, Brown, & Co., 1966).

Excitement

Let's begin by looking at what happens to the woman during the excitement phase. Excitement can result from either physical or emotional stimulation. When this stimulation is received and enjoyed, sexual arousal produces external and internal changes. Dealing first with the external or physical genitalia, we note that the clitoris is probably the most important organ during the excitement phase. As you will recall, the clitoris is a unique organ in the human anatomy in that its only purpose is the receiving and transmitting of sexual stimuli. With arousal, the clitoris becomes engorged or enlarged, just as the penis becomes erect. The clitoris increases in length and in size by two or three times. Hunger for clitoral stimulation may result. Most women report that the caressing of the general area around the clitoris is more desirable than having the head, or glans, of the clitoris directly manipulated.

Other changes that occur in the external genitalia during the excitement phase are in the lips, both the inner and the outer. The outer lips, or the *labia majora,* spread out flat as if opening up in preparation for receiving the penis. The inner lips, or *labia minora,* increase in size, extend outward and become slightly engorged forming a funnel shape. (To identify clitoris, inner lips and outer lips refer to Figure 1 on page 58).

The breasts, too, change during the excitement phase. They usually enlarge, becoming more rounded and full, with obvious nipple erection. This is one of the indications that we encourage a couple to watch for if the woman reports she is not experiencing any sexual arousal. What we often find is that the woman is in fact becoming physically aroused, with both lubrication and nipple erection. However, she is not aware of any feelings of emotional awakening and hence reports a lack of arousal. As she becomes aware that she *is* responding physically, at least in the excitement phase, she can be encouraged to go after the emotional dimensions.

Moving to the internal genitalia, we begin with the vagina, which responds by lubricating within ten to twenty seconds after stimulation is received. This is an obvious sign of readiness for entry, even though entry may not be desired or recommended until later. The lubrication that occurs can be understood by thinking of it as perspiration—little beads of lubrication which form along the walls of the vagina (see

Figure 6). Their simple function is to reduce friction and enhance the pleasure of the penis in the vagina.

The cervix which is situated at the back of the vagina is the opening to the uterus. As the uterus elevates with increased arousal, it begins to pull away from the vagina so as not to be in the way of the penis during thrusting (Figure 6). When the woman happens to have a "tipped" or "retroverted" uterus, this pulling up and away of the cervix

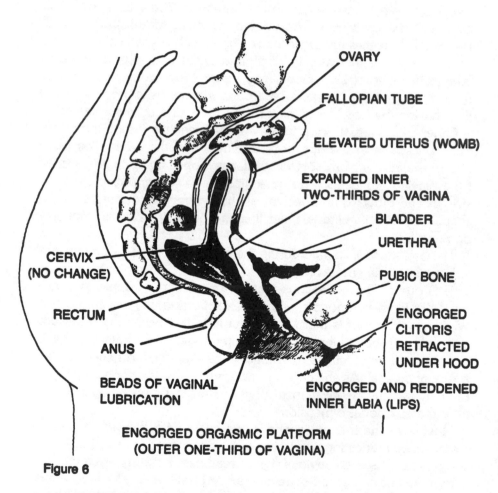

Figure 6

AROUSED INTERNAL FEMALE GENITALIA (SIDE VIEW)

is less likely to occur because the uterus cannot elevate as it is supposed to.

The penis, like the clitoris, is the receiver and transmitter of sexual feelings. The main male response during the excitement stage is penile erection (Figure 7). To define it simply, the unstimulated or flaccid penis becomes erect as the man receives stimulation, either physically or emotionally. The erection occurs as a result of the blood which flows into the penis and is believed to be held there in the veins by valves which keep it from flowing back out as long as there is arousal. Erections can be maintained for extended periods of time without ejaculation or loss of the erection when the man is not anxious, and when the stimulation is varied, both in terms of its type and its intensity.

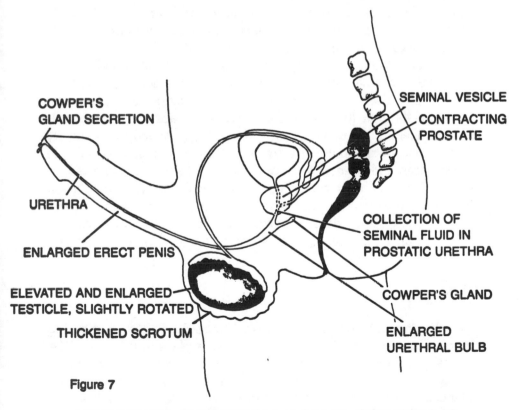

COWPER'S GLAND SECRETION

SEMINAL VESICLE

CONTRACTING PROSTATE

URETHRA

ENLARGED ERECT PENIS

COLLECTION OF SEMINAL FLUID IN PROSTATIC URETHRA

ELEVATED AND ENLARGED TESTICLE, SLIGHTLY ROTATED

COWPER'S GLAND

THICKENED SCROTUM

ENLARGED URETHRAL BULB

Figure 7

AROUSED INTERNAL MALE GENITALIA
(SIDE VIEW)

Note that the intensity of the erection will tend to fluctuate over a period of time and may be lost almost completely. It can be regained. The only factor in the way of regaining an erection would be anxiety about the loss of the erection, or some external event that may have interrupted the sexual experience. Erections are very tenuous. An erection can be stopped very easily when some nonsexual event occurs such as the telephone ringing, a knock on the door, a change in the lighting, or any other interruption. Even a sharp critical comment can make the erection diminish.

The other change that occurs for the man is the thickening of the skin around the testicles. This is believed to occur in order to increase slightly the temperature of the seminal fluid as it is prepared for expulsion and fertilization of the egg.

About 60 percent of men also experience nipple erection. However, since a man's breasts are less prominent, the nipple erection is usually not as noticeable in the man as it is in the woman.

One other bodily change may take place in both men and women during the excitement phase. This is what Masters and Johnson have called a "sex flush." It is a blushing or reddening that occurs over the upper third of the body—the chest, neck, face and forehead. It is more likely to occur in a room where the temperature is slightly elevated and in situations of extreme anticipation. This is observable in some men and women, and not in others. It is not fully understood why the flush occurs for some people; it may be the result of complexion differences. We would hasten to add that it is not a matter of concern whether one does or does not experience the sexual flush; this may simply be an additional sign for some that sexual arousal is taking place.

Plateau

Continuing with the male response, it should be noted that during the plateau phase relatively few changes take place in the penis. The coronal gland or "head" of the penis deepens in color, due to greater engorgement, and enlarges slightly in preparation for orgasm. During extended love play, a small amount of pre-ejaculatory fluid seeps from the penis. This fluid contains live sperm which can impregnate the woman. Because of this, withdrawing the penis from the vagina before ejaculation is not considered a safe method of birth control.

Most of the plateau changes for the man take place internally. The skin of the scrotum continues to thicken and the right testicle pulls in closer to the body and rotates about a quarter of a turn during the mid part of the plateau phase. There is also a significant increase in the size of the testicles (Figure 7). The seminal fluid begins to collect in the area around the prostate gland. As the man moves through the plateau phase toward the point of orgasm, he begins to feel that he is reaching ejaculatory inevitability, or the point of no return (see graph on p. 84).

During the plateau phase, the woman continues to enjoy stimulation. Some prefer a brief time of pleasuring while others prefer a longer period of love play. This is one of those needs or desires that seems to vary from one person to another, and in the same person from one time to another. It is important to recognize that many women experience their sexual arousal in a way that might be best described as "waves." There is a peak and then an ebb or diminishing of the intensity of feelings—and then a new wave of sexual arousal. If a woman lets herself ride the waves, the peaks will tend to intensify. However, if this wavelike diminishing of sexual feelings is thought to be the end of her arousal, the woman may become anxious and thus stop her response from occurring in its natural wavelike pattern. The anxiety fulfills her fear. It, then, *does* end her arousal.

The signs of breast engorgement and the sexual flush which were noted in the excitement phase continue. Most of the changes take place in the internal genitalia. There are a few changes that should be noted externally first. The inner lips become bright red and increase in size. This occurs about one minute before an orgasm. The clitoris continues to be enlarged, but draws up or retracts under the hood and, as the arousal continues, becomes more difficult to locate. It is often extremely sensitive to being touched directly.

Internally, a number of significant changes take place. The uterus becomes fully elevated or pulled into position ready for the orgasm, with the cervix being pulled away from the thrusting penis (Figure 6). The most important changes take place in the vagina. The outer third of the vagina rushes full of blood becoming densely engorged, and contracts forming what is called the "orgasmic platform."

It is as if God designed the vagina to tighten up in the front and expand or balloon out in the back for several purposes. In terms of the reproductive purpose of intercourse, this change keeps the seminal fluid containing the sperm inside the vagina. There is now a small base or pool at the back of the vagina where the seminal fluid can gather, so that, as the opening to the uterus falls back into place after the sexual experience, the sperm can travel up through the cervix into the uterus.

For the pleasure purpose of intercourse, the tightening of the external third of the vagina functions as an extra stimulation to the penis and the vagina. This outer portion of the vagina contracts and produces a grasping effect, holding the penis firmly in the vagina. It is important to note again that since this orgasmic platform includes only the first third of the vagina, or about an inch and a half to two inches, the preoccupation with penis size is of little real consequence. The most important part of the vagina for penis contact is this orgasmic platform area (Figure 6), which at the most is two inches in length and can tighten or expand to any width.

Orgasm

This is the phase that has drawn the most attention in recent years. It is the most intense phase of the sexual experience, yet it lasts the shortest period of time and is experienced most internally or individually. The orgasm does not focus on the relationship. This is often the phase talked and written about as the ultimate and central part of the whole sexual experience. Yet we have talked with many couples who have little difficulty with orgasm, but are very unsatisfied with their overall sexual experience. So as we begin the discussion of the orgasmic phase we want to look at it in proper perspective.

We see the orgasm as an ingredient essential when there is intense sexual arousal. It is important, but not something that is to be focused on to the exclusion of all the other phases. Some women, particularly more passive or low-key women, find pleasuring and affirming more necessary than release. Men over 40 may end a sexual experience feeling fulfilled without an orgasm. The orgasm is a response or a reflex. In Chapter 17 we compare it to the knee jerk. An orgasm is not something we can "will" to occur, but if we allow the right kind of stimulation, then we can expect that the orgasm will follow (Chap. 7).

The Female Orgasmic Response

As a woman moves into the orgasmic stage, various changes happen within the body. The clitoris, inner lips, and outer lips remain basically the same as they were at the end of the plateau phase. The genitally centered feelings of the orgasm (Chap. 17) are due to the strong vaginal contractions in the orgasmic platform. Masters and Johnson have measured three to five contractions for a mild orgasm and eight to twelve contractions for an intense orgasm. These contractions occur at intervals of eight-tenths of a second. This is true for all women and is the same as the spacing of the contractions in the man. As the outer third of the vagina is contracting, the inner two-thirds are expanding even further to form a place for the seminal fluid.

Women have two centers of orgasmic response. The orgasm is experienced not only in the vagina but also in the uterus. The uterus undergoes contractions similar to the first stages of labor. Some women have reported that they experience a dull pain in their lower abdomen. This may be due to the uterine contractions that occur. Once a woman's fears have been allayed through the explanation that this is a normal response, she learns to enjoy the intensity of those contractions rather than to experience them as painful.

We knew a highly intense woman who was very responsive in the initial phases of the sexual experience; but then, as she moved into the orgasmic response, she would draw back from further stimulation to avoid the lower abdominal discomfort. This had been true of the first eight years of her married life, and was particularly noticeable when she was extremely aroused. As she learned to relax and let herself enjoy the abdominal feelings, her experience shifted from sensing the contractions as pain to experiencing them as intense pleasure. This confirms the close relationship of pain and pleasure in our bodies. Just as a very intense pleasurable sensation can easily shift to being painful, a painful sexual feeling may change to intense pleasure.

While the centers of the orgasmic response are in the vagina and the uterus, the sensations that grow out of this center include the whole body. It is analogous to dropping a rock into a pool of water: the most intense reaction is at the center where the rock is dropped, but the reaction continues to move out in wider and wider circles.

These total body responses occur in both men and women. Many of these begin during the plateau phase and reach their peak with the orgasm. Let us enumerate them. The heart rate increases up to 180 beats per minute. The blood pressure often rises measurably. The breathing intensifies, becoming deeper, faster, and noisier (hyper-ventilation). There may be a great deal of involuntary muscular movement— thrusting of the pelvis and spasticlike contractions of the face, arms, legs, back, or lower abdomen. There is a specific response that occurs in the foot called a carpopedal spasm, which is a straightening out of the foot in a clawlike contraction, where the toes curl downward and away from the body (hyperextension). These are all involuntary responses that cannot be controlled.

Many times the contractions of the face, particularly the mouth, are of great concern to women. Some women like to make love with the lights out, because they do not want to be seen making these "unladylike" responses. In the face, the contracting muscles may give the appearance of a frown, scowl or grimace. The mouth may open involuntarily with a gasping kind of reaction that may also include some involuntary sounds or words. Once a woman can accept the fact that all these reactions and noises are a natural part of the sexual response, it may become easier for her to let herself be responsive with her husband. Many women are surprised to find that rather than turning off their partners, these reactions will usually heighten a man's arousal. We have assigned couples simulated practices of these total body responses. In these experiences, they might lie on a bed side by side, with clothes on or off and practice breathing loudly, letting out gasps and moans, and making spasticlike faces and movements. This usually turns into a hilarious event which reduces inhibition and allows these natural responses in future sexual encounters.

Vaginal vs. Clitoral Orgasm

Much has been written and many misconceptions have been passed on about various kinds of female orgasm. It is important to understand the background of these myths. When Freud was developing his psychoanalytic theory, in some of his writings he defined the woman who had only achieved orgasm through external or manual stimulation as an immature woman—in fact, a little girl. He said that as a woman matured into full womanhood she would obviously have her orgasm in the "normal" adult manner; that is, as a result of vaginal penetration through intercourse. These concepts have been disseminated throughout the western world and used to put pressure on women to experience orgasm during sexual intercourse. The research of Masters and Johnson has proven Freud's theories to be physiologically inaccurate, and thus has diminished the potency of Freud's argument from a psychological perspective.

Masters and Johnson found that there is only one kind of orgasm a woman can experience. All orgasms, regardless of the source of stimulation, are exactly the same in terms of their physical components. When a woman has an orgasm, whether it is the result of her thoughts and fantasies, self-stimulation, breast stimulation, manual stimulation by her partner, or intercourse, exactly the same things happen to her body as were just described. There is the formation of the orgasmic platform, the contractions in the outer third of the vagina, the contractions of the uterus. All the bodily responses occur regardless of the source of stimulation.

Some women who have experienced orgasm from both external and internal stimulation report that they find these two to be different from an emotional level. For them the orgasm while the man is inside feels more fulfilling than an orgasm brought about by external stimulation. This is a matter of personal preference for a woman. There is nothing wrong with striving for an orgasm during intercourse, unless that becomes an inhibiting effort. There is also nothing wrong with being satisfied with having an orgasm as a result of external stimulation. In fact, some women report a more intense response when the penis is not in the vagina.

Many times the pressure on a woman to have her orgasm during intercourse is a serious deterrent to full satisfaction. This pressure may come from a husband who feels he is less of a man because he "can't get her to have an orgasm during intercourse." It is as though his worth is dependent on achieving this goal. This mentality is in contrast to our suggestion that each person be responsible to pursue his or her own sexual desires as long as it is not at the expense of the other.

The Male Orgasmic Response

We have said that during the excitement and plateau phases the man's penis becomes erect, the skin of the scrotum thickens, the right testicle rises and rotates toward the body, and the seminal fluid begins to gather.

Stage 1: As a man nears the end of the plateau phase and moves into the orgasmic phase, he begins to notice that some changes are taking place. He senses that he is getting ready to ejaculate. Most men can identify when this occurs, though they usually do not know what is happening to their bodies. They are approaching the point of no return.

A number of changes take place during this first stage of the orgasmic response. Contractions in the prostate gland occur at eight-tenths of a second intervals. The outlet (sphincter) from the bladder closes off so that none of the seminal fluid will be pushed back into the bladder nor will any urine escape during ejaculation. Most men are aware that immediately before or after an ejaculation it is almost impossible to urinate. This is so because the opening from the bladder has been closed in preparation for the ejaculation. Another change now takes place. The left testicle pulls up toward the body and rotates about one quarter of a turn. (The right testicle elevated during the plateau phase, Figure 7). All of these changes take place in a few seconds. They are warnings to the man that he is about to ejaculate. In addition to these warnings, the seminal fluid gathers near the base of the penis in readiness for expulsion during the contractions that occur in the second stage of the orgasmic phase.

Stage 2: When a man reaches the point of no return, or ejaculatory inevitability, the ejaculation *will* take place. There is nothing he can do to stop it. He can try to stop, the phone can ring or a bucket of water can be dumped on his head, but he *will* ejaculate! The ejaculation consists of contractions along the seminal duct system and the penis, which force the seminal fluid out of the end of the penis. In younger men the force is more intense, causing greater spurts. The force of the ejaculation decreases with age. The contractions of the penis and seminal duct system are eight-tenths of a second apart. Men usually experience five or six such contractions, with the second and third usually the most intense. The seminal fluid which is expelled contains between 250 and 500 million living sperm which will stay active within the vagina up to ten hours after expulsion.

Differences between Male and Female Orgasmic Experiences

If it is the first time in a while that a man has had an ejaculation, he will usually experience greater pleasure and intensity. If he has had another ejaculation a few minutes or a few hours before, it may be less intense. Women often experience the opposite: the more orgasmic experiences they have the greater the pleasure.

We want to emphasize the fact again that when a man reaches

the point of ejaculatory inevitability or the point of no return, there is no way his ejaculation can be interrupted. On the contrary, a woman's orgasmic response can be broken into even after it has begun. This is not possible for a man.

Some of the other differences that should be noted between men's and women's orgasms have to do with where the feelings are centered and where the responses take place. For the man, the climax is very genitally centered. Even though there are total body responses, it is as though all the pleasurable sensations are centered in the genital area, particularly the penis. For the woman, the feelings are more encompassing. Her orgasm begins in the genitals and then moves out in waves to the whole body and back to the genitals. This includes not only the physical response of vaginal and uterine contractions, but all the warm feelings that emanate throughout the woman's total body.

Resolution

For the woman the resolution phase varies significantly, depending on whether or not she has had release. If she has had an orgasmic release—whether this has come about as a result of manual stimulation or intercourse—the body goes into a rather quick period of tension loss. Everything moves in the reverse of what has occurred throughout the excitement plateau and orgasmic phases. The whole genital area is relieved of tension and congestion. That is, the extra blood flows out of the area. The woman may feel a tingling sensation as this happens. The vagina, cervix, and uterus move back into their prestimulated stage and the woman's whole body is relaxed.

If the woman has not had an orgasmic release, the resolution phase takes much longer. She may stay significantly engorged for several hours. Some doctors have reported that the engorgement can last well beyond one or two hours. Many women will experience a significant amount of tension during this extended resolution period. A woman may cry, thus providing the physical and emotional release denied her by the lack of orgasm. Her crying may cause her to turn away from her husband in a kind of shame. This turning away is just the opposite of what both she and her husband need. What they need is warmth, affirmation and reassurance. The human body is designed for sexual release; if arousal takes place without release it is likely to cause discomfort. That discomfort can best be handled through mutual expression of care and affirmation.

If you are a woman who consistently experiences arousal without release it is crucial that you share this with your husband. Let him know what your body feels like so that the two of you can move closer together. There can be some relief even in being reached out to. He needs to know what you need.

What about multiple orgasms? A woman's body is designed so that she can have another orgasm at any point of the resolution phase. It can be five seconds, five minutes, or fifty minutes after the previous orgasm. There is no waiting or rest period necessary before she is physically capable of experiencing another orgasm if the stimulation is continued or renewed. Her body does not need to return to its prestimulated state before it can be responsive again. This is not to say that having more than one orgasm is better, or that sexually "together" women will desire this. The point is that, physically, if she desires it and can allow it, the woman's orgasm can be repeated indefinitely.

For the Man

After orgasmic release, the man returns rather quickly to the prestimulated state. His erection may not decrease completely, but the penis is usually somewhat flaccid and the testicles lower. There is a loss in the tension build-up and in the intensity of the feelings. Some men report that the glans or head of the penis becomes very sensitive to touch after an ejaculation and that because of this they want to quickly disengage from their partner. The man may not have told this to his wife because he feels uncomfortable or embarrassed about it. It is important to know that a significant number of men feel this postejaculation pain. If you experience this discomfort, it is crucial to share this with your partner so that she be sympathetic and understanding, rather than taking your withdrawal as a kind of rejection.

It is rare for a man not to experience orgasm. However, there are some men (especially older men) who do not need an orgasm and who do not feel frustrated without one.

Graphing the Sexual Response

The graph below demonstrates the four phases of the sexual response cycle. Throughout this chapter, we have described what happens to men and to women in each of the four phases of this cycle. On the

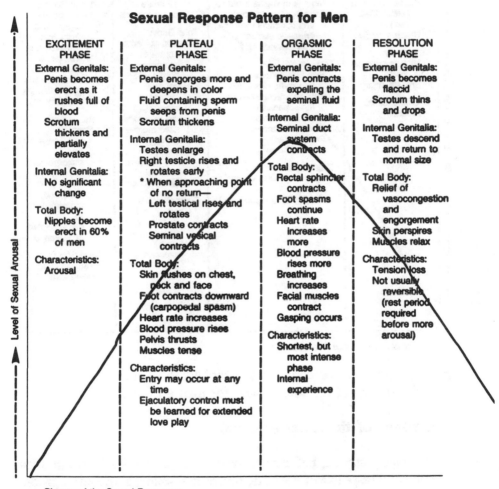

Sexual Response Pattern for Men

EXCITEMENT PHASE

External Genitals:
Penis becomes erect as it rushes full of blood
Scrotum thickens and partially elevates

Internal Genitalia:
No significant change

Total Body:
Nipples become erect in 60% of men

Characteristics:
Arousal

PLATEAU PHASE

External Genitals:
Penis engorges more and deepens in color
Fluid containing sperm seeps from penis
Scrotum thickens

Internal Genitalia:
Testes enlarge
Right testicle rises and rotates early
* When approaching point of no return—
Left testical rises and rotates
Prostate contracts
Seminal vesical contracts

Total Body:
Skin flushes on chest, neck and face
Foot contracts downward (carpopedal spasm)
Heart rate increases
Blood pressure rises
Pelvis thrusts
Muscles tense

Characteristics:
Entry may occur at any time
Ejaculatory control must be learned for extended love play

ORGASMIC PHASE

External Genitals:
Penis contracts expelling the seminal fluid

Internal Genitalia:
Seminal duct system contracts

Total Body:
Rectal sphincter contracts
Foot spasms continue
Heart rate increases more
Blood pressure rises more
Breathing increases
Facial muscles contract
Gasping occurs

Characteristics:
Shortest, but most intense phase
Internal experience

RESOLUTION PHASE

External Genitals:
Penis becomes flaccid
Scrotum thins and drops

Internal Genitalia:
Testes descend and return to normal size

Total Body:
Relief of vasocongestion and engorgement
Skin perspires
Muscles relax

Characteristics:
Tension loss
Not usually reversible (rest period required before more arousal)

Level of Sexual Arousal

Phases of the Sexual Response

Adapted from Masters and Johnson, *Human Sexual Response* (Boston; Brown, Little & Co., 1966).

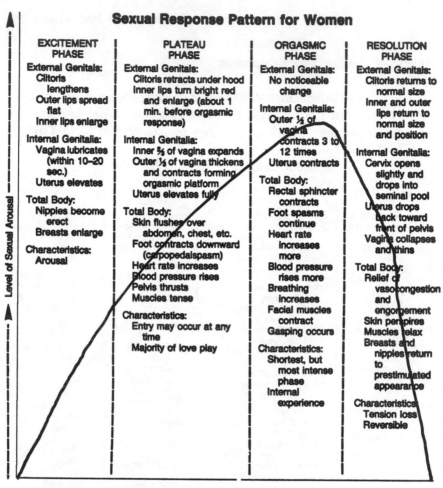

Sexual Response Pattern for Women

EXCITEMENT PHASE	PLATEAU PHASE	ORGASMIC PHASE	RESOLUTION PHASE
External Genitals: Clitoris lengthens Outer lips spread flat Inner lips enlarge	**External Genitals:** Clitoris retracts under hood Inner lips turn bright red and enlarge (about 1 min. before orgasmic response)	**External Genitals:** No noticeable change	**External Genitals:** Clitoris returns to normal size Inner and outer lips return to normal size and position
Internal Genitalia: Vagina lubricates (within 10–20 sec.) Uterus elevates	**Internal Genitalia:** Inner ⅔ of vagina expands Outer ⅓ of vagina thickens and contracts forming orgasmic platform Uterus elevates fully	**Internal Genitalia:** Outer ⅓ of vagina contracts 3 to 12 times Uterus contracts	**Internal Genitalia:** Cervix opens slightly and drops into seminal pool Uterus drops back toward front of pelvis Vagina collapses and thins
Total Body: Nipples become erect Breasts enlarge	**Total Body:** Skin flushes over abdomen, chest, etc. Foot contracts downward (carpopedalspasm) Heart rate increases Blood pressure rises Pelvis thrusts Muscles tense	**Total Body:** Rectal sphincter contracts Foot spasms continue Heart rate increases more Blood pressure rises more Breathing increases Facial muscles contract Gasping occurs	**Total Body:** Relief of vasocongestion and engorgement Skin perspires Muscles relax Breasts and nipples return to prestimulated appearance
Characteristics: Arousal	**Characteristics:** Entry may occur at any time Majority of love play	**Characteristics:** Shortest, but most intense phase Internal experience	**Characteristics:** Tension loss Reversible

Level of Sexual Arousal

Phases of the Sexual Response

next three pages we combine the highlights of the body responses with the graphs of the four phases for men and women.

Variations of the Average Graph

The nicely curved, bell-shaped graph we have used to summarize the physical response of the body to positive sexual stimulation probably would not represent any single individual's sexual response. It is, rather, a general representation of the total population.

The male sexual response pattern might look more like this*:

---

*This and the following three graphs are adapted from Masters and Johnson, *Human Sexual Response*.

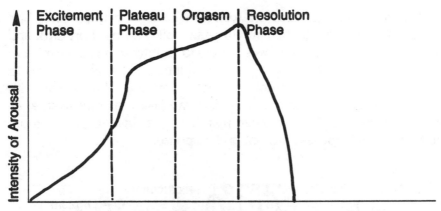

Phases of the Sexual Response—Length of time

There is not much variation in men in the intensity of the response they experience. There is considerable variation, however, in the amount of time each phase might take. Thus the graph might be spread out more or it might be compacted into a briefer experience, but the height of the intensity in each phase would tend not to vary.

This is different for women. Women vary infinitely in both the amount of time each phase might take, and particularly in the intensity of the response.

Using three simplified patterns, Masters and Johnson have represented all the possible ways a woman might respond. These closely represent most of the women we have had graph their experiences.

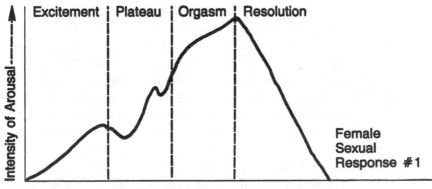

Phases of the Sexual Response—Length of time

This first graph pictures the woman who is quickly aroused. She experiences her arousal building in peaks followed by short dips, and with effective stimulation moves rapidly to an intense orgasmic release. As her build-up is rapid and her release intense, she, also, returns to her prestimulated state (resolution) rather quickly. The woman with this intense response pattern may feel satisfied with one release, as the graph depicts. A few women may have the drive to pursue more love play with repeated arousal and response.

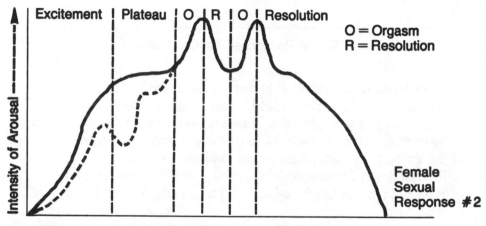

Phases of the Sexual Response—Length of time

The second graph is a description of the woman who enjoys extended love play before she goes after the intense arousal that would trigger an orgasm. Her arousal may intensify upward rather steadily, as the graph demonstrates. One variation may follow the same general pattern, but the woman may experience her upward intensity in waves that have flowing dips, as the dotted-line graph would indicate. As the sexual drive and tension build, whether it is steadily or in waves, this woman experiences an orgasmic release with very little tension loss and she is quickly stimulated to the point of another orgasm. This may happen twice, as the graph shows, or as many times as she desires and her spouse is willing. The orgasms may be pursued in rapid sequence or there may be more let down and relaxation in between orgasms. When she feels satisfied, she allows her body to relax and return to its prestimulated state.

This third graph represents a discouraging dilemma for many women. For them, arousal comes naturally and easily. They hit the peak of the plateau phase, feel intensely aroused, experience waves of arousal but stay pretty much at the same level for an extended period of time. It is as if they cannot quite make it over the hill. Finally, they give up and let down. Because there has been no orgasmic release, resolution takes several hours or more. They often are left feeling unfulfilled and wanting.

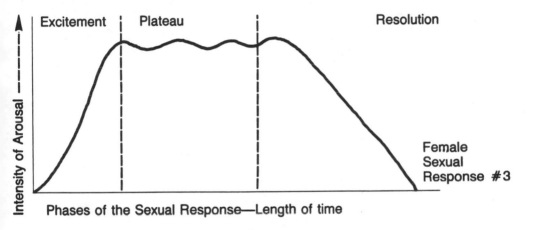

Exercise 6
Graphing Your Sexual Response

Using the graphs on pages 97 and 98 that summarize the primary body responses during the four phases of the sexual experience and the variations just described, we would encourage you to graph your own sexual response pattern. You may choose the graph closest to your experience and then vary the graph line according to your individual situation. After drawing your graph, fill in your bodily responses in as much detail as is available to you.

If you are a person with a sexual problem such as lack of arousal, difficulties with erections, or others, identify at what point your response or arousal stops. What are you aware of happening at that point? What are your thoughts or feelings? What is going on between you and your spouse? What do you sense needs to be different to allow your response to accelerate rather than stop?

We would hope that both you and your spouse would complete your graphs individually. Then share them with each other. Read each other's and have the other person explain his or hers to you. When you are the listener, work hard at sensing what the other experiences rather than defending yourself or describing what you experience. When you are the one relating what you feel, concentrate diligently on talking about your feelings and not blaming your spouse for your feelings. This sharing experience is an important step to understanding each other in a way that can bring enhancement to your sexual experience.

9

Getting Interested

You are pushing your grocery cart down the pet food aisle when you become aware that the song playing on the music system is making you feel bouncy.

You lie down in the warm sand at the beach, and the warmth seems to radiate up through your body. You feel good all over.

As you pay for lunch you see the picture of your spouse in your wallet. You get that yummy feeling inside that makes you want to be with him or her. Desire is being stirred.

How does desire for sexual involvement get started for you? There can be many sources of sexual arousal in your world. You may or may not be aware of responding to these. You might not even notice what stimulates your sexual interest.

Many kinds of outside stimuli may get you in touch with your body. For some people such stimulation includes listening to certain kinds of music, reading a sexual or intimate book, watching a movie or television, being in a setting that feels romantic, or even seeing someone who may be a friend or a stranger.

Sensuous input may also come from within. There may be no particular event or setting that stimulates the sexual desire. Instead, your sexual awareness may grow out of a relaxing, body-oriented time. You might be exercising, bathing or showering, relaxing in the sun, or oiling

103

your body. When "getting interested" is not a problem, sexual desire may be triggered spontaneously by natural internal sexual drives.

Spending time with your spouse is likely to get you interested sexually. This is particularly true if you find the sexual experience fulfilling and free of anxiety. We find that working together or playing together tends to draw us in that direction. This is one of the advantages of writing a book together. As we become one emotionally and mentally, the physical response is automatic. This is particularly true if the times together are not burdened with stress or high expectations. Therefore, we recommend that all couples plan regular times to be together. These experiences must be free of demands such as expectations for sexual intercourse, obligations regarding children, pressures from work, and distractions by other external involvements. Come together without restrictions and without preconceived ideas, so that you can create something special and unique for your time together.

Having sexual energy available to you is necessary for sexual desire. Sexual desire is different from sexual arousal. Arousal is your body's response to stimulation. The four physical phases of sexual response as described in Chapter 8 have to do with sexual arousal. This is a process of change that occurs in the body.

On the other hand, sexual desire is a manifestation of our sexual drive or libido. Some use this sexual energy for creative production such as establishing a new business, being submerged in musical achievement, focusing energy on sports, or other absorbing involvements. When creativity requires a great deal of energy, the person will have little sexual drive left. Therefore, this person will feel less desire for sexual involvement. This lack of desire can be helpful for singles whose moral standards do not permit sexual involvement, but it can be detrimental to a marriage relationship. Stress is likely to develop when one spouse is burning up energy in nonsexual pursuits and the other wants more sexual involvement.

In addition to being used up for creative production, the sexual drive may be burned up by emotional stress such as anxiety, depression, conflict or other disturbances. A person suffering from this sort of stress may have little or no sexual desire.

Since sexual desire is an outgrowth of sexual drive or the energy available in the body, nutrition, exercise, sleep, and hormonal cycles affect the energy available for sexual involvement. Thus, making certain that your body is well nourished, properly exercised, and adequately rested should enhance your sexual desire.

What if you're not particularly aware of getting interested sexually? Your sexual energy is not accessible to you. Chapter 21 addresses problems with sexual desire. If you have a chronic lack of interest—more than just a temporary reaction to your life being too full and not having enough space—refer to that section.

For those who live complicated, busy lives, there may never be a natural time to feel sexual. To correct this problem, you must start by clearing out distractions. Begin the process by making a decision about the television. Many people have the TV on most of the time when they are home together. It is a constant distraction. You may need to turn it off and spend some time alone together.

Outside commitments may interfere. Many of us are busy because of good Christian involvements. Yet, if those commitments crowd our lives so much that we have no relaxed block of time to spend together as a couple, perhaps those involvements are not advantageous. Whether you are a Young Life leader, a pastor, or an involved lay person, your time commitments to Christian organizations cannot replace your time commitment to your marriage. Marriage is a God-ordained institution that does not function effectively when it is not given enough time or priority. Just as a car does not continue to perform at a maximum level if it is not serviced routinely, a relationship cannot maintain its maximum effectiveness if it is not given regular focused attention.

Children can be a distraction. Mothers with preschool children frequently find that their sexual desire has lessened considerably. Their energy is being burned up. Any mother with a toddler and an infant will need to have some relief from the responsibility of caring for the needs of two almost totally dependent children. Even a mother with just one child in either of these age groups will probably feel the need for some time in which she is free of demands. A child with health problems or a behavioral disruption can cause so much stress for the parents that they find themselves having little sexual interest in each other. Very often, getting away from the stressful situation for several days will help the couple revive their physical desires.

In addition to clearing out distractions and, in that process, allowing opportunity for one's feelings of desire to surface, it is important to spend some time identifying what works for you. Think back on your life together. When have you felt the most interested in your sexual relationship? Where were you? What kind of setting was it? What was going on in your life at that time? Was it in response to something you did for or with your spouse, or something he or she did for or with you?

Sometimes there may be a specific action you need from your spouse. For example, one man has a problem with lack of desire. If he and his wife ever do get involved sexually, he has no problem with arousal (getting and maintaining an erection), and he has learned to control ejaculation. But he rarely thinks about sex, and he experiences his wife's suggestions as demands. Thus, they might have intercourse every two or three months. Yet he was very aware of his sexual desire before marriage when sexual intercourse was ruled out because of their Christian standards. Then there was no demand, so there was no anxiety to burn up his sexual energy.

As this man explored his problem, he remembered that his first panic hit when his bride took off her panties on the wedding night. The female genitalia were an unknown, and they represented a demand for performance. He was sure he could not measure up. Thus his anxiety blocked his desire. It would have been helpful to him if his wife had left her panties on until he could cope with the problem, but he did not feel comfortable communicating this to her. His wife would have been willing to cooperate with him had he shared his need.

Think about your own situation. Is there something, however small, that would reduce your anxiety and increase your desire to be together with your spouse in a sexual experience? Communicate this with your husband or wife. Set aside a special time for this sharing—a time each of you knows is designated for talking about your sexual activity. The individual with the need should assume the responsibility for initiating such a talk time.

When couples work to identify what each of them needs in order to feel sexual desire, usually each person knows his or her individual needs, but has not communicated these to the spouse. Often they think, *If I am that blunt about what I would like, it'll take all the fun, spontaneity, and mystery out of it.* There is the idea, particularly among women, that the man should intuitively know what the woman needs. This is somehow a sign of his love. "If I tell him that his bringing me a gift, a flower, or something special turns me on, then I don't think it will work anymore," one woman reported. The fact that *she knew* that *he knew* what she wanted would destroy her response to his action.

We meet separately to talk with wives and then husbands at our weekend seminars for couples. The wives usually have messages they would like us to tell the husbands about what would make their sexual experience more positive. This occurs at the end of a twelve-hour time which has provided regular, structured communication experiences focused on enhancing the couple's sexual relationship. Some women seem to think that it is okay if their husbands are informed about what they desire, but the messages cannot come directly from the wives. Such openness evokes fear of destroying "the mystery" or "the romance." It is ironic that these are usually the relationships in which sex has little or no romantic quality or spark to it.

Keeping secrets from your spouse about what you desire is a *barrier* to sexual fulfillment, not an asset. Let's destroy the "mystery." Humans are unique individuals with emotions that vary greatly from one sexual experience to another—and this fact provides the possibility of continually making new discoveries. The more you know about yourself and about what you desire, and the more you communicate those wishes to your partner without placing demands on him or her, the more enhancement you can expect.

Identify it, communicate it, then practice it. Above all, if you're the one with the need, *you* take responsibility for getting that need met. When it's something you can provide for yourself, do that. If it's something you need from your partner, work it out with him or her so that it is not experienced as a demand. For your need *not* to be received as a demand, it must be clearly communicated as *your* need and not something inadequate about your *spouse*.

The concept of taking responsibility for oneself is *central* to sexual enhancement and *critical* for reversing sexual problems. We will refer to this concept throughout the book, so this is a good place to explain it.

Most Christians have come to marriage with the idea that their responsibility as Christian partners is to *please* the other. Somehow the biblical concepts of love, mutual submission and giving of ourselves have all taken on the meaning of doing the things that will make the other person happy or pleased. There is nothing wrong with our being pleasing to our spouse and bringing him or her happiness. In fact, that is likely to be the *result* when we are loving, giving, and mutually submitting. However, when our goal (rather than the result) is to please and make the other person happy, we are likely to be anxious. This anxiety will cause stress instead of pleasure and happiness.

Because of this tendency to translate "being loving" into "pleasing," and thereby causing anxiety and stress in relationships, we advocate the idea of taking responsibility for your own sexual needs. The sexual response is something that happens in your body. It is personal and loaded with emotions. Each individual differs from every other individual, and each individual differs from one experience to another. You can't count on all women wanting it "this way" or men "always wanting . . . ," or even this particular woman or man responding to the same thing every time. Because of the beautiful and complicated creation you are, there is no way your partner can consistently guess what would please you. However, *you* usually know what you like, so you should take the responsibility to go after that desire.

When a spot on your back itches, you have to tell someone exactly where it itches and how you'd like to have it scratched. There is no way someone else can automatically know exactly where you itch and scratch it just right. Similarly, no one can read your mind to know exactly what will give you the most pleasure sexually at *this* time, in *this* experience.

However, there are some general things you and your partner *can* learn about each other's likes and dislikes, that you can automatically incorporate into your love-making—just as you may know that one likes to be scratched with fingernails while the other prefers fingertips. Taking responsibility for your own pleasure includes honoring your partner's preferences.

This leads to a second point. The first is that each person in the relationship is to take responsibility for identifying, communicating and pursuing his or her own sexual desires and needs. The second is that each partner is responsible to communicate and redirect when the other is doing something violating or negative. This insures that going after your own pleasure will not take place at the expense of your lover. Chapter 12 gives suggestions for nonthreatening ways to redirect your partner.

To summarize this concept of responsibility, you and your partner will be most relaxed together in your love-making if each one pursues the pleasures that give him or her the most enjoyment *so long as* you know these will not be negative experiences for your partner.

Sexual desire or interest is not something someone else can provide for you. It is something already *in* you by creation that you have to *allow* to surface. There may be conditions, as we have discussed, that are necessary for that to happen. Your partner must be cooperative with those, but not responsible for them. Desire is not something to be added on or gained. You don't have to *learn* how to desire. If you don't freely and spontaneously have sexual interest, there is some distraction, anxiety or barrier blocking its free expression in you. You need to uncover these to get to the desire that is in you.

_____10

Having Fun

Sometimes I just want to cuddle—but don't particularly want to make love. Doing this gets my husband aroused—then he wants to make love. What can we do to work this out?

When a couple is dating and getting to know one another they usually play and touch, tease and laugh together. Once married this physical playfulness usually diminishes. We get in the habit of rushing through all the fun and getting down to "real" sex. The cuddling and affection are lost. The playfulness is not fulfilling but is designed to get somewhere. We even often call it "foreplay," as if it is not part of the whole experience. When we can freely and creatively enjoy one another without demand or expectation, our loving takes on a new dimension.

Affection without Expectation

We were giving a seminar at an evangelical church in our community. The message on the surveys from a number of the women were typical of what we regularly hear from women. "How can we have fun together, be affectionate and caring, without sexual intercourse?" "It seems the

111

only interest my husband has in me is to have (get) his sexual goodies. I wish we could take more time to talk and be affectionate."

It seems that men in our culture have been conditioned to sexual release rather than to total body pleasure and emotional intimacy. After some time of living with a husband who is focused only on the physical dimension of the sexual experience, a woman feels used and devalued.

Boys in our American culture learn two things that prepare them to be men who seek fast physical release. The first is that boys are *not* to be tender and emotional. Recently at a swim meet we observed a father with his four-year-old son. This father was affectionate and used expressions like "honey" in addressing his son. The woman sitting next to us mentioned how unusual and beautiful it was to see a father and son interacting with the tenderness one would expect of a mother and daughter. This father is a psychologist, which may contribute to his ability to break out of the traditional role interaction. Or it may be that as a boy he experienced the same emotional tenderness from his father. Whatever the case, boys need more modeling of tenderness from fathers and more encouragement of the expression of feelings from all the significant adults in their world if they are to grow up to be men who can relax and enjoy sexual pleasure and emotional intimacy.

The second message that affects boys is this: the sooner you reach your goal the better you are. This is true of most sports that have, until recently, been limited to boys. In addition, most teaching or modeling of success in business has reflected this attitude. *The focus has not been on enjoyment of the moment, but rather on reaching the goal quickly.*

Girls have generally been given more opportunity for sensuous enjoyment through music, ballet, and other girl-dominated extracurricular activities. In these activities the focus is on the good feeling of the movement and the control and expressiveness of the body. As we have observed in our own children, this is very different from the challenge of getting the ball into the goal area or running to home base with one hit.

Experiencing affection without intercourse is an essential part of marriage. As we mentioned in the theological discussion in Chapter 3, this dimension of our humanness, our potential for relationship, sets us apart from the rest of the animal world. We are made in

God's image. It is the way in which our sexuality is in the image of God.

Cuddling and holding and caressing without expecting or fearing that it will lead to intercourse every time are essential to the well-rounded sexual relationship. If this possibility is not present, the one needing to cuddle will draw back from any affection for fear that it will lead to intercourse. Traditionally it has been the woman who draws back from touch because she is not free to go with what she feels. Often the man pushes for more because he expects resistance from the woman. When both partners are free to let the play go in the direction they mutually desire, knowing that the hesitant one will not be violated, cuddling without demand becomes natural. On occasion, the man or the woman may be left aroused but unfulfilled, but as long as that does not become the usual pattern it need not be a problem.

Freedom and Creativity

A sense of freedom and a desire to be creative are necessary elements in order for a couple to play and have fun together. But a person will not experience freedom and creativity in the relationship if he or she encounters demands. These may be internal demands or demands the spouse imposes. In either case, if the person is concerned about doing it the right way (pleasing one's partner), with "turning on" the other person, or with having a sexual response, he or she is not likely to have much free, enjoyable sexual play.

If either or both of you are aware of these pressures or demands, you need to discuss and deal with them before you attempt to add fun and creativity to your sexual experience. (You will find suggestions for such discussions in various chapters of this book. For example, if you are experiencing demands in the area of initiation, refer to Chapter 11 for help in overcoming those demands.)

How might you as a couple bring about freedom and creativity in your sexual relationship? Even if you are not experiencing any particular demands or stress, your sexual times may lack spontaneity. They may have become routine. Maybe you tend to get together at the same time and in the same place, and you both behave in much the same way. The script is written before the first kiss.

When things have become "humdrum" you need to start with both of you *recognizing* the *need* to change. The next step would be *talking together* about how each of you would like to change. This conversation will be more productive if you talk about yourself, rather than the changes you desire in your spouse. If you start outlining desired changes for the other person you inhibit freedom rather than encouraging it.

It is important, too, that the discussion about changes in your sexual relationship occur away from the bedroom. If you read this section and get the idea you'd like to start talking with your spouse about enhancing your sexual times, it would be best to plan a special time to do this. If you mention what you have read the next time you crawl into bed to make love, it will probably cause a hassle and end that love-making attempt. Your ideas will be much less threatening if you say, "I've been reading a book about sexual enhancement and have some ideas that sound neat and fun for us. I'd love to take you out to tell you about my thoughts and hear your ideas."

Once the two of you agree that you'd like to have more playful fun together sexually, then the door is wide open for ways to make it happen.

A good place to begin is to change the location and the setting or atmosphere of your sexual encounter. The location is the room or area of the house (or the place outside the house) where you get together sexually. The setting or atmosphere involves what you do to or with the location. For example, you can vary the lighting; you can reverse your position in the bed, putting your feet at the "head" end; you can put a comforter on the floor or by the fireplace, instead of having your sexual experience on the bed.

It will add spark to your relationship if you and your spouse take turns choosing the place and creating the atmosphere. This idea provides newness and an element of surprise. (The next chapter provides additional suggestions.)

Sometimes it takes some struggling together to come up with alternate locations and provide the privacy both of you need. One couple, Marilee and Bob, had six children ranging from two to seventeen years of age. The little ones awakened early in the morning, while the teenagers stayed up later than their parents at night. Marilee and Bob found that they were rarely getting together sexually. And when they did, they were under pressure to hurry in the morning or be quiet in the evening. Without a conscious awareness of it, they had developed a routine that took about three minutes. It was entirely predictable from start to finish. Sexual intrigue had left their relationship soon after their second child was born sixteen years before.

Finding new locations and creating new atmosphere took some problem-solving creativity. They organized Marilee's craft and sewing room so that they could add a hide-a-bed and keep the room tidy. This provided an alternate location to the bedroom. The teenagers were enlisted as part of the plan. Marilee and Bob told them that mom and dad needed some "special nights together." From the little smiles on the kids' faces, you could tell they had caught on. There's an example of a great job of modeling by parents!

The plan they worked out was as follows: After nine o'clock two nights a week, the teenagers were limited to the family room, the kitchen and their own bedrooms. In exchange for some favors, they were asked to be responsible to get up with the younger children on Saturday mornings. This gave Bob and Marilee three blocks of time each week free of interruption, thus assuring privacy. They now had two possible locations which alleviated the need to be quiet, and provided the framework they needed to experience some new life sexually. It worked!

When there are no children or other people in the home twenty-four hours a day, any location in the house that is comfortable, free of distraction, and private is an option for creating a new setting. Your van, pick-up camper, or private backyard are other alternatives.

The atmosphere can be varied rather easily. This can be done with lighting. The variations might include: no light, candlelight, dim light, bright light. You might find the visual enjoyment of each other's bodies is enhanced by varying the placement of a candle or lamp. The sheets, blankets, or comforters can be varied. Some couples enjoy the smell of incense burning. Others enjoy the use of perfumes or colognes. Others may prefer the smell of a natural, freshly bathed body.

In addition to having fun experimenting with the setting for playing together, you can enjoy many other areas of experimentation. Clothing can be varied. If you have tended to start fondling each other with night clothes on, crawl into bed some night and let your spouse discover you in the nude. On the other hand, if you are a couple who are in the nude during most of your physical touching time or getting-ready time, you may find it much more arousing to use clothes to add new intrigue. Try a "suggestive" nightgown or nightshirt, a T-shirt, bra and panties, briefs, or a "fig leaf." When nudity is a threat to one or both of you, covering can be used in a fun, playful way to distract from the blatant exposure that triggers anxiety.

You can have fun with using different ways of covering the body to avoid being threatening. It's not necessary to make an issue of trying to overcome an inhibition about nudity. Instead, you can work with it; you can be creative and have fun with it; you can distract from it so that it doesn't get in the way. One couple worked around the wife's inhibitions by developing fun ways to circumvent the problem. For example, she might wear something that covered her and yet was sexy, such as a sheer nightgown. Another idea is to tie scarves around the appropriate places. Try anything—the more fun and the sillier the better—that will help you get past a problem with nudity. Then, if you do want to learn to be more comfortable with your own and your partner's nudity, you can try some of the exercises in Chapter 5. That is work, however, not fun and games. The work you put into the exercises will lead to more freedom with each other, but is not a creative experience in itself. Creativity may follow when you gain added freedom.

Nudity can be enjoyed in many ways. One young couple really enjoyed playing in the nude—playful pinching, poking and caressing—but the man panicked if they were together in the nude to have sexual intercourse. We encouraged them to engage in nude play that involved more and more total body involvement without any expectation for intercourse. We had them go home and roll together in the nude, embracing and interlocking their bodies. They also learned to make some use of coverings that they could have fun with. And that allowed him to be more comfortable. Nude swimming in the privacy of one's backyard pool is enjoyed by many couples. There are limitless possibilities.

Other ways to have fun and to play together with or without leading to sexual intercourse include the *teases that enhance*. It's critical that the teases do not carry a jab or put-down, or pick on a sensitive issue. Rather, the tease has to be for the fun of it, and must not carry a hidden loaded message.

Resisting in a fun way is a tease that can enhance. This is the message that says, "Come on and try to get me," or "See if I'm available," or just pulling away slightly. This can be particularly evocative when used by the person who has tended to be the aggressor. It is not suggested for the person who has been the resister in the relationship, since it might be taken seriously.

The man needs to be as active as the woman in creating new ways to tease and in preparing enjoyable surprises. One man came leaping out of his bathroom without clothing on. He leaped over the bed on which his wife was lying, and then asked his wife to guess what Bible verse he was acting out. The verse was, "Listen! My lover! Look! Here he comes, leaping across the mountains, bounding over the hills. My lover is like a gazelle . . ." (Song of Sol. 2:8, 9). They've had fun with that ever since.

Whatever variation you use—however crazy it might seem—if it creates fun and laughter and does not have to lead to intercourse, you have a good start on keeping alive your total sexual expression with each other.

___11

Initiating

My husband desires me to initiate sex but I just feel so self-conscious and awkward—it just seems like *he* should initiate.

Who Initiates? Breaking Down Stereotypes of Male-Female Roles

It is not uncommon for a woman counselee to be frustrated, crying, and complaining that nothing is happening sexually between herself and her husband. As we gather data and put together a total picture, what emerges is rather interesting. After she describes her husband's excessive involvement in his career and lack of sexual approach to her, we will usually ask, "What keeps you from approaching him sexually, since you're the one wanting it and he apparently doesn't have the drive?" The response is often a blank look or a stumbling for words. Finally the answer comes: "I just never thought of it." She may have given all sorts of subtle hints and become upset because he did not respond. The husband usually didn't even catch on that his wife desired sex. Perhaps she mentioned that she'd like to go to bed, or she wore a special nightgown, or she was waiting up for him when he came home late at night. But she never let him know the *real* meaning of these symbolic, subtle expressions of her sexual desire.

The stereotype is that the man *is* and *should be* the sexually aggressive initiator. The woman is to use somewhat manipulative tactics to get him to approach her. For some couples this works. But there are many marriages for which these expectations are disruptive.

Here again you may need to have a frank discussion with your spouse in which you examine the initiation pattern in your sexual relationship. What percentage of the time do you see yourself initiating, and what percentage do you see your spouse initiating? How does your husband or wife see that? Often there are discrepancies in how each partner answers the question. The husband may see himself as initiating 90 percent of the time; whereas the wife may feel that each one initiates 50 percent of the time. If you discover that your views are quite different, don't try to settle whose view is accurate. Each person's experience and perceptions are his or her own; therefore, the way *each* of you feels is accurate. What is important is to try to "get under the other person's skin" to discover the other's view. Maybe the differences lie in the way each of you defines initiation. For example, the "90 percent" husband may be missing many of his wife's cues, so that he doesn't realize how often she has attempted to initiate a sexual encounter without any response from him.

After you've each discovered how you would define the frequency of your initiation pattern, talk about your feelings concerning that pattern. Is it working for the two of you? How much stress or anxiety does each of you experience around the issue of getting sexual times started? Work through the exercise described later in this chapter.

Approach-Avoidance Games

One typical problematic initiation pattern that develops is the approach-avoidance game. One person sees it as his or her responsibility to get sexual activity going, so he makes frequent approaches to the other—using sexual overtures, dropping hints, or making direct suggestions. He feels as if he has to mention it eight times if it's going to happen once. So he is anxiously suggesting sex far more often than he really wants it. His wife would like him not to bother her, and feels that she never even has an opportunity to suggest getting together sexually because he wants it all the time. She feels bombarded and unable to get in touch with her desire. So she resists or avoids his approaches. You can see how the pattern perpetuates itself. The more she avoids, the more anxious he becomes, so the more he makes advances. This increases her feeling that demands are being placed on her which don't allow room for her desire to build; and so the pattern continues.

This approach-avoidance pattern may have developed as a result of varying levels of sexual drive, interest, or desire for frequency. It may be that one of you has an intense sexual drive, but after a sexual time with your spouse, you have a sense of release and satisfaction for quite some time. Your partner may be the opposite. The release may not be as complete, so there is more ongoing desire, or a satisfying experience may serve to heighten your interest.

You may be a young mother with several preschoolers. Most of the time you are tired. Sexual encounters sound like a good idea, but by the time of day when you're available for such activity you feel exhausted. Therefore, your interest rarely has an opportunity to be expressed. Your husband is probably young and full of sexual energy and can't understand what's wrong with you. This very real difference in sexual interest may lead to an approach-avoidance pattern if the two of you do not talk about the dilemma and plan ways for you to be rested and available.

You may be a 35-year-old businessman or professional at the peak of establishing your career and wealth. Your sexual drive is so used in pursuit of your vocation that your frequency of desire for sexual activity has decreased significantly. In contrast, your wife finally has time and money for herself, and so her frequency of desire has increased. The children are in school. She has time to bathe leisurely, manicure her nails, and play tennis; she is much more in tune with her body. You may experience her "constant" state of readiness for sexual encounters as a demand that makes you feel inadequate.

You walk into the house exhausted. You're late for dinner. Your mind is still going a mile a minute, thinking about the decisions of the day. She is beautiful, well-rested, and in her negligee. The children are in bed. She has a beautiful candlelight dinner set up for the two of you. Instead of feeling appreciative, your mind goes, "Oh, no, not again. I'm just not up to it tonight." But you feel guilty for thinking that, and you try to express appreciation for her caring intention.

After many such events, you experience more and more tension about the demand you feel being placed upon you. You either start coming home later or you "blow up" over the smallest conflicts with your wife. And so another form of approach-avoidance has developed. Talking about your feelings at a time away from the event is the only way to break the pattern.

There are many other versions of this same dilemma. If you have fallen into such a problem, what is your version? How can you break into the situation? You need to take decisive action.

Exercise 7
Resolving Initiation Problems

Here are steps you can take to resolve an initiation problem:

1. Have a casual time together in which you decide you both want to talk about your sexual initiation pattern. If one of you is the initiator in suggesting that there is a problem, do not blame your spouse for it! Rather, *own the problem* yourself. This means that you use "I" statements rather than "you" statements. You say, "I've been desiring intercourse more frequently," not, "You never seem interested in intercourse any more." Tell how the situation affects you and what you bring to the situation, rather than what your partner is doing wrong. "I end up being afraid to take the lead because I don't want to be rejected again." Or, "I don't even kiss you because I'm afraid you'll want more."

2. Plan a time to work on the difficulty. During that planned time, follow the next steps:

a. Each of you spend at least an hour alone writing out how you experience the dilemma. What do you see happening between the two of you? How do you participate in this problem—what is your role in perpetuating the difficulty? What feelings does the entire experience trigger for you?

b. Plan a two-to-three-hour block of time for the two of you to be together when you won't be distracted or interrupted—preferably when you are both at your best, and not when either of you is exhausted. A breakfast or lunch date usually works best—either having a picnic, going to a restaurant, or staying at home without children and with the telephone off the hook.

c. During the allotted time, start by reading each other's writings from Step a. In reading, focus on what the other person is saying about himself or herself. Try to really get "under the other person's skin" and feel how he or she experiences the difficulty. This may take concentration. The more natural response is to see what the other is saying about you, and then to become defensive or start arguing or attacking him. The latter reaction will stifle progress.

d. Apply active listening skills (see Chap. 12) to feed back to your partner what you have understood about him or her from the writing. Work hard on reflecting how you sense your partner experiences the sexual initiation situation.

e. Partner, clarify and expand on what your spouse has learned from your writing, e.g., "Yes, and another way I sense that is . . ."; or "I know that's what I said, but when I hear you say it I realize what I really meant was . . ."; or "If that's what I said, it isn't what I meant; let me try again."

f. Repeat steps d and e, reversing roles.

g. Agree on the need for change.

h. Make a plan that clearly reverses the old pattern. That is, the "approacher" will not make sexual suggestions, just be affirming. The avoider will be responsible to initiate an agreed-on number of sexual encounters in a designated time frame.

Examples of Plans to Reverse Initiation Patterns

1. Problem: Man always initiates.
After discussing what the situation feels like for each of you and deciding on the need for change, you might make a plan similar to this:

a) Set a time span (for example, one week or slightly longer than your usual time lapse between love-making events).

b) Rules for this time span:

For husband: Back way off—no sexual approach, not even a hint—don't bring up the topic. Be confirming of wife—warm, loving, but make no sexual advances.

For wife: Be responsible to initiate intercourse once during this period of time. Be free to initiate by any method that is possible for you. If you are wanting to initiate but having a particular difficulty, you may bring up the topic and discuss your feelings and anything that might be helpful to you.

c) At the end of the time span, set aside a minimum of two hours to talk about what happened or didn't happen, and what it felt like. If the time span elapsed and the wife didn't initiate, discuss a plan for the next time span. Or perhaps she initiated but he didn't catch on. Maybe she sat down close to him while he was watching TV. She snuggled up to him and rubbed his neck in an attempt to get something started, but he just kept on watching TV. They need to discuss what sort of behavior each one perceives as sexual initiation.

2. Problem: Fatigue (for one or both of you)

Before you get into a plan for breaking an old habit, start by defining how each of you sees the problem. Look at your reasons for fatigue (step a of Problem-solving). Are you a mother of little children, getting up at night with a baby? Are you a husband who arrives home late and must get up earlier for work or other responsibilities? Are you depressed? Or is fatigue your way to escape involvement? If the cause is one of the last two (depression or escape), you need some work with a therapist or counselor. If it's a life style problem, then the following plan can be helpful:

a) Agree that time together each week or every other week is a priority. This together time must occur when neither of you is tired.

b) Schedule the specific time: an evening, two hours at lunchtime, two or three hours in the morning, a weekend or day away every now and then.

c) Make sure this time is free of interruption—telephone off the hook, kids at friend's house or down for the night, the two of you away at a motel, or whatever it takes.

d) Plan for adequate rest on a regular basis—have a babysitter come in one hour a day so the wife can nap; the husband may cut down on commitments, and so on.

Once both partners are free to express sexual desires when they feel them, most couples want to enjoy mutual and spontaneous initiation. Mutuality means that both feel equal freedom and responsibility to initiate when the desire is there. It can also mean that the desire grows mutually out of contact with each other. That is, instead of sexual desire starting in one person and that person approaching the other, the feelings grow spontaneously between two people. This may happen while working together, playing together, or just being together.

When the old, demanding pattern is broken so that each of you is free of the negative feelings, the good feelings flow. However, be alert to difficulties creeping in. Plan for correction before negative patterns are formed again. Obviously the most relaxed style is the ability to feel free with your own sexual desires and to be accepting of your partner's. That way either one can express desires as they are felt, without causing conflict.

When "When" Is a Source of Difficulty

The same flexibility and spontaneity that is the goal for "who" initiates is also ideal for "when" sexual encounters are initiated. This is most likely to be possible if neither of you holds rigid stereotypes of when it is appropriate to enjoy love-making. It may be that you always associated sexual activity with going to bed at night. Once the lights have been turned out and you have both crawled under the covers, you will roll over to your spouse and start fondling with the intention of proceeding to intercourse. That's the only time you ever envision as a love-making time. This clearly does not allow for flexibility and spontaneity.

If you are in a rut, you will need to make clear plans to open the door to sexual encounter at other times of the day. Flexibility doesn't usually just happen by recognizing the need or the desire for it. Start by talking about where you learned your limited concepts about when sexual activity should occur. Then plan some times together that are different than your usual times. It's best if planned times are designed primarily for sexual pleasure, with the option of intercourse if that is desired by both.

Little children in the home may limit flexibility. Plan around their schedules, or find ways to be free of them periodically. Maybe you can get away from home, or have the children cared for out of the house. It will be more difficult to allow spontaneous initiation at any time you desire it if you have young children or anyone else present in the house.

There are other ways in which the "when" of initiation can cause tension. Timing can sometimes be used to sabotage the relationship. This usually happens when anger has built up in the relationship or when there is anxiety about performing sexually. The way timing manifests itself varies. It may be that the woman is most alert and responsive in the morning, but the man always initiates sex at night when she is tired. Or he has his fullest erections and is most sure of his responsiveness in the morning, but she says she's just not a morning person, and then complains when he's not responsive in the evening. One partner may insist that sex always has to occur before a certain time.

Whatever the reason, they never seem to be able to get on the same wavelength. We will talk about other forms of sabotage in Chapter 28.

To reverse problems with timing, try scheduling times agreeable to both partners. This may involve compromise from both. Compromise might involve alternating with each other's preferred time. Or it may be that neither time is used, and several new, mutually agreeable times are selected. Again, it is important to make sure that your planned time together will be free of interruptions and pressures. The time period should be long enough so that neither of you feels rushed at either end of the experience together. The goal of the time together must be enjoyment and pleasure, without demands for response or intercourse. Allow each sexual experience to be what it will be!

Where—Creativity with Sensitivity

Finding new and fun places to enjoy each other's bodies can give new spark to a rather "ho-hum" sexual relationship. This is one of the ways to create an ever-changing mood which allows each experience to be a new one. The variety in itself is a delight.

There are really only two limits on where you might plan a sexual nest. One is that the place chosen provides the privacy needed by both of you. For example, your backyard might be an option for you, but would make your spouse feel very uncomfortable. If it's not comfortable for both, then it's not a possible place. However, if you're the one who has always been hesitant about feeling private in the backyard, and you decide you'd like to push yourself a bit, that's fine.

The second limit is that your choice of a place must respect other people. You may be totally uninhibited but your neighbors need to be protected from your sexual activities. They may not appreciate being unwilling spectators.

It can be fun to plan a new place. You can plan together or surprise each other. In all situations remember to be sensitive to each other's need for privacy. A lock on the door of the chosen room usually relieves anxiety about being interrupted. Taking the telephone off the hook prevents fear of intrusion. Closing windows, doors, and drapes can encourage freedom from noises. A secluded yard or area seems to be necessary for outdoor play. Once the privacy needs have been cared for, let your minds run free. The swimming pool at night has been a fun variation for some. A new room in the house, a different bed, a love nest in the family room or living room are all options. Or you may want to be so different as to take your pick-up camper to the grocery store parking lot!

How—Symbolic Messages and Direct Invitations

Different people initiate sexual activity in different ways. Some individuals tend to express themselves with direct physical activity. This may be a combination of kissing, fondling, hugging, caressing, or rubbing bodies together. For these people, their bodies express their desires more easily than words.

Others are direct with verbal messages of initiation. "I'm really feeling turned on. Let's go to bed and make love," for example.

Then there are others who are much more subtle and indirect in their initiation. In our culture this has tended to be true of women more than of men. However, we are finding that the trend is changing, and women are becoming more direct. For some men, a woman's increased directness stimulates a tendency toward hesitancy and timidity.

If you are a subtle initiator, it is important that you take responsibility to make certain your desires are clearly communicated to your spouse.

As long as both spouses are clear about the message being communicated, subtle, symbolic methods of initiation can add spark and intrigue. It may be that you say pet phrases, fix a love nest, come to bed in the nude, prepare a romantic dinner for the two of you, light the fireplace, bring flowers; or, as you get totally free with each other, you may have fun with more ridiculous messages. One man appeared in the bedroom with a bow tied around his penis. Another man took everything off except his white shirt and tie and came in carrying his briefcase and a rose. One woman pasted hearts over the appropriate spots on her body. It's fun to be creative. Remember, within marriage the Bible has no restrictions on your behavior, as long as it's loving. Being "sexy" with your marriage partner is a plus, not a negative!

In summary, it's important to reduce stress concerning who initiates sexual play and when, where, and how that initiation takes place. Then initiation will take a healthy role in the total sexual picture, rather than presenting a barrier or being a source of tension. Initiation can also be cultivated to enhance a merely adequate sexual relationship where more spark is desired. The needed ingredients are removal of demands, freedom within oneself, and unconditional acceptance of each other.

12

Meshing with Each Other's Worlds

The production line broke down at the plant, two secretaries didn't show up and you almost ran out of gas on the way home from work. At home mother-wife has had her own management problems: 8-year-old son punched the neighbor girl, the toilet flooded, and the baby has an eye infection. Now, plan a loving time for the evening.

Meshing with each other's worlds or getting in tune with each other is a total-person process. It is becoming "one flesh" as the Hebrews saw it—uniting spirits, emotions, and bodies. All three are necessary to a satisfying relationship. Sex that is just a union of physical bodies cannot be a satisfying communion experience. God intended it to be much more than just physical release, as we saw in the chapters on the scriptural view of sex. When total togetherness is missing, trouble usually ensues!

Spending time together enables two people to mesh. Having been together, you will be more likely to have a sense of each other's feelings. Meshing takes more effort, care and tenderness when you have come from separate and consuming outside places. You may need to spend time chatting—catching up with each other's worlds. If you have concerns that are difficult to put aside, it may help to share these with each other and in prayer with God. You may have joys, accomplishments, and excitements of the day that you wish to praise God for together as a way of being one. What you have experienced in your day will affect the time and effort needed to feel together in each sexual experience.

You may need to tackle some barriers before the two of you feel free with each other. Perhaps one of you has some negative feelings toward the other that have not been resolved. You need to talk these over.

Aesthetic or physical barriers may also stand in the way of true togetherness. Many people are repelled by bad breath, body odors, or certain aspects of the partner's appearance. Yet they find it difficult to discuss these barriers. If there is something physical about your partner that makes it difficult for you to feel one with him or her, it is best to share it.

When possible, a physical barrier that is a sensitive topic should be discussed at a time other than the actual meshing time. For example, if bad breath really turns you off and your spouse has bad breath every time he eats onions, pick a comfortable time to talk about how that bothers you. Then the two of you can come up with a loving way to communicate about the situation so that it does not interfere with your meshing process. Develop a prearranged symbolic message that will communicate the need to do something to reverse the interfering negative vibes. Something like, "I think we need a mouth wash break," or "A mouthful of peanut butter would help things a lot right now." It's best if it can be done lightly and nonoffensively.

Vaginal odors or infectious discharge can certainly get in the way of sexual togetherness. Keep freshly washed. Try wearing all-cotton underwear, which gives the vaginal area more opportunity to "air out." Sometimes blow-drying the vaginal area or the use of a heat lamp after baths or showers can help keep the vaginal area dry and free of discharge. (Naturally, you will need to be careful not to burn yourself.) If these precautions don't correct the situation, see your gynecologist for assistance.

An annoyance wives often report is that husbands forget to bathe before a sexual experience. If being freshly washed is not important to him, but it is important to you as the wife, take the responsibility to let your need and desire be known. Do not play the game, "If he loves me he will remember." It probably has nothing to do with his love or lack of it. It is simply a difference in what is aesthetically important to each of you. Avoid placing demands on your spouse to remember what is important to you. It will make the atmosphere much more relaxing if a system has been prearranged in which the one who remembers has a humorous way to remind the other to bathe, or whatever is needed.

In the process of learning about her sexual needs, Suzanne discovered that having her breasts stimulated when she was lying on her back felt repulsive. She had always assumed that all breast touching was negative, but found that she really enjoyed having her breasts fondled and kissed when she was on top of Jerry. During one positive pleasuring experience, Suzanne and Jerry were lying side by side on their backs. They were relaxed and enjoying each other. In this comfortable state, Jerry reached over and started expressing his warm, affectionate feelings by caressing Suzanne's breasts. He was not thinking of her previous request, nor did he intend to violate her in any way. Yet, she became irate that he could not remember such a specific request. To her, it was a clear message that he did not value her. She felt violated. Her reaction placed incredible pressure on Jerry. The message he received was that he had better be vigilant and on his toes at all times.

It is best if each of us can realize that our partners *will* sometimes forget the messages we have communicated about what we like. Usually that is not an indication of lack of care. Rather, it is an outgrowth of sexual pleasure and satisfaction being an internal experience. If Suzanne had been able to incorporate this attitude, she could have responded with: "Let me get on top of you so I can enjoy your touching me," or "Right now I do not feel like moving into a more comfortable position for breast play, but I would love to have you roll over and we could just hold each other."

Having taken care of aesthetic barriers, you can start where each of you is and then move together. This tends to create a new mood for each experience. Each time of coming together has discovery in it. Sometimes it may evolve into fun—silly, giggling events. Others may be sad but close. You may experience much tenderness and vulnerability. Intense, passionate expressions may occasionally be predominant in your love-making, or some of your times together may seem like raw erotic expressions. Then there will always be some times that will seem rather functional. That is, one or both of you need the physical or emotional closeness and release, but you experience little more than that. These functional sexual experiences are acceptable and need not be seen as a negative sign about your relationship—so long as they don't become your primary sexual expression.

What role does communication play in the whole meshing process? Effective verbal and nonverbal communication can enhance the process of becoming "one." To feel "one" with each other it is critical that you be able to hear each other. Each partner must feel "heard" by the other. This requires empathy, which is a major part of active listening. Empathy is more than a mechanical technique. It is the ability to enter into another person's feelings instead of defending your own. In addition, it is the ability to communicate with the other person in such a way that he or she feels you are with him or her.

It takes discipline to practice empathy and active listening, to achieve an awareness of our own feelings and reactions. We discipline ourselves to acknowledge our own feelings, to be real about them, but not to let them interfere with hearing and being with the other person. The more emotionally difficult an area is for us, the more disciplined our practice of empathy has to be. The best way to practice empathy is to reflect and clarify. Reflect what you have heard and sensed from the other. Listen and observe with all your senses. Sort out your own reaction and set it aside. Then feed back what you've heard and seen. After that invite the other person to clarify and expand the original communication.

It is most difficult for us to remain undefensive and get with the other person when that person is talking about us. Following is an example of how you might practice empathy even when the message is about you:

Edgar: "You've gotten so much better—you used to have to have sex right when you felt like it. If it couldn't be right then, and if I didn't get an erection right away, then you'd pout."

Linda: "You're feeling less demand from me." (Good reflection and focus on his feelings rather than on what he is saying about her.)

Edgar: "Yes, it seems we've both learned that if one of us isn't turned on we can enjoy cuddling and that's okay."

Linda: "So there is more relaxation in realizing our pleasuring times can be an end in themselves, rather than having to lead to intercourse."

Edgar: "That has really made me want to get together with you more often."

With Linda's consistent reflection of Edgar's feelings, he was able to move from talking about her to talking about himself. For many of us, being an active listener when we are hearing negative messages about ourselves is not easy.

This disciplined, effective, verbal communication does not work well once sexual excitement begins. So this work has to occur before or apart from sexual arousal. We do not hear as accurately when intense sexual feelings possess us. Getting with the sexual process is really flowing with your own internal experience, so it is contradictory to work on empathy once you are into a sexual experience. This does not mean that you switch to being cruel, selfish, or insensitive at the expense of your partner. Rather, you focus on the enjoyment and pleasure of the moment, respecting the guidelines previously learned about what is violating to your partner. We will build on this principle in the next chapter on "Pleasuring."

Because verbal communication is not at its best during sexual excitement, sexual decisions must be made away from the love-making event. In this process of making decisions about what is best for each of you sexually, it is helpful to develop a *nonverbal* signal system. This can then be used during sexual experiences to follow through with decisions made previously.

Here's an example of how this might work. One common discomfort for women is the man's tendency to manually stimulate the clitoris too intensely and for too long a time. Usually the man has no idea that what he is doing is uncomfortable or painful for the woman. After she has shared that she frequently experiences discomfort from manual stimulation, the man will still need ongoing guidance to know what does feel good. You can have an instruction time where the woman shows the man and talks about it. But once you are into a sexually arousing time, that type of instruction will tend to kill the sexual feelings. Instead, use a prearranged nonverbal message that can flow with the feelings of the moment. For example, the woman might gently lift the man's hand to reduce the pressure, or move his hand to another location that feels hungry for touch. This is much easier for a man to take than the verbal message, "You're doing it too hard again."

When there is a particular kind of touch uniquely negative to you, you might decide that a tap on your partner's shoulder is a reminder that those negative feelings are occurring. One man experienced his wife's touch as ticklish. Another woman could not stand to be kissed on the neck, yet when her husband was enjoying himself he might forget. Along with their spouses both of these people developed mutually accepted methods of signaling a need for change.

A positive nonverbal cue can ask for more of a specific action that feels good. A woman might push her pelvis toward a point of stimulation that is bringing her pleasure. A man might move the woman's buttocks when she is in the top position if he needs more movement to keep his erection, or he might stop her movement to control ejaculation. There are many ways we can communicate with each other without using words. The important ingredient is that both the sender and receiver attach the same meaning to the nonverbal message. When positive nonverbal systems are developed with a couple's sexual relationship, the meshing together can be a beautiful, harmonious process.

___13

Pleasuring

You described my sexual relationship with my husband. He gets, I give. What are some positive steps to take to come out of this one-sided relationship?

The Right to Pleasure

"So husbands ought also to love their own wives as their own bodies. He who loves his own wife loves himself; *for no one ever hated his own flesh, but nourishes and cherishes it,* just as Christ also does the church" (Eph. 5:28, 29 NASB, italics ours).

Bodily pleasure is a Christian expectation. The title of Ed and Gaye Wheat's book says it—*Intended for Pleasure.* God created us in his likeness with the capacity to enjoy our bodies. This is analogous to the enjoyment that he finds in his body, the church (see Chap. 4).

People who were raised in a constrictive environment may not be able to experience bodily pleasure. For them, bodily touching may not be pleasurable. Some people feel that they do not have a right to pleasure. This is true whether the constrictions they grew up with were moral, religious or emotional.

Morally rigid persons will often connect the pleasurable responsiveness of their bodies with negative, off-limit feelings. Then they tense up rather than relax and enjoy sensuous feelings. These people develop tight boundaries. "Nice girls don't do such things," they feel. So there is a limit on how far they let themselves be sexual.

A woman who, for moral reasons, kept herself a virgin before marriage may find herself unable to enjoy sex with her new husband. She expected the marriage ceremony to free her magically from a lifetime of constriction and inhibition, but it didn't work out that way. The clergy person's words, "I pronounce you husband and wife," did not unleash a pent-up, sexually charged avalanche of abandonment.

Another woman can let herself become sexually excited only to a certain point, because to go further is out of the realm of how "nice girls" behave. Still others can enjoy sexual pleasure only when it is "naughty"—outside of marriage.

When the constriction has developed through being raised in a rigid religious setting, the problem is a bit different than that for the morally constricted person. The rigid religious environment may convey the idea that bodily pleasure is associated with the fleshly, sinful part of people. People who connect bodily pleasure with sin cannot allow themselves to receive pleasure and feel good about it. Others may be able to experience wildly sexual feelings, but only in narrowly restricted settings or under strict conditions. For example, one woman is not able to enjoy sex on a Saturday night because she will be going to church the next day and she is unable to associate God and sex. For others, the sexual act must occur quickly and in the dark. The man may rush into it, moving rapidly to orgasm, unable to tarry for the pleasures of love-making. Or the wife may become very active with intense thrusting. Thus she brings her husband to ejaculation quickly because that is the only way she can allow herself to experience the sex act: in and out quickly. Unfortunately, in both instances the woman is left frustrated and unfulfilled.

It may be that the person with the religious association of sex and sin can enjoy the sexual experience only when there is risk and guilt involved. Any sexual involvement the couple had before marriage was wild and exciting. However, on the honeymoon both felt strained and tense. The woman could not enjoy herself. The man was anxious and therefore less fun than he had been before. Because of the anxiety and tension around their sexual experiences, he began ejaculating before she or he wanted him to. She became more and more displeased with him as a partner.

At a time of deep disillusionment about their marriage and sex life, the wife happened to be working with a warm, caring male. She found herself incredibly responsive to him, and she even confided in him regarding her "inadequate" husband. The outside relationship incidentally and unintentionally built until they became sexually involved. She felt guilty because of the conflict with her religious beliefs, but the sexual pleasure and enjoyment with this other man were so great that she decided her marriage must be a mismatch. A divorce ensued. She remarried, and would you believe it, the same tense feelings were there. Sex was no longer enjoyable. This is usually the point at which the person or couple comes for help.

Emotional constriction interfering with the ability to allow bodily pleasure is more frequently observed in our male clients. This seems to be due to the cultural impact that says, "Big boys don't cry." Boys are not expected or allowed to be as emotional as girls. Thus, when a boy grows up in a home where either or both parents control their emotions and will not allow emotional expression, he is in double trouble. Not only does he have the cultural input, but also the emotional vacuum at home. Commonly, this man will then choose a somewhat insecure but intensely sexual wife. Maybe he is attracted to what is missing in his own life.

This man will usually not have had sexual intercourse before marriage (whether or not he has Christian standards). The avoidance of sexual involvement has been based on his own unrecognized fear of emotional intensity. Therefore, he has his first sexual experience with his new wife. She is wildly and intensely expressive. He feels somewhat overwhelmed and a little frightened by the whole experience. He starts avoiding, suggesting sightseeing rather than love-making. She, being the emotionally expressive and somewhat insecure person she is, begins to cry because she feels he does not want her. He is not used to this negative emotional expression so, again, he feels anxious. Also he gets the message that she is making a demand he cannot live up to. And, once again, we are on the spiral downward. Sex is a demand, not a pleasure.

Whether the constriction is due to moral values, religious beliefs, or emotional limitations, it inevitably interferes with one's ability to enjoy pleasure in the sexual relationship.

Positive Self-worth: An Essential Ingredient

The "feeling" counterpart to the attitude that you have the right to experience pleasure is *self-worth*. This feeling that you are a worthy person is central to being able to receive sexual pleasure. You must have the sense that you are valuable and that you deserve to have good things happen in your life. Good, pleasurable sensations in your body are to be enjoyed. You can relax and know that your partner is enjoying the experience. When this feeling of self-worth is missing, you will feel uncomfortable with sexual pleasure. You may feel embarrassed or guilty about allowing responsiveness. On the other hand, your lack of feelings of self-worth may take the form of anxiously checking with your partner to make sure he or she is being pleased. You experience no pleasure of your own, only satisfaction that your partner is having a good time. "Who am I to expect a good time?" A sense of worthiness is necessary to the pleasuring process.

Nondemand Pleasuring

In addition to an attitude that you have the right to pleasure and a feeling of self-worth, freedom from demand is essential to the ability to pleasure for pleasure's sake. We explored the idea of removing demands when we talked about the process of initiation. Anxiety due to demand interferes with every emotional phase of the sexual experience. Because of this, we teach couples a process called *nondemand pleasuring*. Nondemand pleasuring has been written about by almost every sexual expert in the country. This is consistent with its importance for finding sexual fulfillment. The chapters that deal with reversal of sexual problems will take you through detailed steps for practicing nondemand pleasuring. Right now, though, we would like to introduce you to the *feeling* of being free of demands.

Demand-free pleasuring experiences are simple to talk about but not always easy to practice. Each love-making time is to be entered with this anticipation: I am here to enjoy myself and my partner. But I will not enjoy this experience if I demand any of the following: that as a man I have to get or keep an erection; that I have to do a certain thing in a certain way; that as a woman I should get aroused and/or be orgasmic; that I should please my partner; or that I must perform in a certain way if the experience is to be satisfactory.

We recommend that you don't even expect intercourse as a necessary part of having a loving, touching get-together. The only criterion is that what you do must be pleasurable to both partners.

Taking Responsibility for Your Own Pleasure: A Two-way System

Enjoying each other's bodies and letting each event take on its own character is most possible when each person feels comfortable pursuing his or her own desire for touch. Each of you takes responsibility to go after your own desire for pleasure. This is not at the expense of your partner. Rather, each of you will develop your awareness and knowledge of what is negative for the other. You will exclude those negatives from your range of options until the other person's perception of that aspect of pleasuring changes from negative to positive. (The idea of going with the conservative partner is found in Chapter 24.) There are usually unlimited possibilities for pleasure without violating your partner.

This is a two-way system. The first part, which we have just described, involves taking responsibility for your own pleasure. The assumption behind this is that you please your partner the most when you are not preoccupied with pleasing, but are fully enjoying yourself sexually and focusing on your own pleasure. This may sound more selfish than pleasing, but we find it the reverse. When you are overconcerned about doing what is best for the other person rather than for yourself, you become performance-focused. This creates anxiety and tension. Your partner will sense this tension, and it will interfere with his or her pleasure as well as yours.

There is nothing more positive sexually than for both persons to take responsibility for themselves, really to enjoy their own and each other's bodies for personal pleasure. This cannot work, however, without the second part of this system: Each person in the relationship must agree that he or she will not allow anything to continue that is negative. This agreement means that you take the responsibility to redirect your spouse away from anything which feels negative, and to something pleasurable. That way, you and your partner can relax and enjoy yourselves, not worrying about whether the other is feeling good about the experience. You can trust that getting into your own feelings is not at the expense of your partner but rather for his or her pleasure.

This two-way contract is incredibly freeing and yet it is most difficult for some couples to accept. We have been conditioned to believe that as spouses (and especially as Christian spouses), it is our duty to determine what is most pleasing to our partners and then work hard to do everything just right. You can see how that can interfere with pleasure for both. Let's look back at the verses we started with. Ephesians 5:28, 29 implies that the best guide for pleasing our partners is to find out what pleases ourselves. The only duty we have is not to withhold ourselves from our spouses (1 Cor. 7:5).

What plan might you set into motion to act on the attitude suggested above—the change from pleasing to pursuing pleasure? The remainder of this chapter will give you some ideas.

Going after Good Feelings

How can you pleasure for your own pleasure and know that this will be the best way you can give yourself to your spouse?

Both of you must believe that you will "please" each other most when you fully enjoy yourselves in the sexual experience. Then you have to know that you will be most able to enjoy yourself when you go after your own pleasure. Going after your own pleasure will work only if this is a mutual commitment. Both of you have to be convinced, and both must cooperate with the plan. You also need mutual trust in each other's commitment. Once the basic verbal communication has been worked out, then it's best to practice some very simple pleasuring exercises. Start with a foot and hand caress. These are the parts of the body furthest away from the genitals; therefore, you are less likely to experience any of the anxieties or demands previously associated with your sexual experience. "The foot caress is the beginning of nonverbal communication. Its primary purpose is to begin to capitalize on existent warmth and positive expression. . . . In addition, it is the beginning of establishing the sensual dimension of human personality. It stresses touching in a warm, loving, and caring way." *

We concur with these authors—the easiest part of the body to start with is the feet.

---

* William E. Hartman and Marilyn A. Fithian, *Treatment of Sexual Dysfunction, A Bio-Psycho-Social-Approach* (Center for Marital and Sexual Studies, 1972), pp. 144–146.

Here are the steps for the foot and hand caress. This is one of the early assignments we give to a couple in sexual therapy. However, we find that these exercises can enhance a couple's sexual relationship whether or not there are any specific sexual problems.

Exercise 8
Foot and Hand Caress

Underlying Principles:

1. Receiving and pleasuring for your own pleasure:

Receiver: Your only task is to "soak in" pleasure and to redirect pleasurer when the touch is not pleasing. Check out your concern if at any point you question whether or not your partner is enjoying himself or herself.

Pleasurer: Lovingly and tenderly touch your partner in a way that feels good to you. Think of radiating warmth through your fingertips and taking in or sensing the warmth and pulsation of the part of your partner that you are touching. Trust that your partner will redirect you if what you are doing is not pleasurable. Express your concern if at any point you become anxious rather than enjoying your partner's body. Caress *slowly. Take time to enjoy.*

2. No experience is preferable to an experience by demand:
When you feel that an experience is a demand—stop doing it and share your feelings and shift the place or person being pleasured. If the demand still continues, talk about the feelings and reschedule the experience, modifying the set-up to accommodate the needs of one or both partners in order to eliminate demand feelings.

3. Varying the setting keeps the experiences interesting:
Select a setting different from that of your usual sexual experiences. The receiver should be seated or reclined in a comfortable, upholstered high backed chair or couch. The pleasurer should be positioned to have easy and comfortable access to the body part being enjoyed.

4. Focus on pleasure:
Sexual arousal is not the expectation of this experience. If arousal should occur, this is an acceptable, involuntary response, so enjoy it. But *do not become concerned if there is no arousal. The purpose of this experience is to learn to enjoy the giving and receiving of body pleasure.* This is not to be a therapeutic massage to get the kinks out, but rather a sensuous touch that communicates warmth.

Steps:

1. *Both:* Bathe or shower, individually or together. Have on comfortable clothes or robes.

2. Decide who will first be receiver and who will first be pleasurer.

3. You may or may not use Allercreme or a similar nonlanolin and nonalcohol lotion. If using lotion, warm it in your hands first.

4. *Receiver:* Get comfortable in the chair or couch selected. Lie back and close your eyes. Breathe in deeply and exhale slowly several times, letting your body sink into the chair or couch as you do. (If your feet are ticklish, you may be highly responsive thus making it difficult to receive the sensuous touch. Focusing intensely on the sensations you are feeling should help relieve the ticklishness and increase the pleasure.)

5. *Pleasurer:* With or without Allercreme, warm your hands. Start caressing your partner's foot. Get to know his or her foot through touch. *Slowly* explore the toes, arch, top of foot, ankle, and so on. If your touch is ticklish try a firmer touch with the total palm of your hand. Always keep contact with the body part being caressed and inform your partner before you move to the next part. Caress one then the other. Next caress the hands, enjoying all surfaces and parts of each hand. Inform your partner when you are finished.

6. *Both:* Reverse roles and repeat steps 4 and 5.

You may want to repeat this experience at several different times in new settings. Change who begins the caress, and vary the location and the additions to the environment—music, fireplace, comforter, animal skin rugs, dim lights, lights on or off, candles, incense, and so on. When choosing accents for the setting, the *pleasurer* may choose the ingredients he or she would enjoy. This follows our basic attitude of pleasuring for one's own enjoyment. For example, if I'm going to pleasure my partner and I like soft music, I will choose soft music unless I know my partner finds it to be negative. In that case, I need to choose something that will enhance my involvement in the experience without being unpleasant for my spouse. When a couple's likes and dislikes are far apart, this takes a more loving effort.

Once the two of you feel free of demand and anxiety and can enjoy the foot and hand caress as both receiver and pleasurer, then you may want to move to the facial caress.

The purpose and guidelines are basically the same for the facial caress as they are for the foot and hand caress.

Exercise 9
Facial Caress

Steps:

1. *Both:* Bathe or shower individually or together. Have hair clean, dry and away from face. Man should be cleanly shaven.

2. *Together:* Reread underlying principles for foot and hand caress.

3. *Receiver:* (a) Position yourself comfortably on a bed or couch, with or without pillow, with your head near the unobstructed edge of the bed or couch. (b) Let yourself relax with eyes closed. Breathe in deeply and exhale slowly a few times, letting your body sink into the bed or couch.

4. *Pleasurer:* (a) Sit in a comfortable chair positioned so that you have easy access to your partner's face. (b) Using a facial lotion or cream (Allercreme is great), close your eyes and focus on the sensation of the touch as you explore your partner's face. Pleasure and explore as if you are a blind person getting to know your spouse through touch. Find eyebrows, eyes, all aspects of the nose, cheeks, forehead, chin, lips. Gently, sensuously and lovingly enjoy the warmth of your partner's face. Inform your partner when you finish.

5. *Both:* Reverse roles and repeat steps 3 and 4.

Giving and Receiving: When There Are Barriers

The barriers that usually surface in these early pleasuring experiences involve giving and receiving. Often it becomes clear that there are two givers and no receiver. Both partners have difficulty believing and feeling that they have the right to receive. It is difficult to let go, relax, and soak in the pleasure. It feels selfish and uncaring. Each imagines that the other is unable to enjoy the pleasuring process. One will think, *I know he's not enjoying himself.* Behind that thought is usually a feeling of low self-esteem: *I couldn't be enjoyable to touch.*

Sometimes one partner can enjoy pleasuring and the other one receiving, but the opposite is not true. Then the giving is no longer a two-way proposition. The underlying principles that we have proposed will not work as well in this situation. The one partner may experience receiving more as a chore than as a delight. If this is the difficulty for you, we would encourage you to practice the role that is most difficult for you. Go at it gradually. Talk about your difficulty with receiving. For the one who has difficulty pleasuring, performance anxiety may be getting in the way. He cannot focus on what feels good because he is so preoccupied with not measuring up—not doing it right—not being able to please a woman. Very often it *is* the man who has this difficulty. A man who has trouble pleasuring is often one who has grown up with a mother who continually expressed negative messages about the father. The son clearly learned that men are inadequate in making women happy.

The woman is probably the one having difficulty receiving. Usually this is a trust problem. She confirms the man's fears of inadequacy because she has learned, "You can't trust a man." She can pleasure him and enjoy his body since she is in control. To be in the receiving role raises all her anxieties about relying on someone else. The man's performance anxiety and the woman's inability to trust enough to receive will probably show up in other areas of the relationship too. Therefore, besides practicing the roles that are most difficult for each of you, you need to watch for similar feelings popping up elsewhere in your lives. Awareness is a major starting place for breaking emotional barriers.

Communicating Likes and Dislikes

After learning to touch and be touched for your own pleasure, a more complicated step is learning to incorporate the likes and dislikes of your partner. To pay attention to those likes and dislikes may feel like getting back to trying to please. That is why it is essential that you feel confident of your ability to give and receive pleasure for your own enjoyment before you move to this next step. Then you can go after your own pleasure with an awareness of your partner's likes and dislikes. Often it will be more enjoyable to do something you know is particularly pleasing to your partner. If total body caressing is delightful to your partner and positive for you, why not choose it even though there may be activities you enjoy more? In this case, it is for your own pleasure that you might like to pursue the activity your partner enjoys most. *The motive is not "trying to please," but rather mutual enjoyment.* As you become comfortable with pleasure for pleasure's sake, mutuality of expression will develop.

If you are going to incorporate each other's likes and dislikes into the pleasuring process, you need to talk about those likes and dislikes at a time separate from the pleasuring experience itself. Each of you probably has likes and dislikes that you have never told the other. Using instruction for positive verbal communication from Chapter 12, set aside a talk time. This talk time is just the beginning. Communicating sexual likes and dislikes is an ongoing process.

Instructing Each Other in Positive Touching

Nonverbal communication about what is pleasurable is another effective tool for learning each other's likes and dislikes. Nonverbal instruction does not carry the demand that verbal instruction can sometimes impart.

Another step can be added to the facial caress to make it a nondemand instruction exercise. While the pleasurer is caressing the receiver's face, the receiver reaches up and gently, lovingly places his or her hands over the pleasurer's hands. (This must be an expected part of the experience so the pleasurer is not taken by surprise.) The pleasurer responds by relaxing his or her hands and letting the receiver guide them. The receiver then uses the pleasurer's hand to caress his or her own face. Another way of saying it is that the receiver guides the pleasurer to demonstrate what kind of touch feels best. The pleasurer's task is to relax and get a sense of where and how the receiver likes to be touched. This can actually relieve anxiety for persons who are anxious about doing it right, or who feel that the ways they touch are never right.

This experience may be followed by a more involved nondemand teaching exercise which includes the whole front of the body.

Exercise 10
Nondemand Teaching

Step 1: Read these instructions together and clarify with each other what each of you understands what you are to do.

Step 2: Bathe or shower together in a way that brings relaxation and enjoyment of each other's bodies.

Step 3: The woman should start the actual experience by sitting in front of her husband in the nondemand position (See Figure 8). Then she places her hands over his hands and uses his hands to pleasure her face, breasts, abdomen and genitals. The purpose of the exercise is for the one guiding the hands to demonstrate what kind of touch she really likes. For the one being guided, his job is to let his hand muscles be relaxed and limp, and to attend to the kind of touch he is being directed to give. He can learn what his partner really likes. This is a particularly good time for both to do a lot of experimenting and communicating about the kind of genital touch that brings pleasure. It is not likely to be an exciting or arousing experience, but more of a clinical and teaching time.

When the man guides the woman's hands to discover and teach the touch he enjoys on the upper front of his body, he may need to slide down and use a modified version of the upper diagram of the nondemand position; for example, he may slide his head into his partner's lap. When the man is guiding the woman in pleasuring his lower body, especially the genitals, we encourage the use of the position shown in the lower diagram.

Step 4: Talk together both about what you learned in this experience as well as any other touching experiences that you have always enjoyed, or that have always been painful or difficult for you.

Once you as a couple are comfortable with guiding each other's hands as a means of instruction, guiding hands can be interjected into any pleasuring, love-making time as a way of ongoing communication. When something feels particularly good you can guide your partner's hand to show that you would like more of the same. Your partner's hand can also be guided to communicate your need for readjustment of the touch when you are taking responsibility for your own pleasure as the receiver.

Variety in Sensuous Touching

When using hands as the pleasuring agent, it is important that the hands be free to communicate inner feelings. The hands become the instruments of loving, caring expression. For this to happen, there are some conditions that are helpful. It is better if nails are not rough or sharp so the receiving person doesn't have to worry about being jabbed. The pleasurer's hands feel best to the receiver when they are

Figure 8

NONDEMAND POSITIONS

smooth, soft and warm. Touch is most sensuous to both giver and receiver when the hands continuously touch the other's body. This unbroken contact provides a sense of continually being in touch with each other's vibrations.

The hands are not the only instruments through which we can sensuously enjoy each other's bodies. In fact, many couples find it most enlightening and exciting to vary the parts of the body used to enjoy each other. The forearms, lips and breasts are particularly sensitive to touch for the pleasurer. Using one of these parts is a positive distraction for the person who has a difficult time pleasuring because of performance anxiety. The hair is a fun sensation for the receiver. Toes can add a spark. The tongue is very sensuous. Light stroking with fingernails is positive for some and negative for others.

A pleasuring exercise that many couples find to be fun is one using no hands. All other parts of the body may be used. Try following the steps outlined; you may find it challenging or hilarious.

Exercise 11
No-Hands Pleasuring

Step 1: Together read these instructions and the underlying principles for the foot and hand caress. Tell each other what each of you understands the assignment to be.

Step 2: Bathe or shower together in a way that brings relaxation and enjoyment of each other's bodies.

Step 3: One of you start the actual pleasuring by following previous underlying principles for body pleasuring *except* this time you may use any part of your body except your hands. Make it an experimental and fun time of discovering what parts of your body you really enjoy using to touch your partner. You might use your hair, nose, eyes, tongue, ears, forearms, breasts, genitals, feet or whatever. When you have thoroughly enjoyed your partner's total body, reverse roles and your partner will pursue the discovery of using various parts of her or his body to pleasure you. Each of you stop when you feel you have thoroughly enjoyed your partner's total body. (A variation may be simultaneous enjoyment of giving and receiving.)

Step 4: Talk about the experience. What felt particularly good? What new things did you discover about yourself? About your partner? What barriers were there for you? What got in the way of maximum enjoyment?

Flowing with the Feelings

Whatever the part of the body you are enjoying, the key is to let yourself flow with your inner feelings. When we take a couple through a total body, general pleasuring experience (Chap. 29, Exercise 16), we encourage the pleasurer to start by placing his or her hands on the receiver's back. Then the pleasurer is to sense the warmth and vibrations of the other's back and begin to move in response to those feelings. Movement is best when it flows from within the person rather than being a mechanical exercise of making sure every inch of the receiver's back was touched.

Summary

You will learn sensuous touching as you are free to flow with the pleasure from your inner self, and as you are open to learning to touch in a way that is pleasurable to your partner. These two factors, plus the ability to allow variation and experimentation, can keep a relationship exciting for a lifetime.

14

Special Treats That Add Pleasure

It was a warm summer day in California. John had been away for a business trip. Sheila was anticipating his return. She felt herself getting aroused as she thought about being with him that evening. Yet the bedroom was hot and uncomfortable. In addition, she knew that she and John would need to spend some time getting back into each other's worlds after the time they had spent apart. How could she plan something enjoyable that would meet her sexual desire, and yet respond to John and his probable need for unwinding from business pressures?

A creative plan emerged. Listening to her inner spark, she balanced it at the same time with the need to give John room to be where he was and not to push herself on him. Planning a simple, light but elegant candlelight dinner, she prepared a familiar meal. She put on their favorite record for relaxing and eating. These were treats she knew they both enjoyed.

What about the hot bedroom? Sheila decided to try a new setting that did not have any past demands or expectations. The family room was the coolest room in the house. How about a love pit? With cushions and comforters, she had a delightful time preparing a place where they could comfortably chat, touch, make love or sleep. All were possible options.

With all her special treats, she was focused on mutual pleasure. It was not an anxious attempt to please, with insecurities about whether or not it would be received. On the contrary, the whole plan was an expression of her own sexuality that left room for John to enjoy what he could. She did not need him to be excited about what she had done, for she already felt fulfilled in her own creation. Therefore, her preparation did not come across as an anxiety-producing demand but rather a true expression of herself.

Unfortunately, we are not always all in touch with our own desires. Nor are we as secure in expressing them without making a demand to have them affirmed. Sometimes it is hard to be sensitive in allowing space for our partner. Sheila's efforts provide a beautiful example of the way special treats can be developed to add to pleasure. In addition to learning to enjoy pleasuring and receiving, there are little extras that make a difference. Three extras we have found enhancing to general pleasuring are setting an atmosphere, sharing sensuous surprises, and expressing thoughtfulness.

Setting the Atmosphere

When we think about setting the atmosphere, the old wedding cliché comes to mind: "something old, something new, something borrowed, something blue."

"Something Old." A sense of warmth is expressed by including in the pleasuring setup some feature that has a positive history for both of you. For example, we light a candle by the bed when we are anticipating getting together for sexual pleasure. This has positive associations for both of us. Also, we use the candle to symbolically communicate with each other that we desire sexual contact.

Providing what we already know is positive makes a great start. For the two of you it might be a special sheet or blanket, a flower, music, fireplace, oil or lotion, or perfume. There are unlimited possibilities.

"Something New." If everything about the experience is old and familiar, regular repetition of that atmosphere will soon cause it to lose its spark. Experimenting with new places, positions, methods of stimulation, or accouterments adds excitement. If you are not used to adding newness to your sex life, it may be difficult to start. You may feel awkward and your spouse may wonder what has happened

to you. We suggest starting with a planned experience. You might find the steps of the following exercise helpful.

Exercise 12
Creative Pleasuring

Step 1: Together read these instructions and the "Underlying Principles for Body Pleasuring" in Chapter 13. Tell each other what each of you understands the assignment to be.

Step 2: Bathe or shower together in a way that brings relaxation and enjoyment of each other's bodies.

Step 3: Each of you bring to the experience one or more items to use to pleasure your partner. Think of things that would feel pleasing and sensuous against the skin. Let these be a surprise for each other. (These might include a piece of fabric, fur, silk, hair, brush, feather, and so on.)

Step 4: One of you start the actual pleasuring by having your partner lie on his or her abdomen. Gently stroke his or her back with the accouterment you chose for this event. If you and your partner both enjoy the feeling of the item you chose, continue pleasuring his or her entire body. When you feel finished, reverse roles. The other partner now does the same thing with the accouterment he or she chose. Each one should stop when you have thoroughly enjoyed your partner's total body.

Step 5: Talk about the experience. What did you enjoy? What would you have liked more of? What other kind of object could you imagine enjoying? What did you learn?

Another way you might vary this exercise is by taking turns setting the atmosphere. For each spouse's turn, that person would be responsible to add something new and sensuous to your love-making setup.

"Something Borrowed" reminds us of an attitude of openness to ideas from others. This may come from talking with a friend, reading a book, or attending a class. Through some outside exposure, you acquire information that can be incorporated into your love-making experience. The borrowed idea enhances your situation.

"Something Blue" speaks of tradition, as in the blue garter at a wedding. Creating traditions that are special for the two of you provides continuity and invites anticipation. Sometimes traditions for a sexual

setting are incorporated as a part of a special event such as an anniversary. Perhaps the husband always buys roses for his wife, or they always go out for an extra-nice dinner. These are fun experiences you can count on, and may enhance your sexual encounters.

If you are the one planning the setting for your next time together, think through these four areas—"something old, something new, something borrowed, something blue." It can provide a framework for creativity.

Planned Surprises

The entire event that Sheila planned in anticipation of John's homecoming was a surprise to John. Planned surprises are often more fun for the doer than for the receiver. The person who is managing the surprise has time to get into the details of the event. He or she also enjoys all the positive feelings of anticipation. The person to be surprised misses the fun of preparation and anticipation, and may not feel ready when the surprise comes. Nonetheless, the right kind of surprise can be a pleasure.

To be sensuous, a surprise does not have to include physical touching. You may want to plan a hike in the mountains, a barefoot walk on the beach, a drive through the country, an afternoon at a cultural event, an evening at the movies, a special dinner. There are many sensuous, nontouching events that promote intimacy and arousal for many couples. It can add a new "zing" to your relationship to plan such an event as a total surprise to your partner. Perhaps there is some activity you've really been wishing the two of you could do together. For some reason, you have not done anything about it. Maybe you're expecting your spouse to take responsibility for the plans. Why not take charge and make the arrangements yourself? Turn it from, "I wish he would think of things like that," or "I wonder why she isn't making those plans" to, "If it's something I'd like to have happen, why don't I plan it as a surprise?"

Just as sensuous events are fun to plan as surprises for each other, so are total sexual experiences. Occasionally it is refreshing for one spouse to take over the entire plan for a time together. For example, say Thursday evening next week is an evening set aside for the two of you. Let your spouse know that you will be in charge. Then plan creatively. Think of setting the atmosphere as we just outlined. You might also become creative in what you do with each other. If your sexual relationship has been limited to intercourse experiences, you might enjoy planning some time for the two of you to be together in an atmosphere that's conducive to chatting and being affectionate without the necessity of intercourse. Make the entire plan an expression of yourself that takes into account your partner's likes and dislikes.

You may not always have the energy or interest to plan a total experience surprise. Most of the time, you may find spark in adding one small surprise to an already planned or anticipated experience. This might be something creative to pleasure with, some sensuous addition to the atmosphere or a new activity focus. Maybe you have both been wanting a new bedspread. You are both clear on what the other likes, so one of you buys it and saves it for a surprise.

Spontaneous Surprises

Spontaneous surprises add excitement, also. Spontaneity grows out of being aware of one's own inner sexual desire and being in tune with each other. A fun surprise that we enjoy pulling on each other is to go to bed nude. We usually wear bedclothes at night, so it is a delightful surprise to find a warm, nude body in the bed. Spontaneous surprises that grow out of the moment give the other person the message that you are desiring him or her—that you are excited about your relationship.

Thoughtfulness That Communicates Care

Thoughtful expressions have much the same effect as planned or spontaneous surprises. For many individuals, it is important that their partners show that they care enough to prepare their bodies. This might involve shaving the face for the man or the legs for the woman. It usually includes having a clean, fresh-smelling body. What is important varies greatly from person to person. This is a sensitive area in which people often do not feel free to communicate their needs.

One woman found herself sexually repulsed by her husband. They always made love in the evening. His work caused him to perspire profusely, and he did not like to shower after work. To her, he was smelly and uncomfortable to touch. He felt her avoidance of him but never knew what it was about. The communication process took some hard work. He was not very open to changing his ways. He saw her as fussy and she saw him as stubborn and uncaring.

Sometimes just talking about the problem corrects the barrier. Other situations may require more investment in the problem. Usually a person is happy to do whatever is needed to correct a negative odor or to prepare oneself in a way that is important for one's partner.

Another exercise of thoughtfulness involves having supplies ready for a spontaneous or previously planned sexual encounter. This might include birth control devices, Kleenex, lubricants, pillow, or special sheets used. Some couples have prepared a love-making kit. Either this kit is stored where it is easily accessible, or both partners share the responsibility of remembering to bring it to their together times.

Preparing the setting is an expression of thoughtfulness even when it is not done as a surprise. Just the idea of taking time to turn on the electric blanket, warm the room, lock the door, dim the lights, or clean up the bedroom is an expression that you care. The sexual relationship between you and your spouse is important and special to you.

Treating yourself and each other adds to sexual pleasure as long as treats do not become demands. Plan a treat because you enjoy doing it, not because you expect a response. Otherwise you will develop anxiety and tension which will detract from rather than add to your pleasure. Treats can also get in the way if you start expecting or demanding that your partner provide them. Keeping score also destroys the pleasure: "I surprised her last time. It's her turn now." Keep it fun, free, and an expression of *your* sensuousness.

_____15

Stimulating

I know how I'm supposed to be able to turn her on, but she's different. She doesn't work like the books said she would.

Stimulating vs. Pleasuring

Why a chapter on pleasuring and one on stimulating? What is the difference? We hope that the sexual stimulation we experience is also pleasurable. But that is not necessarily the case. The extreme situation is rape. A woman who is raped may actually experience physical sexual stimulation, but her feelings are of fear and pain rather than of pleasure.

On the opposite side, pleasuring need not be sexually stimulating to be positive. Sexual arousal and stimulation *may* occur in response to pleasurable touch, but they may *not.*

Creative Variety vs. Mechanical Monotony

Before Masters and Johnson's research influenced the sexual manuals, the three–push-button approach was the predominant premarital teaching. If the man pushed the right buttons in the correct order, he had the key to turning on a woman. You kiss, fondle the breasts, rub the clitoris and she should be ready to go. It reminds us of the instructions for starting our diesel station wagon!

The marriage manual we studied before our marriage in 1963 described it this way:

> The husband must always delay and control his impatient desire, until he has carried his wife through an adequate period of preparation. . . . The most complete response is likely to be evoked if caresses follow a definite sequence, beginning with the lips and neck, then the breasts and finally the sex organs, but women differ and the husband must learn the preferences of his wife instead of relying on theory.*

Fortunately or unfortunately, that "ain't" how it works. Positive sexual stimulation is most likely to occur when two people are free to enjoy each other's bodies with creativity and variety. Any part of the body is responsive to sexual stimulation. Rubbing each other's skin anywhere can be a turn-on. Indeed, a change is often more intensely erotic because it is a new sensation. There is no one standard for what will work. The unfortunate side of the need for variety and flexibility is that it leaves the insecure person without a nice, concise prescription. The fortunate side is that the door is wide open to new discoveries.

Individuality vs. Globality

Creative variety forces us to recognize and allow for individual differences. This includes differences between men and women, from one woman to another, from one man to another, in the same person from one experience to another, and from time to time within the same experience. "Doing it" the same way every time does not account for individual variation. That is why a mechanical routine soon gets to be a bore.

Let's talk about allowing differences from one person to another. Just because a certain kind of touch is stimulating to you does not insure that the same will be true for your partner. Each person needs to be his or her own authority on what is pleasurable or stimulating. That is why it works best for each person to go after his or her own desire. It takes the guesswork out of the game.

---

* Paul Popenoe, *Sex Happiness or Tragedy?* (Los Angeles: Samuel Newman Productions, 1954), pp. 40, 41.

Another way we can get ourselves into trouble and not allow individuality is by imposing lessons learned in a previous situation on our current partners. If you have been sexually involved with someone before your present partner, it is easy to expect the same response. Many couples have had difficulty resolving their sexual tensions because they imposed such expectations on their current spouse.

The situation may go something like this. The woman had been involved sexually as a teenager. Those sexual experiences were exciting and full of vitality. Her partners were usually somewhat older men who swept her off her feet and turned her on. After that she became a Christian. Guilt about her past experiences and her current intense sexual desire plagued her. She resolved never to be promiscuous again—or even to be sexual. By that decision, she chose to turn off her sexual feelings. Then she found a solid, conservative Christian man for a husband. He was most unlike her lovers of the past, yet she expected him to display their kind of charming aggressiveness— traits he would never possess. She also expected in herself (a now turned-off person) the same responsiveness she had experienced before. Not surprisingly, she was disappointed! It took a time of intensive work in therapy to free her up so that she was again able to be responsive, this time to her husband.

In another case, a man remarried after his first marriage ended. His first wife was quickly aroused and intensely orgasmic. His second wife had experienced sexual trauma as a child and so could not freely allow herself to respond orgasmically. She experienced a great deal of conflict about her sexual responsiveness. Though she would become intensely aroused she would fight the arousal and therefore show strain and frustration. The man read this as a message about her feelings for him. He had difficulty comprehending how orgasm could be internally difficult for his second wife when it had been so easy for his first wife.

Besides respecting differences from one person to another, it is important to expect that the same person will change from one experience to another. This is reported more frequently by women than by men. Generally, men report feeling more consistent about what they find stimulating. Women tell us that one time kissing may be highly arousing and the next time they do not even want their lips touched. For the man who believes it is his responsibility to turn on and please his wife, this can be very frustrating. Just about the time he thinks he has figured her out, she changes. This is another example of why it works best for each person to go after his or her own pleasure. When a woman is very changeable, the only way she and her partner can experience freedom and relaxation in love-making is for her to take responsibility for what she needs. There is no way her husband will be able to decide for her what is going to be stimulating.

This is true, too, for changes that occur within the same sexual event. Again women seem to be more changeable than men. We are not sure if this phenomenon is innate, culturally conditioned, or biased by the particular selection of people we work with or teach in seminars. It seems to fit with our culture's tendency to allow girls to express emotions more freely than boys. We hope that this is changing.

A common dissatisfaction that women report is that the man will find a responsive spot and stick with it "until he wears it thin." This approach of finding the correct button does not allow for changeableness.

How might the two of you develop a system that allows individuality and variation? The most effective guidelines we can give are in the chapter on pleasuring. It is particularly important to learn the two-way system. That is, each person takes the responsibility to go after his or her own needs for stimulation; and each person takes the responsibility to communicate in some way when he or she wants a particular activity changed. If you learn some nonverbal communication signals (see Chap. 12), you will probably have a flexible system. The nondemand exercise in the nondemand position is an effective way to learn for yourself and to communicate to your partner what is stimulating for you. In this experience you guide the other person's hands to teach what feels good to you. Even though what you have communicated may vary from time to time, you can learn some basic awareness of each other's tendencies. Then, the same guiding of hands can be incorporated into your sexual stimulation as a way to communicate your changing desire.

Stimulating Touch vs. Irritating Touch

Touch has the greatest potential for eliciting sexual stimulation when the person doing the touching is relaxed and enjoying the other person's body. The less anxiety and stress there is, the more likely it is that stimulation will occur.

Anxiety and tension are communicated in the vibrations we send through sexual touching. This can cause the touch to feel irritating.

Also, individual differences in how people touch can affect one's touch perception. For example, if you get most aroused with a firm touch you are likely to touch your spouse firmly. Your spouse may actually be much more responsive to a light touch. Unless you have talked about this and done some nondemand instructing, each of you may find the other's touch to be irritating rather than stimulating. Too much or too little pressure can make a major difference in your response to being touched. Reaching up and guiding your partner to adjust the touch to meet your needs is an effective means of ongoing flexibility (Chap. 13, Exercise 10).

When stroking and caressing flows, it is more likely to be arousing than when it is abrupt and jerky. Abruptness usually is indicative of discomfort in the pleasurer. Maintaining continuous contact with the other person's skin helps counteract the tendency for abruptness and promotes a flowing touch. For example, even when the pleasurer is obtaining additional lotion, it helps to keep one hand on the partner's body.

Lubricants can add to the stimulating quality of the touch. This is true when generally pleasuring the whole body as well as for genital caressing. Putting a little non-lanolin Allercreme on your hand before stimulating your partner's genitals can be a great feeling for both of you. For men, it feels most like being in the vagina and is very arousing. For the women, it reduces irritations and can add greatly to arousal. The only persons we have found for whom the use of lubricants is not a positive experience are men and women who do not like messes. For them natural genital secretions have been negative, so to add a lubricant that feels similar to these natural juices is a turn-off. We encourage such people to work to desensitize this negative response, because it interferes with their sexual pleasure—not just with the positive use of a lubricant.

There are certain types of problems with touch that are more deeply based than the abrupt touch and the touch with too little or too much pressure. These are ticklishness and forceful, controlling touch.

Forceful, controlling touch is often used by a person who needs to dominate or who is angry. In either case, the person may be too passive to express the need directly. Therefore, it comes out in the way he or she touches during sexual play. The partner often experiences the touch as smothering and as limiting his or her own sexual expression.

Ticklishness is thought to be indicative of intense erotic responsiveness that is blocked. In other words, the extremely ticklish person feels the partner's touch intensely, but instead of perceiving the touch as arousing, the erotic feeling is blocked and the ticklish feeling is substituted.

Gerald had this difficulty. He and his wife came to us because of his impotence. During the foot caress we discovered that his ticklishness interfered with the pleasure of the caress. We had him focus intensely on the sensation of the feeling, at the same time being aware that he was not allowing himself to take in the sensuous touch. With practice, he was able to allow himself incredibly sensuous responses to foot caresses. The same thing surfaced as Gerald and his wife, Susan, went through the nondemand instruction for positive genital stimulation. We learned that Susan had stopped touching Gerald's penis years before. There was no way she could provide him positive genital stimulation without tickling. No wonder he was unable to get an erection! First we worked through some emotional barriers that had never allowed him to feel anything intensely. Then the couple practiced some experiences that allowed Gerald to focus on and receive sensuous stimulation. As anxiety about erections was reduced and stimuli received, erections became a regular response.

Kissing is a part of stimulating touch that is often not addressed. We have been surprised to find individuals and couples who have never kissed passionately. Their kissing would not be considered stimulating; it is a friendship peck. It has been a challenging experience to teach couples how to kiss! We discover that kissing has never been a stimulating part of a couple's love-making. Neither of them has ever experienced passionate kissing with anyone. They have never used tongue, teeth, or anything but lips. In our professional role we do not see ourselves as acceptable models, and *for sure* not surrogates. So there we are, explaining with words how to enjoy using tongues and teeth and *really* kissing. It has been fun and rewarding for us to help a couple to find a whole new area of sexual stimulation—their mouths.

If one or both of you find yourself fitting into the nonpassionate kissing category, talk with each other about how you would like to grow, and then start experimenting. At first it may feel rather awkward, but stick with it. Start by teasing with your tongue against your spouse's lips, then tongue against teeth and finally tongue to tongue. Eventually the whole mouth can get into the act. Once the passion and arousal is experienced, further mouth involvement will happen spontaneously.

Exaggerating vs. Withholding Natural Body Responses

When we sense our bodies becoming sexually stimulated, we can react in two ways. We can let ourselves take in and express those responses or we can tighten up and prevent the stimulation from following its natural acceleration.

For the person who has had some difficulty in flowing with his or her body's responses, there is a need to exaggerate positive sensations. This is done to counteract years of conditioning that taught the person to withhold natural sexual responses.

Start by listening to your body. This is not an evaluation of your body—not standing outside yourself and checking your response. Rather, listening to your body means crawling inside and "getting with" your inner self—going with your good feelings, focusing on the good sensations of touch. Sometimes this includes moving in a rhythmic pattern. The rhythmic pattern might be a response to vaginal or penile throbbing. It may be a response to your clitoris wanting rhythmic pressure or your penis wanting rhythmic stroking. If you are aware of your inner desire for such a rhythmic experience, become active in setting the rhythm in motion. Exaggerate the natural desire of your body by acting intensely in response to it.

The same thing can be true with breathing. A number of women who have had difficulty responding orgasmically have discovered that they stop their natural exaggerated breathing when they get highly aroused. Deeper and more rapid breathing is a natural body response to sexual stimulation (Chap. 8, p. 91). When we cut off our body responses, we inhibit the potential for release. So if you find your breathing intensifying, breathe even harder.

Noise can also be exaggerated or withheld. Sometimes external conditions hinder your freedom to let out all the sounds that you feel like expressing. The most common inhibitor is children in a nearby room. This is a realistic interference. If it causes conflict for you, try to find some times away from children where you can both really let loose.

Another natural response to stimulation is to move our bodies towards stimulating contact. Often this means pushing one's pelvis toward some point of stimulation. Listen to yourself on this, too. If you notice yourself pulling away from points of contact, consciously attempt to reverse that withholding pattern by actively moving your genitals toward positive sexual stimulation.

The more we can open up and allow ourselves to take in and respond to stimulation, the more responsive we will become. It is important to get with our bodies, to enjoy God's creation in us, and to freely celebrate our sexuality within our marriage.

_____16

By Invitation Only

I don't understand why my wife gets so upset when I get in her. I always check to make sure she's moist, yet she says I enter her whether she's ready or not. I'm confused.

When?

Somewhere in the process of sexual stimulation entry is likely to occur. The act of entry is what changes a sexual experience from sexual play to sexual intercourse. However, entry is not necessary for sexual enjoyment and release. For many couples entry is not an automatic part of every sexual experience. When entry is not possible—in cases of prolonged impotence for the man or vaginismus for the woman—couples can learn totally satisfying sexual play without a full intercourse event. (Vaginismus is a tight contraction or spasm of the vagina.) There are some advantages to sexual play without intercourse. All of us would benefit from learning to enjoy the pleasure of each other's bodies totally.

When entry is possible, it should occur when both partners feel ready and desirous of having the penis in the vagina. Entry is not likely to be desired until there is intense sexual stimulation for the man and the woman. In fact, women may experience release through external bodily stimulation before entry.

There is no one correct time for entry. The only physical criteria are vaginal lubrication for the woman and an erect penis for the man. Even these are not entirely necessary in that a man and woman can learn to stuff a slightly erect penis into the vagina. A lubricant can be used to substitute for or add to vaginal lubrication. So the right time is your time.

The physical signs of readiness do not always insure emotional readiness. The man may learn to want extended love-play for quite some time after he has a full erection. Women often do not "feel" ready even though they have plenty of lubrication. If a woman is feeling tense, she will not be desiring entry. This may be demonstrated by stiff legs or a withdrawing from sexual stimulation rather than reaching for it.

The woman needs the man to back off when her body is ready but her feelings are not. She needs room to allow her feelings to catch up with her body's response. This can happen only if she is free of the demand to be ready.

When the feeling of readiness is there, the woman knows it! It might be described as the opening up and reaching out of the vagina. There are actual physical changes occurring during the plateau phase (Chap. 8, p. 88 f.) that correspond to this opening sensation. The labia majora (outer lips) have thinned and are folded back out of the way of the vaginal opening. The swollen inner lips gap widely to create a funnel into the vagina. A woman is only minutes away from an orgasmic release when she is experiencing the sensations of these changes in her genitalia. She may or may not pursue entry at this time. It is her decision. The woman is the only one who can decide when she is ready.

Why Entry by Invitation?

We all have a sense of territory. All of us feel somewhat protective and possessive of our space. Children go through a time starting somewhere around age ten when they feel extremely violated if a brother, sister or even father or mother enters their room uninvited. When we are in our bedroom or bathroom with the door closed, we request that our children knock and wait for a response before entering. We give them the same courtesy. This is what it means to respect each other's territory.

Have you ever had an energetic salesman come to your door? You barely have the door open and he's already standing in your entry. You have to back up to have room to talk with him. An automatic response to that kind of invasion is to want to push the man right out the door.

The same principles apply to sexual intercourse. Entry is an act of the man entering the woman's body. If he is going to feel welcome there, he must wait for an invitation. All of us feel much more comfortable when we *invite* someone into our space. This is true of our homes, our rooms, our feelings and our bodies.

The invitation need not be formal. It might be a nonverbal message that communicates positively for both of you. That might be the woman reaching for the penis with her pelvis. It might be her inserting the penis into the vagina. It might be a pet word the two of you enjoy. There are many possible ways the woman can let the man know that she is ready.

Why the Woman?

It is the woman's body that is being entered. By physical anatomy she is the receptacle, which tends to be a more passive position. She can easily experience the sense of invasion that you might have felt with the aggressive salesman. The man, on the other hand, has the penis with which he tends to take aggressive action to move into the vagina. But aggressiveness is not necessary. In fact, a man can lie passively on his back and a woman can move her body over his erect penis, thereby inserting it into her vagina. Positions and roles are then somewhat reversed, even though the vagina is still a receptacle receiving this responsive, aggressive part of the man's body. However entry occurs, the man will feel better about being in the woman when he senses a warm, desirous response from her, rather than a rejection because she feels invaded. Husbands do not like to feel that their wives would like to throw them out the door.

What about Biblical Symbolism?

We have studied the way in which Christ compares himself to the bridegroom and the church to his bride. In Ephesians 5 Paul instructs the man to love his wife as he does his own body, even as Christ loved the church.

Christ offers himself to us. He is ready to enter our lives and to guide us to the extent that we his people will ask him to be there with us and for us. Christ does not invade. He gives, loves and cares, and waits to be invited. What a beautiful model of entry by invitation.

After Entry?

Is entry the beginning of the end? No, entry is not a final event. Much love play can occur after the penis has entered the vagina. The penis can be withdrawn for more total body play. Then reentry can occur. When the couple is having fun together, the focus can be on total enjoyment. The mentality does not have to focus on entry and thrusting to the point of ejaculation and orgasm.

During an extended love-making experience with focus on the enjoyment of the process, a person's level of arousal may vary in intensity. The level of arousal will tend to be experienced in waves, with intense surges and then a fading away. As long as the person isn't standing back watching and evaluating arousal, it is fun to ride the waves. However, if a person is in an evaluative role, a dip may cause anxiety which will interfere with the possibility of another intense surge. It is the *anxiety* about the dips, not the dips themselves, that gets in the way of continued responsiveness.

The freedom to enter, withdraw, and reenter will also help a man last longer. This allows him to have dips in excitement level so that he doesn't ejaculate before he is ready.

Flexibility and freedom add fun to sexual encounter. Let entry also be a fun part of the total sexual event. This can best happen when you communicate your own feelings of readiness, respect each other's feelings and territory, and focus on the process rather than on a specific intercourse goal.

_____17

Letting Go

I think I have orgasms, but I've never been sure. What does it feel like? My husband doesn't think I ever have.

What Happens?

For most men the orgasmic response has been rather obvious because of the concurrent ejaculation of seminal fluid. It is an external happening. There are internal feelings, however, that accompany the more obvious event. In fact, there are some men who report being able to experience the sensation of letting go, the orgasmic release, without ejaculation. Almost every time we teach our seminar to groups of 80 to 150 people, at least one man reports that he can experience an orgasmic release without an ejaculation.

When we took you through the physiological body responses of the sexual experience, we talked about the male orgasm having two stages. The first stage occurs between the time of warning that the man is approaching the point of no return and the point of ejaculatory inevitability (see Sexual Response Pattern graph, Chap. 8). The second phase starts with the point of ejaculatory inevitability or the actual point of no return. The feeling sensations for the man compare with these two physical stages. There are anticipatory tingling sensations which warn the man that he is approaching the point of no return. These might be described as pleasurable burning sensations. There is the sense of wanting those feelings to last forever, and yet the urge to rush on with intense thrusting. Along with this, there is a feeling that warmth from the total body is being drawn into the genitals; the sensation becomes primarily genitally centered. As the man moves from this first stage to the second stage, he experiences a momentary sensation of being held in suspension. This is followed by the letting go with the rush of the ejaculation, and a warm flowing feeling inside the penis.

Because the orgasmic physiological happenings for the woman are all internal, there has been much confusion about the woman's orgasm. Women have had more difficulty allowing release than men. This, also, has caused more focus on the woman's orgasm than on the man's.

Graber and Graber in their book, *Woman's Orgasm* (Indianapolis: Bobbs-Merrill Co., 1975), have thoroughly described the letting go experience for the woman.

They compare the orgasmic response to the reflex response of the doctor tapping a person's knee with a rubber hammer. The tap (the sensory input) occurs at one point of the body, the knee. The jerk (the muscular response) occurs at another point of the body, the lower leg. Similarly, the clitoris may be stimulated (the sensory input) and the pubococcygeus muscle in the vagina contracts (the muscular response).

There is an initial spasm in the orgasmic platform (the lower third of the vagina) that occurs two to four seconds before the actual orgasm. This sensation is comparable to the man's warning that he is approaching the point of no return. This may be the point at which many women cut off their orgasmic response. That spasm is the warning cue that sets off their panic, fear, or conflict about letting go.

Graber and Graber go on to describe the orgasm's three stages. The first one begins with an initial momentary feeling of being suspended in air. Then there is an intense, pelvically centered sensual awareness. Finally, there is a feeling of opening up. We think of it as a very vulnerable sensation of all the woman's nerve endings being exposed. This can be frightening to a woman who has difficulty trusting.

The pelvic sensitivity and opening up moves the woman into the second stage, with the flow of warmth spreading from the pelvis to the rest of the body. This experience is just the opposite of what men describe as happening to them. We might picture the difference with a diagram.

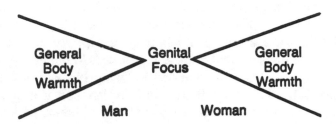

The flow of warmth for the man starts with the general pleasure and flows to the genitals. The woman's starts genitally and flows outward with general body warmth.

For the woman, however, there is a return of attention to the pelvis with vaginally centered pelvic throbbing. This is the third stage. A complete illustration of the woman's release might look like the following diagram.

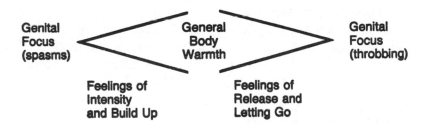

We have two personal descriptions of the orgasmic response that we would like to share with you. The first is from a woman's journal. She shared this with us and gave us permission to share it with you. This is her description of what happens to her:

> It is beautiful! It's as though my being withdraws from my extremities and is compacted in the clitoris. Everything recedes—there is nothing but this intense build up of pleasure—nothing else exists. Then there is this tremendous explosive release that radiates outward in waves. I breathe in rhythm with the waves and my muscles contract. . . .

The second description came from our twelve-year-old daughter after a sex education evening for parents and their junior highers. Following the evening we had a special communication time with her. During this time we wanted to allow her to ask further questions and get feedback from her about what she had heard and understood. Her first question was, "When the doctor was answering the questions we handed in, he used regular language except for answering the questions about girl's masturbation and woman's 'organism'—or whatever you call that. Then he changed to using big words I couldn't understand. Why did he do that?" Our explanation was that those are answers some parents do not want their children to know. So he used accurate technical language that the parents could reinterpret for their children if they desired, or avoid talking about if the information was not comfortable for them. We then proceeded to answer her questions about how girls masturbate and what an orgasm is. Using the effective communication skills we wish we always practiced, we had her feed back to us what she understood. Her description of an orgasm was delightful.

"You get all good feelings down here (holding her hands on her pelvis). Then you get all jazzed (panting). Then you let it all out (sigh) and then you just sit there feeling good all over."

What better way to say it!

A question often asked is, "Does not an orgasm during intercourse feel different than an orgasm as a result of external stimulation?" We talked about the fact that there is no physical difference between orgasms (see Vaginal vs. Clitoral Orgasm, Chap. 8). In terms of what happens to the body, an orgasm is an orgasm. Women do report differences in feeling, however.

Many women talk about an orgasm from external stimulation as being more intense, but not feeling as emotionally satisfying. There are possible explanations for each of these differences. As we understand it, the vaginal contractions during an orgasm are more intense when there is no penis in the vagina. The muscle has nothing to bump up against. Therefore, its range of expansion and contraction is greater. The empty feeling seems to relate to the readiness for entry that we described in Chapter 16. When the outer lips are out of the way and the inner lips are engorged, making a funnel into the vagina, many women experience an intense desire to have their husbands inside them. When that is not possible, it leaves some women frustrated and dissatisfied. This is a difficult feeling for the wives of impotent men. It seems less noticeable for women who are choosing to have an orgasm with external stimulation rather than during intercourse.

When Does It Happen?

Letting go can be allowed during love play before entry, after entry with the penis in the vagina, or after withdrawal of the penis from the vagina. Let us talk about each of these possibilities.

The source of stimulation (the sensory input or knee tap) for the release that occurs before entry can vary. It may be manual stimulation around the clitoris for the woman and on the shaft of the penis for the man. There could be oral-genital contact—the woman sucking or licking on the man's penis and the man using his mouth and tongue around the woman's clitoris and into the vagina. There might be a release during general body and/or breast caressing. Or there may be no direct physical stimulation. Some women experience orgasms while reading love stories. Some men ejaculate while looking at pictures of nude women. Therefore, letting go before entry has many possible sources of origin.

People's responses to release before entry vary. Sometimes both spouses desire it. Perhaps intercourse has become a demand. Entry is associated with many negative feelings. One means of relieving those pressures is for the couple to become comfortable with letting go without entry.

Some women find they are freer to respond before entry. Once entry occurs they feel more demand. Or they might start to worry that their husbands will ejaculate before they have a chance to let go. These feelings interfere with their natural sexual responses. They soon develop a style of being unable to let go when the penis is in the vagina, so release before entry can be a valuable alternative.

On the other hand, when a man accidentally experiences release before entry, he usually feels like a failure and leaves his partner frustrated. Neither one of them planned for him to "come" that quickly. This is called premature ejaculation. We will deal thoroughly with this dilemma in a future chapter (29).

Letting go after entry with the penis in the vagina has traditionally been accepted as the ideal time. Indeed, many couples prefer this. The woman may enjoy the feeling of the man's penis in her vagina during the contractions of her orgasm. However, when a man insists that both the man's and the woman's release must happen with the penis in the vagina, this need is usually tied up with his concerns about his masculinity. It confirms him as a man if this orgasmic timing is possible for them. But for the woman who has difficulty letting go when the penis is in the vagina, this need of her husband puts an incredible demand on her. It lays on her the responsibility to have an orgasm at a certain time so that he can feel good about himself. This is a sure way to prevent her from freely letting go when they are having intercourse. This is true whether the demand is felt from the husband or within herself.

Many women want more sexual stimulation after withdrawal of the penis from the vagina. This may be because the husband does not have control of ejaculation. He cannot remain in the vagina long enough without ejaculating for her to let go of her built-up sexual excitement. This may be true whether or not she has had a previous release. If she has become rearoused, she may need to let go again. Another reason for the woman wanting more stimulation after withdrawal of the penis from the vagina may be her internal drive for repeated orgasms. Or it may be that she did not have a release before entry, she could not have one during, and so this is the first time in the experience that she is ready to pursue an orgasm.

For the man who has already ejaculated, the woman's need may be experienced as a demand. He is so relaxed it is difficult for him to have the energy to pursue his wife's body. The tendency is for him to fall asleep. This is a natural reaction. If this is a regular conflict for the two of you, talk about it at some objective time. Explore all possible ways for the woman to get satisfaction without its being a demand for the man. Maybe learning ejaculatory control is the answer. Maybe all the woman needs is the man's body close to her, his arms around her and his hand available for her to use to bring herself a release. Discover your own options that resolve this problem.

It is important to mention that some men experience retarded or inhibited ejaculation. Sometimes this can occur after drinking alcoholic beverages. Or it can happen when a man is very tired. A small percentage of men need a long time to be able to let go. If there has been extended thrusting with the penis in the vagina the woman may be getting tired and sore so she needs the man to withdraw. He may still want a release. Sometimes manual or oral stimulation may be used to bring about his release. If this is not possible and the pattern continues, professional help is necessary.

If the couple is withdrawing to ejaculate as a means of birth control, we would say, forget it. As we mentioned in describing the four phases of the sexual response (Chap. 8), some seminal fluid with sperm will often be secreted before the total ejaculate is expelled. These can impregnate the woman just as easily as the sperm in the remaining ejaculate.

How Many?

What are the possibilities for letting go? Men are usually limited to one release per experience. This is due to their need to have a rest period of at least 20–30 minutes, and probably more like several hours, before they can become rearoused after a release.

The men who experience release without an ejaculation are an exception to this pattern. They report being able to maintain their erections after their release and continue love-making with repeated releases.

Women are different from most men in this regard. Physically, women have the potential for many orgasms within one event. These may occur in rapid sequence without any relaxation of sexual excitement. They may also occur after a brief letdown followed by more stimulation.

It is important to recognize that repeated orgasms are a physical potential for women but should not be the goal. When orgasms become a goal rather than a reflex response, they are less likely to happen.

This same principle applies to couples who desire simultaneous orgasms. By that we mean the husband and wife letting go at the same time. Even though it is a delightful experience if your sexual activity can flow that way, simultaneous orgasms are far from necessary for a fully satisfying sexual relationship. They must remain an exciting option and not become a demanding goal.

Letting go is an important feeling in the whole sexual process. It is the most individual aspect and the part of sex when the partners are least aware of being together. A person becomes totally caught up in his or her own being. It reminds us of soaring. Letting go requires being able to take a risk—to let yourself be totally you in the presence of another person.

We skied downhill for the first time this past winter. Joyce recalls,

"The closest sensation I have ever had to orgasmic release happened with skiing. There is one moment that particularly captures that 'letting go' experience for me. I was at the top of one big rolling hill with a flat area below and then an incline beginning another hill. There was a feeling of building excitement as I got my skis parallel and flat, flexed my knees and pushed off with my poles, ready to let my skis take me as fast as the momentum could build on the decline. The ride down was a beautiful, risky feeling of flying through the air, totally letting out all the stops. The flat place felt like soaring across open territory. I had already taken the risk, but there was still more speed to enjoy. The incline felt like the satisfied sigh; I made it and it felt good."

What experiences have you had in life where you have risked, soared, and had the satisfaction of releasing yourself to that situation?

_____18

Affirmation Time

When he's done he rolls over and is gone. I lie there wanting more contact. I need him to touch me and talk to me. I need to know he loves me. When he falls asleep I feel like he got what he wanted and I don't matter. First I'm hurt, then I get mad, finally I just cry.

The emotional affirmation phase compares to the physical resolution phase. Affirming one another meets emotional needs. Resolution describes what happens to the body as everything reverses itself to return to the prestimulated state. We dealt with the resolution phase in Chapter 8. Now let us see what is happening emotionally.

After physical and emotional sexual release, both men and women experience a peaceful, relaxed feeling. The more complete the tension release, the more sleepy a person will be and the less he or she will need continued physical touching.

Some people feel their letdown very rapidly. Men report this more commonly than women. There is an intense release and an almost immediate falling asleep. A woman's tension release may occur just as intensely and rapidly as a man's or it may be more gradual. The more gradually the body returns to its prestimulated state (gets rid of its vasocongestion), the more the woman needs touching and affirmation.

The affirmation time is a time of confirming one another's nakedness. To be naked, open or vulnerable and not ashamed is the essence of sexual trust. This was the quality of the man-woman relationship before the Fall. The intense intimacy involved in allowing oneself to let go totally with another person can trigger strong feelings of vulnerability. This elicits the need to know that the other person still cares and will not take advantage of the exposure which has occurred.

What meets one person's need for affirmation may be very different from what meets another's need. Once again, communication is the place to begin. What are your feelings? What would each of you like? How might you resolve your differences or meet the needs of both of you?

When Is Affirmation Needed?

The need for affirmation depends both on the degree of physical release and on the emotional need. This is true for both men and women.

Physical sexual release has often been compared to a sneeze. That is, there is the full tingling feeling of blood rushing into the area. This is followed by the good releasing feeling of the "ah-choo." The more intensely a person lets out the sneeze, the more rapidly the relief of the congestion occurs. Similarly, the more intense the orgasm, the more rapid the release of the pelvic congestion. When you stifle a sneeze, you can feel an uncomfortable congestion for some time afterward. The same uncomfortable congestion occurs in the pelvis when you do not allow a release.

Since more women have difficulty letting go, and since women have the potential to be restimulated to need further release, women more than men commonly find themselves wakeful after a sexual experience. They either want more stimulation, as we mentioned in the previous chapter, or they want to be held and affirmed. When the pelvis is engorged with blood and fluid due to sexual arousal without total release, there is a feeling of tension and irritability. The person will not feel relaxed and ready to fall asleep.

Emotionally, the need for affirmation varies with the degree of trust in one's partner and security with one's own response. A man may be as emotionally in need of affirmation as a woman. The trust and security issues are usually brought with the person from childhood and past experiences.

The idea that all women need to be caressed after withdrawal of the penis from the vagina is not necessarily accurate. Women may need it more often than men if they have been left unfulfilled. But when a woman is physically satisfied because she has had one intense release or the number of releases she has desired, she is likely to feel like falling asleep rather quickly herself. On the other hand, if a man is feeling rather unsure of himself and uncertain that he can trust his wife, he may be the one desiring a close, gradual unwinding.

This need can vary from time to time. Some experiences provide more intense release than others, and a person may be more or less vulnerable from time to time. These conditions will affect the person's desire for touch and closeness in each encounter. Thus, each couple needs ongoing communication.

What Problems Interfere?

Tension within the relationship concerning the affirmation time usually has to do with failure to communicate and resolve individual differences.

The common dilemma is the man who falls asleep, leaving the woman needy. We talked about ways to work on that in the previous chapter. Both people's responses are entirely legitimate. Having had a full letting go of the tension, the man's body is ready to drift off into peaceful sleep. Needing more release, the woman's body is irritable, tense and wide awake. This is a situation of opposite individual needs in a mutual relationship. Both will have to look at what they can do to resolve the difference.

Other individual needs or differences may arise. Some men have an urgent need to urinate after intercourse. They may jump up quickly after withdrawing from the vagina. The man may never have told his wife why he gets up immediately. She is left feeling vulnerable and hurt. She feels that she exposed herself to him and he does not even care enough to stay with her; all he wants is his release. Communicating the reason for his hasty departure and making a plan to come back will usually turn this from a painful happening to a building time. Some men experience pain in the penis after release. They need to share this and plan to withdraw, but to stay close.

Because of the anatomy of some women's genitals, they have a high susceptibility to bladder infections if they do not get up and wash right after intercourse. Again, this may be perceived as desertion.

Usually the man feels that the woman was dissatisfied with the sexual experience. He then sees himself as inadequate.

Tensions concerning the need for affirmation after release, or after sexual arousal with no release, can usually be resolved if there is open communication and a caring relationship.

The process of affirming can be the most valuable, beautiful part of the total sexual experience. It can be a time of tenderness, of closeness, of having shared something extremely intimate and personal, and of having been out of control with each other. Sexual release is probably the most total expression of one's emotional and spiritual being without mental control. Thus there is a feeling of vulnerability, yet with intense caring and intimacy.

_____19

Cleaning Up

Is This Normal?

It was our first time teaching our seminar on Christian Perspectives in Sexual Enjoyment to a younger, newly married group. At our first break a young woman led Joyce off to the side to talk privately. She said she and her husband had been married for three months. After they had intercourse there was always a mess to clean up. She was wondering if that was normal and what other couples did about it. Since that time, it has become a rather common question. We now routinely address the issue of normal excretions and how to handle the cleanup.

How much discharge should you expect? The man's seminal fluid will be about one teaspoonful. Women's vaginal lubrication varies considerably. We really cannot give even an approximate measure. Maybe we can picture it for you. When the man withdraws from the vagina, his penis will usually drip with the secretions. If the woman were to sit up on the sheet and let the discharge run out of her vagina, it would probably soak a spot one to five inches in diameter. This is a combination of her own vaginal lubrication and the seminal fluid that has been deposited if her husband ejaculated while in the vagina.

Is this a turn-off? Should you let your spouse see it? Most men get turned on by vaginal lubrication. It's a sign of the wife's responsive-ness which many men take as a compliment. Besides, most men get turned on by a turned-on woman. They love it!

An exception to this might be some men who have extreme difficulty even touching the vaginal area. They think of it as messy and do not like messes. Some women have a similar response to the man's ejaculate. To them it is repulsive. They avoid it as if it will contaminate them. These are the exceptions rather than the norm.

For most women, the ejaculation has a positive, warm, intimate feeling. It is a symbol of the intimacy shared.

Since the usual response is positive, we encourage openness about the discharge. It is clean; it has no germs. There is nothing embarrassing or innately repulsive about it. The result of a beautiful act, it gives life. This is the way God made us and intended us to be.

If it is a turn-off to one of you, that person should talk about it and possibly even get some professional help. Removing that negative barrier from your sexual relationship could open up a whole new world of freedom for the two of you.

How to Handle It

There is really no prescribed, correct or proper way to take care of the sexual juices. Usually you can start by talking about what, if anything, you would like to do about it. What is comfortable for each of you?

Some couples bring a box of tissues to their love-making spot. Others like to have a wash cloth or towel. Some have their special love-making sheet or blanket they put under them. Still others feel no need to take care of the discharge. If they make love in bed, the sheets absorb the discharge and that is comfortable for them.

Sometimes the cleaning up time can become a pleasant, familiar ritual. The item(s) brought to the experience can be included in the "something old" part of setting the atmosphere (see Chap. 14).

When the "Norm" Varies

A small percentage of women experience an expulsion of fluid that is not vaginal lubrication. Robert C. Kolodny, M.D., from Masters and Johnson's Institute has researched this phenomenon. He has reported on this at a workshop and in a personal telephone call. A large amount of fluid—approximately a cup—is expelled from the urinary bladder, but it is not urine. The woman can urinate immediately before a sexual experience. She can have every drop of urine removed from the bladder with a rubber tube called a catheter. Nevertheless, if she has an orgasm within even a few minutes of having a totally empty bladder, she will expel this clear, watery fluid from the urinary bladder. This evidently happens in intensely orgasmic women. Apparently the pituitary gland causes fluid to be withdrawn from the cells of the body and fed into the blood, and from there to the bladder.

Even though this discharge is not usual for most women, it need not be a negative experience. Extra preparation will be required to protect the surface on which the sexual experience occurs. Otherwise, the area would be rather wet afterward. The fluid is clean, warm, and need not be repulsive. Some women who experience this fluid expulsion have withheld their orgasmic response because of their embarrassment. They feel as though they have lost bladder control. Getting accurate data and sharing it with each other can free the woman to make the necessary preparations before love-making and to allow herself to let go orgasmically. It has helped some women to think of letting themselves go with the flow of the fluid. This helps them gain a warm, positive association with their body's responses, rather than tightening up when they feel it coming. For them, this is the body's normal response. It is something to go with, not fight.

Summary

The sexual organs, orifices and discharges are clean. They are free of disease-producing microorganisms. As you are able to integrate the sexual parts of yourself into your total being, you develop positive feelings toward all aspects of your sexual expression, rather than feeling hesitant toward or repulsed by them. Your positive associations contribute to natural comfort in handling the sexual dimensions of your life.

20

Enhancing the Sexual Response

Keeping in Shape

Research data to document the effects of sleep, nutrition and exercise on the sexual response is greatly needed. We are convinced that these three areas of a person's life style are extremely important and merit more attention than has been given to them by researchers up to this point.

A woman comes to us with orgasmic difficulties. In the initial assessment and throughout the therapy process, we become increasingly aware of imbalances within her system. She has difficulty falling asleep at night, becomes depressed before her menstrual period, and starts showing signs of premature menopause. Tranquilizers are used to modify these symptoms. We refer her to an endocrinologist and a biochemist-nutritionist. The work-ups reveal that she is not producing adequate levels of hormones. Her estrogen level is very low. There are also indications that her body is not absorbing nutrients properly. As her diet is revised, an exercise program activated, and sleep is regulated without drugs, her system begins to show signs of clearing. Along with the clearing comes increased sexual responsiveness. We cannot prove that the increased responsiveness is caused by the changes in nutrition, exercise, and sleep. But knowledge of how our bodies work has led us to formulate some theories about this.

Nutrition and Sleep

Currently there is an increased emphasis on the ways in which food affects our physical and emotional health. There has been a particular concern with sugar and its relationship to hypoglycemic depression, sleep disruption, and learning problems in children. Artificial dyes and additives in food have also received attention.

We know that carbohydrates (sugars and starches) affect our insulin production, which in turn affects our metabolism. This is directly related to our energy level.

We are also becoming more aware of the way nutrition influences hormonal production. When our bodies are not getting the nutrients they need, our sex hormones will be the first to be affected. Premature menopause can be related to reduced estrogen production due to malnutrition. This malnutrition may be caused by poor eating patterns or by malabsorption due to the body's intolerance of a particular food. Gluten is a common offender.

Many have wondered about the effect of alcohol on sexual response. Alcohol is an inhibitor. Therefore, if a person is anxious a small amount of alcohol can enhance sexual activity by reducing the anxiety. Anxiety is always a sexual inhibitor, so lowering the anxiety will allow people to get with their natural body responses. However, large amounts of alcohol will inhibit the sexual response. Many men report experiencing difficulty with erection or ejaculation after they have had too much to drink.

"Chronic abuse of alcohol frequently leads to deterioration of sexual functioning in both men and women. . . . Chronic alcoholic men display a reduction in libido as compared to their previous levels of sexual desire, even if allowances are made for age differences. About 40 percent of alcoholic men are impotent and approximately 5 to 10 percent have retarded or inhibited ejaculation." [1]

Women are also affected by alcohol. "Thirty to forty percent of alcoholic women report difficulties in becoming sexually aroused, and

---

1. Robert C. Kolodny, William H. Masters, and Virginia E. Johnson, *Textbook of Sexual Medicine* (Boston: Little, Brown and Company, 1979), pp. 239, 240.

approximately 15 percent of female alcoholics experience either loss of orgasmic responsiveness or significant reduction in the frequency or intensity of orgasm." [2]

Be alert to the way you are affected by what you take in. What do you sense about your sexual feelings after eating a heavy, starchy meal? How does such a meal affect your sleep? What about alcohol consumption for you? Does it help or hinder? Wines are usually more tolerable than distilled, hard liquors which go directly into the bloodstream. Protein eaten *before* drinking slows its absorption and its effect on the body.

The area of nutrition and sexual responsiveness intrigues us. It is wide open for exploration and research. We believe that nutrition has a greater impact on us than anyone realizes at this time.

Our beliefs about the impact of nutrition on our bodies have developed through a trying personal family experience. Sharing this experience with you will lead us to the effects of disrupted sleep on sexual desire.

When our youngest child, Kristine, was ten days old, we started her on a few drops of vitamins. She screamed for four hours. Since she had hardly cried in those first ten days, we all took notice. When she was two months old, we planned to take her with us to Spokane, Washington, where we were going to teach our seminar. As she was still being breast-fed, she needed to be with us. Thinking it would help us carry her through our lecture times, we started her on baby cereal. About an hour after her first teaspoon of cereal, she started screaming and screamed for four hours. We tried other cereals. Others did not seem to affect her so severely. However, her sleeping patterns changed. She had been sleeping from her 10 P.M. feeding to her 6 A.M. feeding. By the time we were ready for the trip, she was waking up anywhere from five to ten times a night. On the trip she developed respiratory symptoms. We obviously had a child with extreme food intolerances.

Our pediatrician was very supportive and provided guidance. Nevertheless, not much seemed to help. Most of the food that even allergic children can usually tolerate upset her.

When she was seven months old, our pediatrician referred us to one of the best children's allergists in the country. We were both ex-

---

2. *Ibid,* p. 240.

hausted. Kristine had been sick most of the time during those five months. The allergist took Kristine off everything she had been eating and put her on a very limited diet. Joyce was to follow the same diet or discontinue breast-feeding. There seemed to be nothing in the house Joyce could eat. She was weak, tired, and overwhelmed, so the decision to stop breast-feeding soon became obvious.

Kristine's health began to improve, but the struggle was far from over. Food trials were tedious. The majority of the foods we tried still caused reactions. Reactions meant disruption of sleep and often susceptibility to infections which could last up to two weeks. Diarrhea became an almost constant problem.

We felt we had not found the real clue to the problem. The UCLA medical clinic was our next attempt, when Kristine was about eighteen months of age. The physicians there suggested an extended hospitalization. We could not accept putting our little one through that separation and emotional trauma.

One day Joyce stopped by the store where she buys her clothes. Not really having energy to make decisions about what to buy, she shared her frustration about Kristine's health and our disrupted sleep. The woman in charge had become a friend over the years Joyce had shopped there. Hearing our story, she suggested we visit a biochemist and nutritionist who had been a tremendous help to her husband, who also suffered from food intolerance.

A biochemist! That's it! We had often felt that a chemical analysis of some sort would be helpful in guiding us in our food selections for Kristine. There must be some way to find foods that worked.

Our next reaction was, "How ridiculous! We have access to the best medical care in the world. Here we are listening to the manager of a dress shop who knows next to nothing about medicine."

We decided to try it, since we were desperate. Also we had enough confidence in our own knowledge of physiology that we would not take any potentially harmful advice. Up to this time, we had not been able to find any form of protein that Kristine could tolerate. We had ruled out any dairy products because of her intolerance to milk. We soon learned that cottage cheese, string cheese and yogurt do not contain lactose, the sugar in milk which makes it intolerable to many people. The first change we made was to take all sugar out of Kristine's diet and start giving her string cheese six times a day. This was based on the biochemist's suspicion that Kristine's lack of protein and her high carbohydrate intake was setting off overproduction of insulin, with the resulting low blood sugar causing her to wake up frequently during the night. Within a week she was sleeping most of the time. What a difference we discovered in two areas—the difference nutritional and biochemical balance made in Kristine's health and sleeping pattern, and the difference uninterrupted sleep made in our sexual interest!

We share all of this to show how, in our own personal experience, we have witnessed the effect of food on the emotional state. As a result of this experience and the many sleepless nights we also know how the lack of sleep affects us sexually.

Sleep research has shown that we have sleep cycles. Just as sexual responses such as vaginal lubrication and penile erections occur every eighty to ninety minutes during a normal adult's sleep, so there are other psychological and physiological involuntary processes that occur in cyclic patterns while we sleep. When sleep is disrupted, we lose more than just the actual time that we are awake. We break our body's rhythm. This can affect our energy level, emotional stability, and sexual responsiveness.

Exercise

We have often been asked, "Does being in good shape physically, that is, exercising regularly, increase one's sexual responsiveness?"

There are many other factors that could be influencing sexual responsiveness at the same time an exercise program is started. Thus it is difficult to be certain that the exercise has made the difference.

However, there are several ways in which exercise is helpful, and we suspect that there are even more positive effects than just these.

First, regular exercise that increases your cardiovascular functioning (heart rate, blood pressure, and so on) will enhance your circulation, increase mental alertness, reduce stress, and improve muscular tone. Since one body system cannot change without in some way affecting the other body systems, those changes will indirectly influence sexual functioning. In addition, circulation, muscular response, alertness and reduction of stress are all a direct part of sexual responsiveness.

Second, exercising often improves how people feel about their bodies. This improvement in body image will often affect general feelings of self-worth and sexuality.

Third, exercising will get people in touch with the sensations of their bodies. This inevitably increases awareness of sexual feelings. So this is another way in which exercise can enhance sexual enjoyment.

We encourage regular exercise for cardiovascular improvement— such as jogging, hiking, swimming or whatever you find works for you. In addition, we have a list of body awareness and breathing exercises used with women. All of these may also be helpful to men. We recognize that a man does not have a vagina to contract, but he does have the same pubococcygeus muscle that is used to start and stop urination. That muscle can be tightened for practice that is comparable to the exercise we call "vaginal contractions."

Exercise 13
Body Awareness and Breathing

Breathing:
1. Panting (increases oxygenation and energy level):
Draw air into chest, above diaphragm; blow out six times, as though blowing out a candle; exhale slowly and completely. Do ten times at beginning of exercises.
2. Chest—slow, regular, smooth, relaxed breathing. This is good to do between exercises and may be helpful during intercourse.
3. Abdominal or "deep" diaphragmatic breathing:
Take in maximum amount of air slowly through nose, with your chest rising first and then your abdomen. Hold breath to count of four. Exhale slowly through slightly separated lips. Let go of all tension and let all air out.
This is done with all exercises. Try using it during intercourse.

Body Awareness and increased muscle tone in pelvic area:
1. Pelvic bounce: Lie on floor, knees slightly bent, pressure on soles of feet. Pushing with your feet, bounce buttocks up and down.
2. Pelvic rock:
    a) Get on your hands and knees.
    b) Inhale slowly through your nose as you arch your back and tense it; hold your breath in this position to count of four.
    c) Exhale slowly through parted lips as you sag back.
    d) Repeat ten times.
3. Pelvic lift (great for increasing orgasm potential):

a) Lie on your back on a firm surface with your knees bent and feet flat on the floor.

b) As you breathe in slowly through your nose, align your back with the floor, starting with your lowest vertebra and moving up toward your neck.

c) As you slowly exhale through parted lips, lift your pelvis and your back off the floor, one vertebra at a time, again starting at your coccyx (tail bone) and moving toward your neck. (You may actually move to a position of resting on your feet and head, with your fists holding your heels). Work up to this point slowly.

d) Come back down, one vertebra at a time, from neck to coccyx.

4. Vaginal contractions* (to increase friction and sensitivity during intercourse and prevent complications due to loss of pelvic muscle tone that can occur after childbirth or with aging process):

a) Tighten the pubococcygeus muscle, the muscle used to start and stop urination.

b) Hold as tightly as you can to count of ten.

c) Relax muscle.

d) Do a minimum of twenty-five daily (for a person with a particularly loose vagina, two hundred a day may be necessary).

e) To help you remember, connect this exercise with some other activity—driving, ironing, washing dishes, and so on.

Regular exercise, good nutrition and adequate sleep should help to banish the excessive fatigue that can block togetherness. If you get in shape but discover that you and your partner still are not getting together sexually, maybe you need to work on keeping in touch.

Keeping in Touch

Even as the gourmet cook is always looking for new recipes, the sexually aware person is alert to discover new feelings, sensations, and ways to bring pleasure. The cook may create a new recipe or experiment with one devised by someone else. Even so, your new discoveries may be created through experimentation in your own relationship or through trying ideas you have found somewhere else.

Reading is one avenue to new ideas. Read individually to gain new

---

* Extremely important!

ideas to try when the two of you are together, or to get in touch with your own sexual feelings. Read together as a couple for fun, education, stimulation or experimentation. The Song of Solomon in a modern translation may be the best literature available. Many other resources are suggested in the Annotated Bibliography.

Buying special sexual treats can help you keep tuned in to your own sexual desire and in touch with each other. These include special clothes, body paints, perfumes, oils, satin sheets.

Planning special times for yourself—taking time to rest, to pamper your body, to wash and lotion yourself, to manicure your nails—can build sexual awareness of both men and women. This is particularly needed when life's pressures do not allow room to get with your sexuality. These are the times when you need to lie back and relax. Since such times don't happen naturally, you need to plan and set aside the time you need. Make it a priority.

Special times for the two of you are a must! You may say, "But we can't—we have little children." Those children can survive being left with a caring adult for a day or two on a regular basis much better than they can survive living with parents whose relationship is neglected. Or you may say, "I can't leave my work." Which is a priority for you? What if you could predict that taking regular time away from the pressures of work to focus on your sexual relationship would help your marriage survive? Would you be able to find time?

The two of us are not exempt from the external pressures that get in the way of our own relationship. It involves constant planning ahead to make certain we have enough free time allotted for ourselves and each other. Ed Dayton, a friend of ours who writes about time management, taught us years ago that time scheduled for each other and for family members has to be treated just like a work appointment. If someone else wants to see us during that time, we already have a previous commitment.

This together time needs to be planned into most couples' lives if they are going to keep in touch. Planning ahead and scheduling may not be necessary for all couples. Maybe your life style is such that you naturally have hours each week already focused on each other. You are the exception rather than the rule! In most homes, activities, church, children, work, television, books, and exercise all get in the way of focusing on each other. We've talked about how to plan for and schedule times together in Chapter 11. Use those guidelines to plan time to communicate, touch, and have fun together. Use external enhancers to keep in touch sexually. Listening to music can help keep you alert to your internal feelings. Set up a special environment for a sexual experience. The tidiness of the room, the temperature of the room and the security of knowing you will not be interrupted are all external conditions that can make a difference.

Some people are almost continually aware of their sexual feelings. Others have to work at it. They need to focus on keeping in touch with the natural responses of their bodies. Keeping in touch with yourself and your partner takes effort, just as keeping in shape physically takes individual discipline. But both are well worth the effort.

I'm Not Interested

In order for two people to get together sexually, they must make a choice to do so. People usually choose what they desire. Thus, if people do not particularly desire sex, they are less likely to choose to get involved in a sexual experience.

This lack of desire, or lack of interest, is one of the most common of the sexual difficulties. To maintain interest in sex, a person must gain some satisfaction from sexual encounters. Lack of satisfaction leads to lack of interest. And lack of interest leads to lack of sex—unless the person chooses to be involved in sex because of a sense of duty, or habit, or a desire to please one's partner.

In this chapter we look at various situations that lead to lack of interest, and discuss some ways to solve this most perplexing and elusive problem.

The Uninterested Woman

In the past, the woman who is not interested in sexual activity was often called "frigid." In more recent years, particularly since the Masters and Johnson studies, we have tried to use this term less and less. "Frigid" is a critical and judgmental term, whereas we prefer to be supportive. In addition, the term has been so misused that it has come to mean almost any kind of sexual problem that a woman might have—problems with interest, arousal, or release. For this reason, we normally choose not to refer to any woman as being frigid, but rather to define her problems more precisely.

Good sexual feelings are often referred to as erotic feelings. Erotic feelings are usually a combination of physical and emotional sensations. The woman who lacks interest or desire is sometimes one who experiences little or no physical arousal and almost no emotional pleasure in sex. She does not experience the sexual act as a way of giving or receiving love. Usually she is not eager for a sexual experience except to please her partner. In terms of the actual physical signs of arousal, such as lubrication or nipple erection, she may have some slight sensations of pleasure, but these are usually far outweighed by the resistant emotional feelings that go with them.

We might ask, then, why a woman would engage in an activity that has so little positive and so much negative in it for her. We might compare it to going to the dentist. Sorry, dentists! People go to the dentist even though they hate having their teeth drilled, because they recognize that the consequences of not doing so will be harmful. They are willing to subject themselves to the distasteful experience of the dentist's drill for the long-term benefit of controlling tooth decay. Similarly, a woman usually has some understandable reasons for putting up with sex even though it is a negative ordeal for her. The main reason is to carry out her duty as a wife; she feels she must meet her partner's needs to maintain the integrity of her marriage. If she is a Christian, she may see this not only as a marital duty but also as a Christian duty.

Other women who don't enjoy sex prefer to avoid it rather than perform their duty. But they are not usually very direct. Few women will just say, "Hey, I hate sex, so forget it, buddy." Rather, they will find more subtle ways to get around it. The standard excuse is the headache. Even though there are many jokes about it, such a physical complaint is often used to avoid contact. Another way women avoid sex is to develop a busy schedule. The woman goes to bed or gets up later or earlier than her husband, and thus avoids being around when he might be sexually interested. A third common ploy is to initiate a hassle around the time when a sexual encounter might take place. Many couples report that they have their biggest fights at the times when sexual involvement would be most likely. After a while, the man may, without realizing it, slip into the pattern too.

Let's look at some specific reasons why a woman might be uninterested in sex.

One reason why a woman might avoid sex is that she does not experience her partner as warm and caring about her needs for sexual pleasure. As we have .already said, it is essential for a woman in any sexual experience to feel loved and cared for, to feel some tenderness, some concern for her thoughts and feelings and her current situation. Without this atmosphere she is not likely to allow herself to be intimate and emotionally vulnerable. If that emotional support is regularly lacking, she will be regularly uninterested.

Closely connected with the lack of emotional satisfaction is a lack of interest due to problems with arousal or release. If the woman does not become aroused during sexual pleasuring, does not go from the excitement phase to the plateau phase, does not experience lubrication and clitoral and genital engorgement or response, any interest she may have had in sex will wane. Even if she experiences arousal, consistent failure to reach a climax will eventually squelch her interest in sex. It's no fun to have your body and your feelings prepared for an orgasm over and over again, and then to experience only frustration. This causes such intense discomfort that it's no wonder a woman's interest fades away.

The graph for the woman who often becomes aroused without release is shown below. At one point her experience would be charted by line 1, in time it resembles line 4.

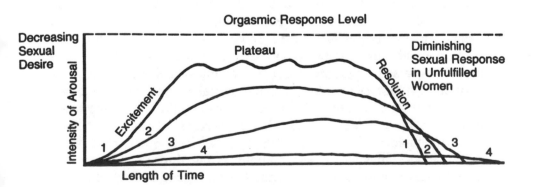

When a woman does not experience satisfaction even though there is arousal, over a period of time the arousal is likely to diminish. You will notice that the bottom line on the graph is almost a straight line. The way it usually goes is something like this: a new bride is delighted and excited about being involved with her partner, and finds herself becoming very aroused. She may have felt a similar arousal during hugging and kissing before marriage. However, when she has no orgasmic response, and hence feels no satisfaction, the arousal takes her nowhere. Because of what this does to her, she begins to slow down.

You will notice on the graph that it takes a little longer for her to get aroused and she does not become quite as aroused. Then as time goes on, arousal takes even longer and is even less intense. It also takes longer for her to return to her unstimulated state. This is usually a period of discomfort. Finally, she experiences almost no arousal and hence no desire. She goes nowhere in the whole experience.

This flattening out of the curve will often occur between the fifth and tenth years of marriage. The timing is sometimes related to other events in life, such as having children and being occupied with heavy responsibilities. The pattern is certainly reversible, but the woman may need some professional help. If you are in this sort of situation, and you want to reverse it, you must identify yourself as being in this pattern. You and your partner must communicate with one another about your understanding of how this developed and the fact that you want to do something about it.

The pattern may have been caused by the fact that the man ejaculated prematurely, not allowing enough time for the woman to respond with an orgasm. Or it may have come about because the woman could never allow herself to experience an orgasm, so she was left hanging in her preorgasmic state regardless of how long the man could maintain his erection. Whatever the original cause, the pattern must be reversed if you are going to feel any sexual desire.

Another major cause of decreasing sexual interest in the woman is the boredom that may set in because of mechanical or goal-oriented sexual activity. By this we mean that a woman's interest is not likely to be maintained if the couple has adopted a standard routine for love-making—what we've talked about as the three-push-button approach—the woman is passive while the man goes through the standard procedure like an airplane pilot checking to see if the airplane is ready for flight. If a man follows this kind of procedure and the woman does not go after variation or creativity, then it is not likely that her interest will be maintained. By goal-oriented activity, we mean sexual activity that is always aimed at having an orgasm rather than having as a goal the expression of love and care and affection, the joy and delight present in the relationship. Lack of interest is likely to develop after a couple has functioned together under these circumstances for some period of time.

Another major cause for lack of interest in women is emotional ambivalence. A woman may find herself being intensely responsive, but she cannot accept this response as part of herself. Something in her training or her upbringing, some fear, an experience in her past, or a general discomfort with pleasure interferes with her enjoyment of sex. She will probably not want an activity that causes her inner turmoil. Because of this conflict, some women will cut off their natural and God-given sexual responses. As a result of cutting off their sexual feelings, they will experience less pleasure, and when they experience less pleasure, they will lose interest. They end up in the same place as those who have little or no intensity in their arousal to begin with.

Other women enjoy full, intense arousal and response once they are actually sexually involved. Nevertheless, those good erotic feelings of arousal and release do not lead to future interest or initiation. The conflict about allowing those good feelings seems to block the desire. Their graph might look like this:

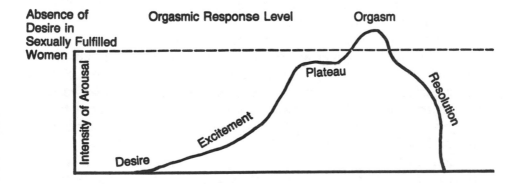

There is no interest or desire, in fact continual resistance. It takes a long time to get into the experience. Arousal may be slow. But once they are aroused, the arousal is intense and the release fairly rapid. Resolution follows rather naturally.

There are other psychological reasons for lack of interest. These include anxiety or depression. Any continuous tension or stress can also reduce desire. Sometimes the causes are much deeper; these are unconscious barriers. Helen Singer Kaplan, a sex researcher and therapist, has cited unconscious reasons such as fear of success, fear of intimacy, oedipal conflicts, deep long-term anger, and other interwoven, complicated psychological problems.

The Uninterested Man

It may come as a surprise to some that we would even include the category of the uninterested male, since all men are "supposed" to be vitally interested in and even preoccupied with sexual activity. How can it be that there are men who are not interested? We have found that men who lack sexual interest fall into three main groups. There are those who are what we would call "sexually naïve" or uninformed; there are those with serious emotional barriers; and there are the entrepreneurial or goal-oriented men whose interest in sexual activity diminished with acquiring a wife. Let's look at each of these in some detail.

The sexually naïve or uninformed man is usually one who has grown up in a very protected, almost overprotected environment. He was usually either a mama's boy or a somewhat frightened child. Such a boy had relatively little exposure to the normal sexual stimuli that most children receive in growing up, whether they receive it in the home, classroom, church, or on the streets. He may have been warned against the evils of sexual activity and never been taught about the joys and pleasures of this part of life. Probably little physical affection was shown in his home, either between parents and children or between mother and father. He may have heard several warnings about the dangers of masturbation; any type of sexual interest or exploration was dealt with briefly but conclusively.

A man who was very successful in his professional career, had been married for fifteen years, and served as a deacon in his church had a severe problem of impotence. This impotence had been with him almost from the beginning of his marriage. As we explored the situation with him and his wife, we discovered that he lacked much of the basic information necessary for normal sexual experience. He found any kind of genital touching of himself or of his wife to be extremely distasteful; he tended to engage in sexual activity mainly to please his wife; he was reported by his wife to be someone who really didn't know how to do anything in bed. He didn't know how to kiss, and she could never seem to teach him; he did not touch her in a way that was comfortable either for her or for him. Evidently he had failed to learn about these activities at the appropriate time in his life. Now he found it extremely difficult to change.

The sexually naïve man will often be perceived by his wife as a cumbersome and inadequate love-mate who is never even able to kiss her in a satisfying way. It is gratifying to be able to help couples move beyond this point. The main ingredient necessary for change is the willingness to accept his limitations and learn the basics. This requires a cooperative wife.

Another group of men who are uninterested in sex consists of those who have serious emotional blocks or barriers. Often the barrier is unknown to the man and may be somewhat difficult for a counselor to uncover. This is often the result of repression in some earlier part of the man's life. One example is a handsome young youth leader who married his college sweetheart. They met at a Christian college where she was the star cheerleader and he was a leader in student government. As they dated, they both seemed to have plenty of sexual interest, but because of their Christian commitment, they decided to wait until after they were married to consummate the relationship.

As soon as they began their seaside honeymoon, the new bride sensed that the man was really not very interested in pursuing any sexual activity. This came as a complete surprise to her and caused her much dismay. In exploring the man's background, we discovered that he had been raised in a home where the family was clearly divided. The children were aligned with the mother against the father. He had never really identified with his father and learned to be a man, and so he had great difficulty being a man with his new wife.

There are other reasons why men have emotional barriers. These usually have to do with some distorted relationship with the mother or with some other significant adult woman which the man experienced as a boy.

The third type of man who is uninterested in sexual activity is the goal-oriented, or what we might call the "entrepreneurial" male. He has seen the process of acquiring a wife as a goal to be achieved; once he has done that, he moves on to other projects, even as he moves on from one business venture to the next. These men are highly successful *initiators* of business projects who turn over the day-to-day operation of each venture to someone else while they move on to a new project.

It is not uncommon for these men to have selected extremely attractive, bright, and confident wives who will be good mothers for their children and who can function very adequately in the social scene. But soon such a woman finds herself emotionally starved because the man she married and had all her hope in, the man who romanced her in a most successful manner, now spends little or no time or energy to bring her the continued emotional fulfillment she needs. This lack of energy in the relationship also includes a lack of interest in sexual activity. The energy that the man may once have had for sexual activity is now being put into other ventures.

Some men, on being confronted with their entrepreneurial approach, decide to change their priorities to a more human, less business-oriented manner of life. They decide to go with the more loving side rather than the material side of their life. This obviously fits in with the Christian perspective: we are to be more concerned with human relationships and loving concerns than we are with business success. Other men say, "No, if she chooses to live with me, she's going to have to recognize that this is how life is going to be." This places the woman in a dilemma and forces her to make a difficult choice. Such a man can change— if he *chooses* to change. His change may require professional help.

How does a man's lack of interest in sex show up? Because the man in our society tends to be the initiator, what usually happens is that there is simply little initiation of sexual activity. Then the dissatisfied and unfulfilled wife expresses her concern about her husband's love for her and her concern about her own desirability. This may lead to some attempt to deal with the problem. Often the man will, in a brief flurry of activity, initiate sex a few times, which will bring temporary satisfaction to his wife. But then things will drift off to the same state in which they were before she complained.

Over a period of time, a pattern will often develop with the unsatisfied wife exploding every several months, followed by sexual activity, and then a period of little interest during which the woman again becomes increasingly disgruntled until she explodes again. The difference between the situations with an uninterested man and an uninterested woman is that if the woman is disinterested, the man may still be getting his satisfaction. But if the man is disinterested, the woman will usually be left frustrated.

Tension and Anxieties Which Produce Lack of Interest

When the bedroom has become as somber as the funeral parlor, it is likely that there will be little sexual interest. For many couples, because of the various factors that have led to problems, there is a kind of sober, serious, sacred atmosphere connected with any kind of sexual activity. This can come about as a result of sexual stress and dissatisfaction, or as a result of tension within the relationship.

It is important to note that any stress or tension in the family or in the relationship between husband and wife can cause sexual interest or desire to diminish, even though normally the couple is responding satisfactorily and enthusiastically. Unless two people are functioning harmoniously, it is improbable they will be able to get together in bed in a way that is pleasurable, relaxed, and releasing for both of them.

Another reason for tension and anxiety that results in lack of interest is the fear of pregnancy. For some couples, particularly for women, this is a strong, conscious fear. Others may not be aware of it until they do become pregnant or change to another form of birth control, and then realize what a relief from tension has occurred. If you are concerned about getting pregnant and are using a method of contraception in which you are not really confident, and if you are finding that your interest in sexual activity has diminished or that your arousal is not as intense as it once was, it may well be because of this fear.

Another common factor that reduces interest is an external project into which we direct all our energies. This may be an educational experience such as pursuing an additional degree. It may be building a business, working extra hours, remodeling the family room, adapting to a new baby, adjusting to a new job, or a change in roles such as a mother starting back to work. Anything that captures a major portion of our interest and energy is likely to diminish our sexual interest. About the only activity contrary to this is something both husband and wife are enthusiastically involved in together. Such a joint commitment may in fact bring greater closeness and lead to more sexual intimacy. An example of this might be writing a book together. We have found it so.

What if you are a person for whom desire does not surface easily or spontaneously? How might you discover or be more aware of your sexual feelings?

In Chapter 10 we talked about building desire. We emphasized that sexual desire is a natural bodily feeling. It can surface most readily when you clear out distractions, identify what works for you, communicate openly about your needs to your spouse, and then take responsibility to get what you need to arouse your interest. The issues of feeling and expressing sexual desire within the relationship have to be clearly and openly discussed between husband and wife. That is the first step toward remedying problems with desire.

Let us assume for the moment that the man is the one who lacks interest. We would encourage a thorough and open discussion about how the man feels in this situation, what he thinks gets in the way of desire, and what he perceives to be his duties and obligations as a husband, lover, and Christian. Then the wife should clearly communicate how this whole issue of his lack of interest leaves her feeling. Sometimes this process makes it clear what is getting in the way and causing the lack of interest. In other situations it is much more difficult, because at the conscious level a man believes he is interested. Yet he rarely shows any interest. An unconscious barrier gets in the way and causes the lack of sexual pursuit.

When the barrier is unconscious, and the couple is not able to identify what is getting in the way of feeling or expressing sexual desire, they should seek professional counseling. Kaplan's work on problems with sexual desire shows that unconscious barriers to feeling the need for or interest in sexual involvement stem from early childhood environment. Because of the strong impact of early influencing factors, an individual is not likely to be able to resolve the problem without the help of a professional.

Where the problem with desire is related to an obvious stress, it may be dealt with between the two of you. Talk about how the lack of desire feels to each of you. Then determine together how you are going to bring about changes that can allow the natural desire to surface.

Allowing for desire requires giving space to the person who lacks the feeling. Giving space means that the other partner needs to avoid initiating sex or communicating expectations which will be felt as demands. The steps for reversing who initiates, as defined in Chapter 11, should be helpful.

Once the person with a desire block feels the sense of space, it is important for that person to find ways to enhance sensitivity to sexual feeling. You will need to find, or make, time for this. Maybe you need to reduce outside pressure. With this pressure-free time available, look for sensuousness in your world. Use some of the natural external stimuli mentioned in Chapter 10. Read the Song of Solomon every day. Leave yourself notes to remind you to turn on sensuous music while you're driving or working around the house or yard. If you are a woman, get acquainted with your own genitalia as described in Chapter 6. Ask God to free up your feelings for sex, and praise him every time you feel even a fleeting urge. Spend time looking in the mirror and thanking God for how he made you. Focus on listening to your body. Be aware of touch that has a tingle. What we're saying is to give yourself a good tune-up.

Since each problem of lack of interest is unique, each couple will have to be creative in finding their own variations for working out the details. Levels of interest can change, and thus any couple who experiences lack of interest should begin working at it, and should seek help if necessary.

22

Differing Sexual Needs

No two people are born equal. No two are raised in exactly the same circumstances. All of us have different experiences. These three major areas—what we inherit genetically, where we are raised, and what we experience—will cause us to come to marriage with different levels of needs in every aspect of life. For some couples, these differences show up immediately upon marriage. More often, though, differing needs take time to surface. The years go by, and the marriage moves along from the excitement of the first years to the distractions of child rearing, establishing a home, building a career, forming a solid financial base. During these years differing needs—including varying sexual needs—emerge and make themselves known.

Basic Differences

To begin with, we must state that there are some very basic differences among normal, healthy people. There is not necessarily anything wrong with a person who has a greater or a lesser need for sex. Such a variation is not necessarily the result of life experiences, positive or negative. Rather, just as people vary in their need for food or activities or hobbies, people will have a greater or lesser drive for sexual activity. When we are trying to understand a difference in need, we must consider the normality of such differences.

Energy Differences

As a couple moves through their years of marriage, the amount of energy they have available for sexual activity changes. Often during the first years of marriage when they are excited about being together and the honeymoon is not over, the energy available for sexual activity is almost unlimited, particularly if both partners are experiencing satisfaction. But then the couple decides to have children. The woman may still be working when she becomes pregnant, and so she experiences a great deal of fatigue. Or she may have some adverse physical reaction as a result of the pregnancy. Thus, even during the part of the pregnancy when she could still be sexually active, she backs off because of fatigue or physical problems. She just does not have the energy for sexual activity.

Then the child is born, and there is the usual four-to-six-week period of physical recovery before intercourse is advised. But even after this time the new mother may be getting up many times at night. There may be adjustment problems or sleeping problems with the child. Mother is adjusting to all the extra work and stress, so even for a year or two after the child is born she may not have much energy for sexual activity. It doesn't have to be like this, but usually when we review people's sexual history, they report that the change in sexual activity occurred around the birth of the first or second or third child.

A man or a woman who is building a business or a career, or even just struggling to make ends meet as the family grows, may have little energy left for sexual activities. Perhaps the man is trying to start a small business. He leaves early to go over the books, works long hours, comes home tired, and is preoccupied because of various business problems and struggles. He finds that he does not have the energy he once had for sex when he was working at an eight-to-five job in which he had relatively little responsibility. The same thing could be true for a woman. If she is trying to build her career as an executive, teacher, shopkeeper, nurse or whatever, energy is diverted toward that and away from sexual activity.

Fulfillment Differences

Differences in sexual drive are determined in part by the level of sexual fulfillment. It is not uncommon for a woman who never feels sexually fulfilled to have a diminishing awareness of her sexual need. From a logical point of view, this makes good sense. If she is not being satisfied through sexual activity with her spouse and self-stimulation is not comfortable for her, she will shut down her sexual feelings. This is not to say that her basic, God-given sexual need is absent from within her. However, because it is never being satisfied, it is not likely that she is going to be able to stay in touch with that need. Let's consider an analogy: All of us have a need for social contact, and in the church we have a need for community. If I go to a church and no one greets me, I may go back the next time, and if no one greets me again, my interest may lessen a little bit. I may wonder what's wrong with me, and why no one is interested in me. I may go back again in a couple of weeks, and if, once again, no one attends to me, I may decide I'm at the wrong place. So I may go to a class; and if I'm left alone one more time it's likely that my interest in attending that particular church will diminish. This is not to say that my need for social relationships, my need for fellowship, my need for community had diminished in any way. Rather, I have simply not experienced anything fulfilling in that particular church. In the same way, if a wife never experiences anything fulfilling in the sexual act, regardless of how much she needs it, she will experience a lessening of the awareness of that need, because it doesn't bring her any satisfaction.

If it is a man who is not being fulfilled, he may experience great sexual need. This desire may be in excess of his normal need, because he is always wanting and yet rarely receiving sexual satisfaction. It may seem as though he experiences satisfaction one out of ten times; he is in a state of perpetual hunger, like a person who is rarely able to eat a full meal. He is always hungry, and even when he does have a meal with enough food, he is anxious about the period of hunger to follow.

We are not certain why women tend to shut down when they are unfulfilled sexually and men tend to feel more sexual hunger with lack of fulfillment. Our suspicion is that the difference relates to self-stimulation habits. More men tend to masturbate than do women. The men we know who have shut down with lack of sexual fulfillment have all been men who were not comfortable with self-stimulation. The few women we know who have unfulfilled sexual relationships with their husbands but still feel intense sexual need all masturbate.

A full presentation of our view on masturbation is expressed in Chapter 24.

Emotional Differences

There may be differences due to varying emotional intensities of the partners. Some individuals are very low-key, relaxed and easy-going, experiencing little stress or tension. At the same time they feel little intensity. This is the type of person who is seldom angry or excited to any degree. Their experience in life will usually be relatively stress-free, but also relatively excitement-free. Other individuals experience life at a high level of intensity; they move from one intense experience to another. When they are active sexually, they are involved with all of their being and with great intensity. When they are playing a game or cooking a meal or studying the Bible or whatever they are doing, they do it at a level of involvement that includes their whole being. When you put together one person of low intensity and one of high intensity, you are likely to experience different levels of need. This obviously can produce tension in a relationship, particularly when the low level of need is interpreted to mean that the individual loves the partner less.

Adjusting to Differences

Obviously, if the couple is going to survive differing levels of sexual need, they must find ways to adjust to these differences to reduce the impact on their relationship. As with any problem, the starting point must be communication. Until a couple has clearly defined what they understand the problem to be, there is no way to resolve it. In this kind of communication, it is important that each one take responsibility for himself and his own feelings. He must define those feelings clearly, rather than criticize his partner. Openness is crucial here. Anything that can be done to reduce defensiveness will help make this kind of discussion more productive. When people feel accused, they become defensive. If they feel that what they are saying is being received and understood and reflected, however, they are likely to be able to continue the exploration (see Chap. 12 on communication).

Once the couple has communicated, they must identify the life-style changes that will enable them to adjust to their differing levels of sexual need. For example, if a man is frustrated because his wife is always too tired, it does little good to tell her to stop being tired. Rather, the two of them must work out ways to lessen the fatigue so that she can get in touch with her own sexual need. (If the fatigue is just an excuse, a cover-up for the real reason for lack of interest, the plans that are made will be sabotaged. The cover-up will be discovered quickly.) If a woman is frustrated because the man is expending all his energy on weekend softball games or building his business or watching sports events on television, the change in life style necessary must be something to which both can adapt. Radical solutions usually don't work. Moving the television into the garage will only produce frustration and anger rather than greater sexual desire.

Keep in mind another thing in adapting to differing levels of needs. There are many ways to satisfy sexual needs, and many different types of sexual needs. For example, many women report that they do not necessarily need a full sexual experience, but rather are hungry for cuddling and touching. Many men would be willing and happy to be involved in such caring and touching experiences if they knew that this was as far as it needed to go. The same is true of women. Many times they would be willing to participate in an experience if they knew there was no demand for a response from them that they didn't feel up to at that particular moment.

When a woman is not feeling up to a full sexual experience, she may be happy to pleasure her husband to the point of release through manual stimulation. She can enjoy that process. This is one more way to meet the man's sexual desire without forcing the woman into something which violates her at a particular moment. Many women report that they would be most willing to satisfy their husbands in this way on occasion. Similarly if a man does not feel the need, he may be willing to pleasure his wife to orgasm if that is her need.

Finding ways to meet one person's need without making a demand on the other is the crucial dimension in resolving this issue of different levels of sexual needs. As with so many other problems that happen in a relationship, partners need to discuss the issue, make plans, experiment, and be open to move toward finding fulfillment without demand. Even in the sexual experience, Philippians 2:4, 5 can well be used as a guideline: "Do not merely look out for your own personal interests, but also for the interests of others. Have this attitude in yourselves which was also in Christ Jesus . . ." (NASB).

23

Never Enough Time

As we travel around the country talking to various church and educational groups about sexual adjustment, we always take a survey. One of the questions on that survey allows the respondents to check various areas of concern which they would like to work on and improve in their relationship. One of those categories has to do with the matter of time. Roughly 75 percent of the several thousand people who have filled out these questionnaires have reported that time is one of the greatest areas of frustration for them in their sexual experience. It is difficult for partners to find significant amounts of time to be together. In addition, it is difficult to coordinate the times that are available. Finally, it is difficult to be consistent about time together unless it is planned for. This chapter will focus on time—not on how the time is used, but rather on finding the time to be together.

Defining the Time Conflict

There are two main ways in which the matter of time together is an issue: overscheduling to avoid sexual encounters, and inadvertent overscheduling. Overscheduling can be used as a way to avoid sex. Because it is difficult for people to deal directly with the feelings which prompt them to avoid sexual activity, they design their lives so that there is seldom enough time. The distractions that are employed are usually for good purposes. For example, the wife may become a compulsive housekeeper. She may be preoccupied with always having the dishes done immediately after dinner, getting the children's lunches ready for school the next day, setting out their clothes, and making sure that everything is ready for the next morning. By the time she is ready for the next day, it is 10:30 or 11:00 in the evening. She may be seen as a good homemaker and may take pride in this reputation. But when such preoccupation takes precedence over the couple's time together, then obviously it is being used to avoid sexual contact.

Maybe a man is just starting an accounting business. He is at the office until 7:00 or 8:00 in the evening. He then comes home, spends a little time with the kids, has dinner and is ready to drop off to sleep. Again, all those are worthwhile and laudable activities, but if they either are designed to or inadvertently do cause a couple to avoid each other sexually, then they are a way of avoiding sex without dealing directly with the problem. In some situations both partners unconsciously collaborate to avoid sex; they design their lives in such a way that they are both overly involved; they never get together sexually because they have found no satisfaction in their previous sexual encounters.

Most often, however, hectic schedules inadvertently crowd out or cramp this important area in the relationship. In busy families children's activities, civic activities, church and school, sports, education, and entertainment gradually crowd in so that the couple's sexual time together becomes just a quick encounter between two exhausted people at the end of the day.

We should not be hard on ourselves for letting things develop this way. The matters that take up our time are usually good and wholesome activities. Often they have to do with various forms of service in which we are involved. Sometimes they are for personal development. One man always goes to bed at 8:00 because he likes to get up at four in the morning to have an hour of quiet time with God, to study and meditate and pray. This is obviously a wholesome and beneficial activity, but it still has the effect of causing sexual problems in his marriage.

Differing Time Needs

One of the things that almost inevitably happens as a couple moves along in their marriage is that one person's time has many more demands on it than the other's. A couple was experiencing difficulty in just this area. The man was in charge of a growing business. He was earning enough money so that his wife didn't have to work outside the home, but could care for their two children. His business was expanding, so it demanded much time if he was to run it adequately. At the same time, the wife now had a great deal of time and more energy available for sexual involvement. This kind of difference in the demands on your time will often lead to stress, particularly when the one who has extra time is the one who is eager for more sexual activity. The man we just described may have been just as interested in sex as his wife was, but he had many other demands on his time. He was just not available to his wife.

It may be that the woman is loaded with time demands because she is working and has to come home and cook and clean and care for the family. The man may not feel as much concern for perfect housekeeping, so he's willing to let things go, and is certainly not willing to spend all his evenings tidying up the house. Thus this wife's available time to be together is extremely limited, and usually occurs when she is most exhausted. She, then, is the one not available.

"I'm an evening person and he's a morning person" is often the way a spouse will define the sexual difficulties a couple is experiencing. Some people wake up at the crack of dawn and are ready to roar into life. By 8:00 they have been producing for three hours. We'll never forget the woman who came in at 8:00 for a psychotherapy appointment: she had already jogged her ten miles for the day. In contrast, there is the person who comes in an hour later, still trying to get her eyes open.

There is nothing right or wrong about being a morning or evening person. It only causes problems when it doesn't coincide with your partner's system. Some people are night people. They get going by about seven in the evening, and are then ready to continue until two in the morning. These are their most productive hours. We could go into all the reasons why people have various body chemistries, but the differences will still be the same. People are going to marry other people who operate on different time schedules. One of the places where this obviously causes some difficulties is in the sexual realm. Some men love to wake up in the morning and make love. If their spouse happens to be a morning person there is no problem. But the chances of that are minimal. Many women complain about husbands who wake them up in the morning to start their day with a sexual experience. Often these same men are dozing off to sleep in front of the television by 9:30. Yet this is the time when the woman may be ready for some involvement. What can a couple do about this?

Sex: A Time Priority

If the time issue is going to be resolved for a couple, both partners must be ready to make a commitment to each other that they are going to make their sexual experience a priority. It is of utmost importance that this decision should not be an edict which comes from either the man or the woman; rather it should evolve from the two of them together. It is easy to make a commitment verbally, but it is another thing entirely to make it work in day-to-day life together. What does the man do at 5:50 P.M. when he has promised to be home by six, but gets an important long-distance call that is going to take an hour? Does he say, "I've got a commitment"? Or does he stick with his business? It's easy to decide ahead of time that one is going to be committed—but it is sometimes difficult to carry out that commitment. It is the same way for the wife. She can make a time commitment, but then is she willing to let the work at the office go? Or to let the ironing pile up? Or to have the house in less than perfect order?

The man and woman have to determine a process by which they are going to make their sexual relationship a time priority, given the life style and the time demands that exist for them. This must be a very practical kind of priority. The couple must spell out exactly how it will be worked out. Some couples choose to have brief sexual experiences at home, and then go away for a few days at a time every several weeks for more intense times together. Others find that this leaves them frustrated, or that they are unable to do it because of financial or family limitations. Each couple has to work it out in their own special way.

You might be saying, "Why all this preoccupation with time? If it's important to a couple they will get together." That may be true, and yet there are no outside pressures that demand sex. When we agree to work for a certain company we're expected to be there so many hours a week, or to complete a given project. When we work for a committee at the YMCA or at the church there are other people to whom we are responsible, and we have deadlines. If we are involved in some kind of sports activities there are practices to attend and games to play. There is no such accountability in the sexual relationship. Decisions to make this a priority have to come out of desire and the recognition that this is a crucial area of life which needs fulfilling and is not happening without a plan.

Busy life styles may require times together "by appointment." This is true both for vacation times and sexual times. First-time responses to this idea are often, "But that takes all the excitement and spontaneity out of it." This is usually said by people who have not tried it. Sexual experiences do not work simply because they are begun on a spontaneous impulse. They work because of what happens between two people once they are together, whether this is by impulse or as the result of scheduling. Normally when people begin to schedule their time together, the quality of those times and the satisfaction from those times improve measurably. We are not ruling out the possibility of spontaneous times together. Scheduling is done only to assure that there will be extensive time for the two to be involved. Spontaneous times together tend to be relatively brief. They tend to satisfy primarily the physical needs, rather than meeting all the needs present when a couple comes together. These include the need for sharing, extensive touching, enough time for arousal, for repeated arousal and release if that's what the woman desires, and a time of affirming afterwards.

One thing vital to scheduled time is that it be planned without a demand for intercourse. Of course there is the possibility that a full sexual experience can grow out of the scheduled time. But any time people approach an experience with an expectation or demand it can get in the way of their freedom in that experience. Many couples allow the possibility that they are just going to talk, particularly when one person has the need to converse and to be held. This reduces much of the pressure they would feel if they came to the experience merely with the intent to have an active sexual time together.

One other ingredient necessary in making the sexual relationship a time priority is that the times together must be free of interruptions.

It is amazing how many couples report that their sexual experiences are interrupted by the ring of the doorbell, a telephone call, the cry of a child or disturbance by a pet. As much as possible, it is necessary to remove all possibilities for distractions. Taking the phone off the hook is absolutely necessary. If you live in an apartment complex where people are forever dropping by, put a "Do not disturb" note over the doorbell. Teach your children that there are times when mom and dad have to be by themselves without interruption. It is important for children to learn this in terms of respect for parents' wishes. It is even more important that they learn about a husband and a wife and the priority that their time together should have. Rather than shutting them out of your world, you are providing them with a good model on which they might choose to base their married life in the years to come.

Making sure you have time together is the responsibility of both partners. It takes forethought, planning, effort and recommitment. There is no way it will happen automatically. If there is to be time together—you will have to make it.

24

You Want to Do What?

What Is Appropriate? Common Areas of Tension

Questions of where, when, why, how, with what, which part, how long, and with whom all involve conflicts regarding the appropriateness of sexual activity. In this chapter we are not addressing the issue of moral right or wrong but rather the question of what feels comfortable to each partner. We are primarily talking about the emotional and personal acceptability of various kinds of sexual activities rather than about their rightness or wrongness from a moral or biblical perspective. However, when certain sexual activities do involve the moral area, we will look at the biblical view. For those interested in further study of biblical sexual ethics, we suggest the book *Sex for Christians* by Dr. Lewis B. Smedes (Grand Rapids, Michigan; William B. Eerdmans, 1976).

Traditional vs. Experimental

The problem of appropriateness can be thought of in terms of the traditional versus the experimental. Some common kinds of sexual activity have evolved over the years as the "natural" positions, styles, or stimulations. These traditional approaches are often thought to be the "right way" to make love, while everything else is labeled as weird or deviant. Many people are uncomfortable with such practices as oral sex, masturbation, and total body freedom.

Places

"Everyone knows that there is only one right place to make love. That is in bed, under the covers, with nightclothes on." Right? Not necessarily. That may be the most frequent place of love-making. It may be the most comfortable and it may be the most private, but there is nothing sacred about that location. A newly married couple experienced difficulty with this issue of tradition versus experimentation. The woman was an experimenter and the man was a traditionalist. Whenever his new bride tried to initiate an activity that was out of the ordinary, the man felt uncomfortable. One day she engaged in sex play on the bear rug in their den. He laughed nervously in response to this apparently deviant behavior. She felt judged.

Is it really strange or unusual to want to experiment? Keeping a love-making relationship alive requires experimentation and variety. Yet, unless both people are open to new approaches, such attempts may cause more stress than stimulation. They may bring about more tension than freedom. When a couple is learning to live together, it is usually best if experimentation grows out of communication. Once you have made some decisions about the approach you are going to take, you can experiment together. That is not to say that one person cannot surprise the other. Surprises are a delightful part of the whole process, so long as you are sensitive to your partner's preferences.

Experimenting with locations will often make an amazing difference in the excitement and pleasure that you experience. Even switching directions on the bed can bring a whole new perspective that moves you out of your rut.

In choosing new locations, the key criteria have to do with privacy from the outside world and comfortableness for both partners. Given these guidelines, there are really no limitations. Some couples enjoy shifting to another bedroom and a different bed. Others prefer a couple of comforters on the bedroom floor or in front of the fireplace. Outdoor locations include the swimming pool, the backyard, the beach or the forest. When there is adequate privacy, these locations bring an exciting quality that can be quite delightful. Anything from being on top of "Marabel Morgan's" dining room table to being underneath it or anywhere in between can be a possibility, even though your main preference may still be the bedroom.

Looking for new places will work only when both partners are comfortable with the idea. Pushing something onto another person will only produce tension. When you experience stress about experimentation, discussion is the best way to resolve it. Many couples find that one person is clearly more experimental than the other. The experimenter must be willing to take the initiative, but at the same time must be considerate while the partner attempts to overcome his or her hesitancy. So whether it is your pickup camper or your attic, it will take some holding back by the experimenter and some stretching by the more conservative partner.

Positions

So much has been written about experimentation with positions that a word of caution may be a good way to begin here. Many times the varying of positions is seen as a necessity to keep your sex life from becoming boring. The two of us, having grown up in constricted settings, were determined that our marriage should not get into a boring rut. During our five-day honeymoon we attempted to make use of every position we had read about or could imagine. Before we had mastered the basic kinds of sexual involvements we were already experimenting with more advanced possibilities. It was like a beginning piano student trying to play a Chopin concerto before he knows the C major scale. It didn't cause us any particular harm, but it certainly was not necessary, nor was it beneficial to us at that point in our relationship.

An extensive focus on positions communicates an attitude that is not helpful. When the emphasis is on getting into various positions, mastering them, following a check list of the forty-seven most desirable positions, then love-making ceases to be an expression of good feelings between two people. Such an overemphasis on position may be likened to a still photograph, stilted and lifeless. But when experimentation with position grows naturally out of the couple's enjoyment of being together, it is like movie film, filled with motion and life.

The most traditional position for making love is sometimes called the "missionary position." It apparently received this name from the Hawaiians, who somehow observed this behavior in the American missionaries and thought it strange. In this position, the man is on top of the woman, with the woman lying on her back. There is certainly nothing wrong with making love in this way. Many couples prefer it. One of the advantages of this position is that it permits more solid clitoral contact when the man is inside the woman. Because derogatory statements have been made about this position, some couples feel embarrassed or unsure about their enjoyment of it. You can certainly choose whatever position you enjoy, and you need not be concerned about anyone else's preferences, about the national averages or the trends of the day.

There are valid reasons, though, for the current push to experiment with new positions. When you engage in any activity, even an enjoyable one, in exactly the same way every time, it will become boring. If every time you went to a concert you heard Beethoven's Fifth Symphony, as great a piece of music as that is, you would eventually be bored by it. If you went to church and always sang exactly the same great old hymns and heard exactly the same excellent sermon, you would become bored. If you went to your favorite restaurant and ordered your favorite meal three times a week, week after week, that too would grow old. Sex is no different. If you behave in exactly the same way time after time after time, it will become ho-hum and humdrum. Many couples find that after becoming adjusted to one another and getting used to the idea of love-making, they want to branch out and be creative.

The natural first attempt at experimentation is to have the woman on top—just a reversal of the "missionary" position. There are many advantages to this form of love-making. Often the woman needs a great deal more stimulation and more specific stimulation than does the man. The man can be thoroughly aroused with rather general, nonspecific stimulation. When the woman is in the top position, she can be more active in going after the specific stimulation she needs.

Some women and men have serious doubts about the appropriateness, the rightness of a woman going after her own pleasure. They accept a double standard: it is acceptable for a man to be active in the pursuit of sexual stimulation, but it is less acceptable for the woman to do so. With the woman in the top position, the focus is on her having control of her own pleasure. If that is uncomfortable for her, she will not feel as free as she might in some other position. Each couple needs to work through their views on the woman's right to have pleasure. Sometimes this awakens memories of events or comments that occurred while she was growing up.

Another problem that sometimes arises is this: the man feels his manhood and leadership are threatened by the woman-above position. This man probably would not feel dominated if he and his wife were hanging wallpaper together and she was on a stepladder while he was standing on the floor. But somehow the symbolism of the woman being above the man in the sexual act has more meaning. Very often, the concept of submission that Paul talks about in Ephesians 5 is used to support the man's insecure feelings. This passage is misused to interpret the woman's submissiveness as a physical position rather than a response to a man's leadership. Misconceptions about submission have caused a great deal of stress and turmoil in people's lives. Couples need to get their views in the open, study them together, and talk about new ways of understanding the concept of submission.

Other intercourse positions fall in between having the woman or the man on top. One of the most common and helpful is called the lateral position. Both partners are lying on their sides with one person straddling one of the other person's legs, rather than being between them. The reason this position is sometimes beneficial is that some women experience more stimulation when the penis directly strokes the side of the vagina. The woman experiences more arousal as the thrusting takes place at a slight angle. There are obviously four variations of the lateral position. The man may be on top straddling the woman's right or left leg, or the woman may be on top straddling the man's left or right leg (see diagram).

Standing or sitting can provide interesting variations. A fully pregnant woman might lie on her back on the bed while the man either kneels or stands at the side of the bed, holding her legs, so that he does not rest on top of her. Sometimes couples find that the rear-entry position, in which the man enters the vagina from behind the woman's legs rather than from in front of her, is most arousing for the woman. There are some advantages to this position. It allows easy access to the breasts and clitoris for direct stimulation. However, there is the disadvantage of the lack of face-to-face contact, which can be essential for a feeling of intimacy. Some women find the rear entry position intolerable because of air pressure that builds in the vaginal cavity.

Figure 9

THE LATERAL POSITION

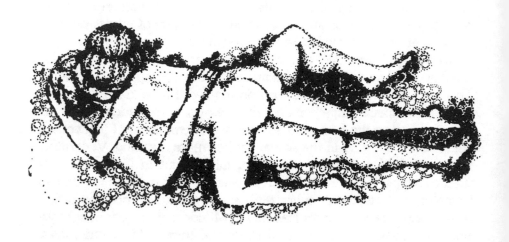

Develop an attitude of openness and freedom so that you can let the choice of position grow out of the feelings of the moment. Thus you will not be overconcerned with the question of which position to use. We like to think of letting positions evolve out of the experience, rather than "getting into position," as if you were on the scrimmage line in a football game waiting for the whistle to blow.

Style

Another question of appropriateness has to do with love-making style. When a couple is having serious difficulty or is getting bored with their sexual experience, they usually develop a routine style of love-making. At 5:00 in the morning the man wakes up and rolls over, experiencing his morning erection: he does certain things to his wife and she gets the message that he is interested. They go through a ritual, entry takes place, and they move to orgasm—or at least he does. Once they have ritualized this pattern, they seldom deviate from it unless they are out of town on vacation by themselves. People often behave in noticeably different ways while on vacation, but as soon as they return home, they fall into the same old pattern.

While both men and women can easily get into a boring style of love-making, it is most commonly initiated by the man, with the woman going along with it. When a man believes he is the one responsible for the couple's sexual functioning, he may become unsure about how they are doing. If he finds a method that works, he will stick with it. The woman participates in the process, but usually in a more passive way. She simply goes along with it; she doesn't object to the routine or suggest any variations. The pattern then becomes established. It is usually followed very carefully.

If this is your situation, whether you are the man or the woman, do some experimenting. If the ritual is offensive to you, talk about it. But if it is just boring, take the initiative without even talking; plan some new events. Some time when your husband is taking a shower before bed, prepare the room with candlelight and your favorite music. Or don't wait until bedtime; "seduce" him into a love-making session at some other time. Start by focusing on pleasuring his body rather than waiting for him to pleasure yours. If you usually make love in the dark, turn on the lights. If you usually make love in the light, turn off the lights. Anything that will bring some change and variety is likely also to add a new spark.

Stimulation

The matter of stimulation and the form it takes flows out of style and ritual. Very often, the ritual is most clearly followed when it comes to stimulation. We have talked in other places in this book about the "three-push-button" approach, but we want to mention it again here. Many of the older marriage manuals assumed that it was the duty of the man to "turn on" the woman. The way to turn on a woman was to kiss her, stimulate her breasts, and massage the clitoris; then she should be aroused and ready for activity. This is a rather impersonal and ineffective way of making love to one's beloved.

The fact is, most women are not aroused by that particular pattern, nor by any particular pattern. One day a woman may enjoy kissing; the next day she may not. One moment she may enjoy direct breast stimulation and the next moment she might prefer it very indirect. One day she might enjoy having her breasts nibbled on or sucked, and the next day that might be painful. Sometimes clitoral stimulation will be most enjoyable when done directly; other times, very indirectly. Part of the delight of the love-making process is learning how to respond to the feelings of the moment. This moment-by-moment discovery about oneself and each other adds spark and spirit to a sexual encounter.

The kind of stimulation that the person enjoys will vary from one person to another, from day to day and even from moment to moment. This can be true for both men and women, although it is more often reported by women. At the beginning of the love-making time, the person may feel like kissing, but by the end may need more freedom for total body movement. Kissing may be too constricting. On the other hand, a person may not feel like kissing at the beginning of the love-making time and may feel like it later because it best expresses his or her total self. There is nothing "right" or "wrong" about this kind of a change; in fact it is very normal. Each person and each couple must learn to go with the various feelings and moods that occur in the love-making process. When each person takes responsibility for going after his or her own enjoyment, getting with those varying feelings need not cause tension between the partners. It will not be a guessing game of trying to read what the other one is wanting. Rather, each person will be using the changing feelings to initiate variety.

Some men may be satisfied with a routine pattern of love-making. However, once a man learns the delights of variation, teasing and moving from one kind of stimulation to another, he will usually prefer that kind of loving. He finds it to be the most expressive and caring. It is also more exciting and less boring.

Another form of stimulation that can cause a lot of stress occurs when the man or woman finds a place that is arousing for the partner, becomes attached to it, and never lets go. This is particularly frustrating for a woman when a man attaches himself to the clitoris and tries to stick with it until the woman has some kind of an orgasmic response. This is almost sure to bring irritation rather than orgasm. Most women find stimulation much more arousing when it is varied in terms of its location and its intensity. Whenever we speak in public, women asks us to tell their husbands three things: (1) not to be in such a big hurry, (2) not to stick with the "hot spots" until they're worn out, and (3) to be able to caress and stroke each other without any specific sexual expectations.

For some people, the method of stimulation seems relatively insignificant. Others experience so much dismay and disappointment that they feel, "If I have to go through this same routine one more time, I'm going to scream or quit forever." Instead of screaming, try some effective communication: a letter, a tape recording, or a direct message. Communication is not as likely to shock your partner as is a scream. He is more likely to hear you. You will need to repeat your communication more than once. Do not expect that because you have changed the routine for a week the two of you will not slip back into old habits. Just like any learning experience, sexual change will take place over a period of time rather than in an instant.

Accouterments

Accouterments are small items that can communicate special care for and attention to one's lover. For example, some people are especially responsive to touch from soft articles such as fur or wool. To pleasure your partner with a small piece of soft fur may be just the kind of experience to bring special joy and delight.

It is important to use an accouterment that will be pleasing rather than offensive. And we are certainly not suggesting a deviant use of external objects. But you can communicate your love in a new or different way through the appropriate use of something enjoyable. When couples begin to experiment with accouterments, they are often surprised at the new delights they can experience together. They use everything from various kinds of fabric to fans, feathers, or rolling pins (for stroking, not for hitting!) as a special source of touch that brings bodily pleasure. Such items bring newness, variety and humor into the sexual loving process.

Even as you will be most totally fulfilled when you allow yourself to enter the sexual experience with abandonment, you will also be most fulfilled when your time together can include complete bodily freedom with one another. Not many couples can begin life together with such total freedom, but over time they become more and more intimate. The couples who are most satisfied are those who are moving toward greater levels of bodily freedom with one another. Total freedom means that there are no boundaries, no limits, no areas that you call a "no-no." This is quite a contradiction to those who feel most comfortable making love in their bedclothes, under the blankets, with the lights out and the curtains drawn.

Major Conflict Areas: Oral Sex

"Biblically speaking, is there any sex technique which is not acceptable, i.e., oral sex?"

Everywhere we go to speak, whether it's to a mother's group, a high school group, seminary students, college students, doctoral students, couples' groups or an interview by a Christian journalist, the one question we can count on is, "What about 'oral sex'?" Oral sex or oral stimulation is the stimulation of your partner's genitals with your mouth, lips and tongue. The man may stimulate the woman's clitoris and the opening of the vagina with his tongue, or the woman may pleasure the man's penis with her mouth. There is a great deal of interest in and at the same time a great deal of doubt regarding this activity.

Solomon in the Song of Solomon refers continually to enjoying the delights of his lover's body. He speaks of feeding among the lilies (4:5). His partner says, "Awake, north wind, and come, south wind! Blow on my garden, that its fragrance may spread abroad. Let my lover come into his garden and taste its choice fruits" (4:16). In the following verse King Solomon says, "I have come into my garden. . . . I gather my myrrh with my spices. I have eaten my honeycomb and my honey; I have drunk my wine and my milk" (5:1). His lover responds, "Eat, O friends, and drink; drink your fill, O lovers." Many references speak of the oral delights of one's lover and the enjoyment of her full body. Every part is talked about: hair, lips, neck, breasts, stomach, legs, feet. The lovers usually refer to the genitals as "the garden of spices." The book speaks of total body involvement. For some of us this freedom seems strange, unusual, and not part of the natural order.

In thinking about using our mouths to find enjoyment and bring pleasure to our lover, there are usually three questions that people ask. First, is it natural? Second, is it right? Third, is it clean?

When we ask whether or not something is natural, we are trying to discover the internal purpose for our creation. We are striving to avoid the violation of that perfect plan of creation. Some people find it easy to describe what is natural for themselves. However, their idea of what is natural is usually based on their own experience and does not necessarily represent what others might describe as natural. These are often "God-fearing" people who have a clear commitment to faith, truth and "right" living. But how do we determine objectively what is natural? The Bible is specific in providing guidelines to restrict sexual activity to marriage, but within the marriage relationship there are no guidelines. Nothing is said directly about what is acceptable in our love-making activity. Hence "what comes naturally" must be the product of what we feel inside us, how we have been informed by the Scripture as a whole, and the sense of God's Spirit directing us in relationship to our spouse.

From our perspective, oral activity becomes clearly unnatural if one of the partners is violated by it. It does not violate anyone to avoid oral sex, but it certainly may violate someone to be pushed into it. Here again we follow the principle of going with the most conservative partner. This might be compared with Paul's concern not to offend a brother by eating meat that has been offered to idols—even though from a strictly technical point of view Paul does not find this eating of meat to be a sinful act. The sin would lie in the offense to the other person, not in the act itself. So naturalness will ultimately be defined between partners.

Is it right? We refer to the Bible as our authority for rightness. As we said earlier, the Bible does not speak specifically about love-making activity within the marriage relationship and thus does not at any point refer directly to oral-genital involvement. So if we are going to say it is right or wrong, we must look for some indirect scriptural teaching rather than looking for a quote about oral sexual activity.

Some have thought that oral sex was included in Paul's statements regarding men or women leaving their God-given ways and engaging in unusual acts. However, careful reading of these passages will usually show that there are references to homosexuality, not to oral activity.

The Scriptures are not clear on the matter of oral sex, and so it is one of those gray areas where various biblical teachings will come into play. The principle of what is loving and caring for the other person must be addressed. On the other hand, the teaching that our bodies are each other's to enjoy must also be incorporated.

One thing we would caution against. Many people use Christian or moral arguments to defend against an activity which is personally troublesome for them. Often their moral arguments, though relatively weak, keep them from dealing with the *real issues* of emotional conflict. By finding some obscure passage or unique interpretation they avoid working through their own personal reason for the position they hold. While it is sometimes easier to call on an outside authority, this can cause a person to avoid facing the genuine issues that are present and need to be discussed with one's spouse.

The final question has to do with cleanliness. Is it clean? In an earlier chapter on the body we referred to the fact that there are three types of systems in the genital area: sterile, clean and contaminated. The urinary system is sterile: that is, it has no microorganisms. The reproductive system, which includes the penis or the vagina, is clean. It is free of any disease-producing microorganisms. Finally, the rectal area and the mouth are contaminated with disease-producing microorganisms. Therefore, if the body is cleanly washed and there are no infections present, contamination of the mouth from the genitals is impossible. If contamination takes place because of infection, it will usually be communicated from the mouth to the genitals rather than from the genitals to the mouth.

It is important to keep in mind that just because something is not clearly wrong or dirty or unnatural, does not necessarily make it right, natural, or necessary for you. Rather, the factual data given in this chapter is intended to clear away myths and distortions concerning oral sex.

Our hope is that with the facts, you will be free to discuss your own personal beliefs and feelings about this form of sexual contact. This is a personal issue and can ultimately only be resolved between you and your spouse. Communication continues to be the essential way to arrive at a congenial conclusion. To the one who desires oral activity but is inhibited by the hesitancy of your spouse, we offer encouragement. Many couples change over time, and what was uncomfortable for one becomes more natural as that one is cared for and loved without judgment and without demand.

Masturbation

"One night as I was sleeping, my heart awakened in a dream. . . . my hands dripped with perfume, my fingers with lovely myrrh . . ." (Song of Sol. 5:2, 5, TLB).

What part does masturbation play in marriage, if any? Is it a sign of not being fulfilled, or can it be used during a separation period without guilt feelings? I mean for a husband or wife.

Whenever the subject of self-stimulation is raised, it inevitably brings anxiety, tension, sometimes fear, and occasionally disgust. It is one of those topics that virtually everyone has thought about, yet many have never talked about. Unless you have lived an extremely sheltered life, you have found it necessary to make some kind of decision about it. The data that you received while growing up is usually what has most clearly shaped your view of masturbation; and yet that input may be difficult to remember. The reason it is so hard to remember is that it often began before you reached your first birthday.

It is inevitable that children will reach for their genitals in the process of discovering their own bodies. When they do this, regardless of their age, they will discover that touching themselves genitally brings pleasure. It is natural, therefore, that they will want to do it again. This is often the moment when the first messages about sexuality are communicated. If the child reaching down and touching the penis or the clitoris causes the mother to move the child's hand away, this is a unique experience. There is nowhere else that child is not allowed to touch himself. He can poke his fingers in his ears, his belly-button or his nose without a negative reaction. However, there are areas around the household that he is not supposed to touch because they are "bad" (dangerous). Pulling the hand away from the genitals, therefore, may also be connected with "bad" or dangerous. The next message may be "No, no." It may be because a little boy is playing with his penis while he's getting his bath; or the "no" may come as a result of the little girl lying on some towel or object on the floor and rubbing herself against that object in a way that stimulates the clitoris.

These activities can make the parent uncomfortable. So the negative messages begin early. Throughout childhood, children are *appropriately* taught, "Don't play with yourself in public," but they are also taught that it's wrong to enjoy touching themselves in private.

Parents may give warnings about what will happen if the child does engage in any kind of genital self-pleasuring. In times past, these warnings were extremely severe. Self-stimulation was said to cause warts, insanity, or the loss of one's hair. It was suggested as the source of impotence and of congenital defects in children. We now know that there are no physical effects from self-stimulation. However, the emotional effects may cause distress. When you have been conditioned throughout your lifetime to think of an activity or feeling as wrong or dirty, evil or uncivilized, it is natural that similar behaviors or feelings will set off some immediate primitive guilt. By primitive, we mean deep or old, having a long history. This usually has its roots in your childhood.

It is not our intention here to deal with the subject of masturbation in children. That will have to wait for a subsequent book. Nor is it our intention to discuss in detail the morality or ethics of masturbation. That has been handled very effectively in other places.* We will focus on self-stimulation for the married adult. Let us explore just what the Bible says on the matter, the use of self-stimulation in a marriage relationship, and how to struggle with it as a couple.

The Bible and Masturbation

In times past, various Scripture passages were used to condemn masturbation. Virtually all current biblical expositors, however, believe that these passages have nothing to do with masturbation. Still, it may be of help to take a brief look at them.

The first two passages are Leviticus 15:16 and Deuteronomy 23:9–11. Moses is writing about behavior that is acceptable "within the camp." Leviticus 15:16 says, "Now if a man has a seminal emission, he shall bathe all his body in water and be unclean until evening" (NASB). The Deuteronomy passage reads, "When you go out as an army against your enemies, then you shall keep yourself from every evil thing. If there is among you any man who is unclean because of a nocturnal emission, then he must go outside the camp; he may not re-enter the camp. But it shall be when evening approaches, he shall bathe himself with water, and at sundown he may re-enter the camp" (NASB).

In the past, these references to a man's "wet dream" were thought of as references to masturbation. We now know that wet dreams occur without being brought on by masturbation. They are the body's way of taking care of the buildup of seminal fluid that occurs, particularly in young men, and are often connected with erotic dreams. They are an automatic response that cannot be controlled by the individual. It is important to let adolescent boys know this.

If we look at the whole context of the passages, it is clear that the writer was thinking of nocturnal emissions as a natural body function, because he deals with other emissions from the body that occur for both men and women, including the women's menstrual cycle. If we want to say that this is a passage condemning masturbation, then

---

* Lewis B. Smedes, *Sex for Christians* (Grand Rapids: Eerdmans, 1976).

we would also have to say that the same passage condemns the monthly menstrual flow.

The primary passage used to condemn masturbation is Genesis 38:8–10. This is the story of Onan. "Then Judah said to Onan, 'Go in to your brother's wife, and perform your duty as a brother-in-law to her, and raise up offspring for your brother.' And Onan knew that the offspring would not be his; so it came about that when he came to his brother's wife, he wasted his seed on the ground, in order not to give offspring to his brother. But what he did was displeasing in the sight of the Lord; so he took his life also" (NASB).

Let us put this in context. The custom of the day was that if a man died without an heir, it was the duty of his living brother to provide an heir for him by means of a sexual union with the widow. When the son was born he would be considered the son of the deceased brother, rather than the son of the biological father. Apparently Onan did not like this idea. He wanted to operate in his own way, so in the middle of the sexual experience with his brother's widow, he withdrew and "wasted the semen" or ejaculated outside the vagina.

This has most frequently been used to condemn self-stimulation, even though this was not an act of self-stimulation, but rather intercourse and withdrawal. It has also been said that the Lord was so angry with Onan for masturbating that he slew him. This was used to indicate how severely the Lord disapproved of his behavior. Yet the exegetes agree that this was a reference to the Lord's displeasure with him for refusing to do the duty of a brother-in-law, rather than for the supposed masturbation. In times past, masturbation has sometimes been referred to as *Onanism,* in allusion to this particular passage.

The Scriptures we have examined are the three main Old Testament passages used to condemn masturbation; but as we can see, they provide no basis for that condemnation.

In the New Testament, 1 Thessalonians 4:3, 4; Romans 1:24; and 1 Corinthians 6:9 have at times been used to condemn masturbation. All three passages are now understood to be references to homosexuality or immorality, not to self-stimulation. Hence, we must conclude that the Bible does not deal directly with the subject of self-stimulation in either the Old or the New Testament. Any biblical guidelines we could bring to this subject would have to come about as an understanding of some other principle taught in Scripture. Here we think particularly of the principles of love, of self-abuse, and of lust.

Is It Loving?

Since this is the guiding principle of all of our behavior, it is obviously a question we must ask. To determine whether self-stimulation is loving, we must first clarify who is going to be the evaluator or the judge of that behavior. Now obviously the Lord is the judge; the Spirit within us is the judge; and we can usually determine what is loving in a practical sense toward one another. If our adult self-stimulation takes something away from our partner, then the behavior is not loving. On the other hand, if one partner desires a great deal of sexual activity and the other is less frequently interested, the couple might decide that masturbation is the most loving act the highly interested person can do, so as not to put the spouse under pressure. There may be periods when abstinence from intercourse is necessary. At such times it may be most loving and adaptive to enjoy a sexual release brought about either by self-stimulation or by mutual stimulation. Some of these occasions might be during extensive periods of separate travel or illness. When there is extreme outside pressure for one individual either relationally or vocationally, that person may prefer that the other take care of his or her own sexual needs. Or there may be times when one partner needs to be free from the pressures of sex for emotional reasons. So while it is possible that self-stimulation could be an unloving act, there is also the possibility that using it to relieve pressure would be the more loving act, not only for the self-stimulator but also for the partner.

Even though self-stimulation may be a loving option, many couples find that the most satisfying approach is to stimulate each other (without entry) rather than one person having a sexual experience alone.

Is It Self-Abuse?

On occasion, masturbation has been spoken of as self-abuse; and yet, from a technical, physical point of view, we know that there is no difference in the physical response that occurs whether the arousal is the result of self-stimulation, mutual stimulation, fantasy, or sexual intercourse. The physical, bodily responses are the same. Now if someone is masturbating ten times a day, this obsession would suggest a rather emotional deprivation and a need for help both psychologically and spiritually—whether the person is married or unmarried, Christian or unbelieving. If masturbation is used as a way of avoiding contact with one's partner, this, too, is a deviation from the norm. It would indicate that some kind of help is necessary to get past the problem.

But if self-stimulation occurs on occasion, not as a replacement for contact with one's partner, but rather to provide some physical release, then it would not seem to fall into the category of self-abuse. It is not likely that healthy married adults, male or female, are going to enjoy self-stimulation more than intercourse with their partner. If they do, then something is amiss.

Self-stimulation may be a way for the woman to discover what brings her the greatest bodily pleasures. If she can learn by touching her own body what brings her satisfaction, then she can communicate this to her partner. This learning could hardly be seen as either self-abuse or an unloving act, since it is designed to bring greater pleasure to their experience together.

Is It Lustful?

The Scriptures say that if one so much as looks on a woman to lust after her, he has committed adultery (Matt. 5:28). The question is often asked, is not all masturbatory activity a lustful act? We have talked with many people and have found that this is not necessarily so. Many people report that during self-stimulation they never think of anyone as a sexual partner. Others report that their thoughts are focused on their husband or wife. Still others may imagine someone else, but only in peripheral, still-life way, not with the intention of acting on the thought. Of course, there are many who *are* actively involved in lust in their masturbatory activity. So we must be careful not to categorize all self-stimulation as lustful, but rather would need to determine from each person in fact what is happening in the event.

Freedom without Enslavement

In Romans 14:14–23 Paul teaches a principle that is also repeated in 1 Corinthians 10:23–31. The simplest way to sum up this principle is to say that many things in and of themselves are not evil or unclean, but rather become sin in their context. Romans 14:14 says, "I know and am convinced in the Lord Jesus that nothing is unclean in itself; but to him who thinks anything to be unclean, to him it is unclean" (NASB). He then goes on to talk about consideration for the other person—how we are to follow the principles of love in determining our behavior. He continues, "Do not tear down the work of God for the sake of food. All things indeed are clean, but they are evil for the man who eats and gives offense. It is good not to eat meat or to drink wine, or to do anything by which your brother stumbles" (vv. 20,21, NASB). We include self-stimulation under "do anything" here. It can be offensive and cause a great deal of stress in a relationship.

In 1 Corithians 10:23, Paul says, "All things are lawful, but not all things edify" (NASB). Earlier in 1 Corinthians, Paul gives almost the same teaching: "All things are lawful for me, but I will not be mastered by anything" (6:12b, NASB). Other translations talk about not being *enslaved* by anything. The principle enunciated here is that we must be sensitive to the needs of the other person. We are to be cautious in doing anything that causes someone else personal turmoil. If we are loving in how we behave we will be understanding of our partner. We should not be possessed, mastered or enslaved by our sexual drive, but rather keep it in its proper subordinated place in our life. The sexual drive in us in a natural, God-given drive. But it is not a drive that must be fulfilled regardless of how it makes others feel, particularly within the marriage. The principles in these passages provide us with a way to think about handling masturbation in our marriage relationship.

In summing up this topic, it is important to note that masturbation relieves the physical need and may be helpful in self-discovery for some women. However, as we have seen earlier, any person's sexual need includes far more than just the physical release. It is true that all of us need physical release. But if that is the only need being met, then we are not living up to all we were created to be. So masturbation can never be seen as a total fulfillment of what we were made to be, but rather as a temporary, incomplete, but sometimes necessary pleasurable physical release, or a step toward reaching greater satisfaction with our relationship. Whenever we speak of masturbation, whether we are discussing it as a couple, teaching our children, or attempting to struggle with the issues surrounding it, we must see it in its proper perspective. We might think of it as a "snack" that will tide us over until the real need can be met.

Exercise 14
Resolving Conflicts

It is vital for us to continue to struggle with the biblical principles regarding relationships. The number one principle is to do what is loving. That is, we are not to violate the other person. This principle speaks to the person who is wanting more, or wanting something different than the other. For the hesitant partner, the best focus is on the principle presented in 1 Corinthians 7:5. It says that our bodies belong totally to our spouses. If the more experimental, exploratory, creative partner focuses on loving and not violating, and the hesitant partner focuses on learning to give his or her body more and more fully, then growth is sure to take place.

In addition to the two underlying principles just mentioned, we suggest using four steps to resolve conflict about what is acceptable or appropriate. These are described below.

Step 1: Communicate. To resolve a problem, you need to define clearly what the problem is. This process includes communicating how each person views the difficulty. Whether you are the hesitant one or the interested one, communicate your feelings about the activity that concerns you. This communication may include your history with this practice—the experiences you have had in the past, the teaching you received, the discomfort you feel regarding it, and anything else that may have a current effect on how you feel. If you are the one who wants to move ahead and experiment, and you are bored with the current limitations, share those feelings. Talk about your feelings concerning your present sexual relationship. Suggest where you would like to gain increased freedom in the future.

In the communication step, it is important to deal with your moral and Christian perspectives. If you view something that your partner wants as "sinful," explore your ideas together. Determine where the ideas came from. Find out if the behavior actually is evil or if your reluctance comes from a part of you that is hesitant to be free and open. As you are both able, make this area of conflict a matter of study and prayer.

Step 2: Go with the conservative member. Whenever one person introduces a new idea which the other finds negative, we recommend that the decision be made in the direction of the more hesitant one. In this way, no one is violated. This is not to say that the one interested in new experimentation must be resigned to being stuck with the status quo. Rather, the conservative one is less likely to build up resistance if the negative feelings are respected. People do change, and the hesitant partner will be more likely to loosen up if he or she is not nagged, bullied or shamed.

Step 3: "Pusher" retreat. When we have a desire, it is natural to want to pursue it until we get our way. It is natural to want to keep going after it by mentioning it frequently, thus riding the other person about it almost to the point of harassment. This usually does not help resolve the problem. It only builds resentment on both sides. If the person who is interested in expanding can back off for a time, this will usually relieve pressure and allow the possibility for change to take place.

Step 4: "Hesitant one" stretch. If you are the one who is resistant to new ideas, try to discover why. Is it because of some old conditioning that took place while you were growing up? If your father was very demanding of you, for example, requiring you to clean up every speck of food from your plate, and was slow to praise, you may be hesitant to experiment in life. Is it because of some past experience you had before you were with your current partner? Does it have to do with previous experiences with him or her? What is the hesitancy about? Experiment on your own without his or her encouragement. Stretch beyond your current limit and see how that feels. Perhaps you will discover that what you fear will not happen. Throughout all of this stretching activity it is of vital importance to keep talking, struggling, reading, writing to yourself, and praying in order to grow. If you reach a point that causes severe stress, sometimes brief conversations with a good friend or trusted professional can bring a new perspective in those areas of tension.

So whether your concern about appropriateness has to do with positions, places, style, self-stimulation, oral sex or anything else, share about it and make plans on how to handle it in the days ahead. These four steps may help.

25

Excluding God from the Bedroom:
A Christian Dilemma

A Little History

When a person comes from a narrow, somewhat rigid, conservative religious background where there are many direct and indirect messages about the sinfulness of sex, God is often excluded from that person's sexual experience. One woman talked about this exclusion of God as something that happened very literally for her: when she walked into the bedroom to make love with her husband she felt she left God outside the door. We have shown that God through the Scripture sends a positive message about human sexuality. Yet many of our fears and inhibitions about sex have been connected with God in order to justify the existence of such negative feelings.

Problems That Result

There are many ways in which this separation of God and sexuality can affect us. The most likely way is that it will impede our freedom to enjoy sexual pleasure. If we understand God to be a punitive parental figure who towers over us menacingly when we enjoy ourselves, obviously we are going to be inhibited in our sexual expression.

This inhibition occurs both in the area of excitement and in the process of letting go for a sexual release. Many people find that as they move close to the point of release, fear sets in. This is a message they send themselves about God's disapproval of their activity. Some find that the only way they can let go is to put themselves in a sinful, "risking" setting. Sexual pleasure is not condoned by the teaching they have received, so they can only experience arousal and excitement in "unacceptable" places or with "unacceptable" partners. They have great difficulty responding in the condoned married situation.

Invite God to the Bedroom

If we are to destroy the pattern of separating God from our sexuality, we have to become active in that process. This attitude of inviting God into the bedroom may take many forms, but it starts with the individual person. It means including one's sexual life and feelings in one's prayers as a matter of concern. A woman came up to us in tears following a seminar because we had closed the session in prayer after speaking of some very explicit sexual issues. The connecting of those two events—prayer and overt sexuality—was so foreign to her that she found it a very jarring experience. Yet as she voiced her thankfulness to God for her own sexuality, she found that God was no longer excluded from her bedroom; she experienced him as an approving God.

Another way to change the tendency to exclude God from sexuality is to study what the Bible teaches about sex. It is easy to go to those passages which talk about limitations on sexual activity rather than to study the other portions of Scripture that suggest the positive view. We have introduced some of these topics earlier in this book; they could be used as a launching pad for a more complete study.

You might consider including the topic of sexuality in a series for a small group in your church. If you are actively studying together, sharing and praying as you discuss this openly, you can often learn from your fellow Christians' viewpoints. This can have the effect of reducing your resistance to recognizing that God is a part of the sexual you. Various films and seminars also promote a healthy sexual message with a Christian perspective.

Invite God into Your Sexual Experience

Begin by thanking him for any sexual feelings that you experience during the day. Then, as you are with your partner and you begin to make love, do not draw back from your feelings, but offer a quiet inner prayer thanking God for those pleasant, exciting, satisfying feelings. Recognize that God approves of these feelings. Pray together before or during pleasuring as a way of admitting to one another that the enjoyment of sex is a part of your Christian life.

Include God in your activity as you become more aroused; know and admit to yourself that the ability to experience excitement is something God has given you. Actively thank him for all these delightful feelings. You are a sexual person. He made you that way.

If the struggle continues and you are unable to break through this barrier, select someone to help you. This person may be from your church or your community. He or she should be a mature Christian with personal integrity and an openness and ability to deal with the whole area of sex. As you talk with this person, share your need to allow God to be a part of the sexual dimension of your life. Listen willingly to his or her responses. As you and your friend discuss the matter and as you hear this respected and trusted person's responses, he or she becomes God's ambassador to help you break through the barrier regarding your sexuality.

God is in the bedroom whether you invite him there or not. God has made you the responsive person you are whether you acknowledge it or not. Your body is designed for pleasure whether you let it experience pleasure or not. You begin to reach the point of enjoying all the pleasure for which you are created if you recognize that he is with you.

26

I Don't Love Him Anymore

When the "Feeling of Love" Is Gone

After several years of marriage, when a couple has had children and has survived the first few traumatic years of parenting, and when the couple is established solidly in some business, profession or vocation, then there is again time to focus on the marriage relationship. The couple may discover that what was once a very loving, caring relationship no longer exists. The two people are together because they are married, have children, and own a home. They have a history, they plan a future, they go on vacations together, but without the feeling of *love*. How does this happen?

Pain-filled Relationships

Whenever a person experiences a great deal of pain as a result of his or her marriage, it is likely that the feeling of love will drift away. That pain may come about because the person feels the partner is unattentive to his or her needs for emotional care, physical help, spiritual guidance, or sexual fulfillment. Somehow the partner does not respond to what this person is looking for in the relationship.

Pain may also result from a more active response such as anger.

A person may come to the marriage with accumulated anger. He or she may have received little affection as a child and may have become somewhat calloused. He or she expresses this anger by blasting his or her partner. These outbursts actually say more about the angry individual than they do about the partner. Nevertheless, the mate may feel hurt and pushed away.

Think, for example, about the law student whose wife was helping him through college. He was raised by a punitive father who never showed his care for the son. Even though his mother was very expressive of her love, his father's behavior left him feeling he was without worth. Whenever the wife did anything that could possibly be construed as having some negative reflection on him, he became angry and put her down severely. This left her feeling that she wanted to get out of the marriage.

When a husband or wife has been deserted for another person or for any other reason, the pain may be so severe that the feeling of love will diminish. If the unfaithfulness or desertion continues over a period of time, the partner's trust, commitment and love may disappear entirely. If the wandering one returns, a long struggle to rebuild trust and regain love will probably be in store for the couple.

Drifting Apart

Sometimes a husband and wife drift apart because of external pressures. Probably the single most common external stress pulling people apart is the conflict and pressure associated with child-raising. The likelihood of this happening increases with long-term child behavior problems or chronic physical illness. Such a problem is so subtle and long term that its effect is often missed, even though its force is potent.

The stress caused by children may begin with the pregnancy. Some morning sickness during the first three months is likely to make the woman less interested in any sexual experience. When she gets past that point into the second three-month period, her figure will begin to expand. Her body image may now be at stake. Doubts about her appearance may trigger hesitancy sexually. In the last three months, the size of her abdomen may interfere with her comfort in love-making. During the last month she may avoid sexual activity almost totally. It is important to point out that there are no physical reasons a healthy pregnant woman should not be able to make love. What we are talking about here is an emotional response or physical discomfort rather than physiological reasons for not being involved.

The man may have some difficulties with the idea of making love to a pregnant woman for fear of hurting her. He may not understand how well protected the baby is inside the uterus. And he may not be able to come to terms with the idea of being sexually involved with a pregnant woman, the woman who is carrying his child.

After the baby is born, it will usually be four to six weeks before the couple will be given approval by the doctor to go ahead with sexual intercourse. Even then, the wife may still be very tired. Her body may not yet have fully recovered, or she may experience some vaginal pain. In addition, she now has the distraction of the child who is totally dependent on her. This mother-child relationship will often bring about major changes in terms of how the woman sees herself and how free she feels to respond sexually. It is not uncommon for a woman to experience uncomfortable emotions in contemplating sexual involvement as a new mother. Some couples find this to be more true if she is breast-feeding. It is as if sex is a desecration of the beautiful mother-child-nursing-caring relationship. Even if there are no attitude difficulties with mothering, fathering, pregnancy, or nursing, the major commitment of time and energy necessary to get a child through the first few months is a disruption in any relationship. As beautiful and delightful as children are, and as much joy as they bring into our lives, there is no doubt that readjustment is a major event for most couples, even when the children have been planned for. Many couples will not consciously deal with this readjustment together and hence will begin drifting apart.

Usually about the time the couple is ready to renew their sexual relationship they begin thinking about having the next child. Often the whole experience is repeated, and then the mother not only has a nursing child but also a jealous two- or three-year-old. If the couple stops with only two children, there will be a four- or five-year period in which the relationship cannot maintain the closeness that existed before the first pregnancy. If they have more children, the time period lengthens with each new pregnancy.

We are not saying that every child introduced into a family will bring distance and the loss of love. But there is a very serious possibility that the sexual relationship will be interrupted to some extent. It is crucial that the couple be aware of this likelihood. Sometimes by the end of this five- to ten-year child-bearing period, a couple will no longer feel or experience much of the love that was present before it all began.

School, Career, or Business

An intense focus on college, graduate school, seminary and any other specialty can so capture one's energy and interest that there is little time left over for the expression of the love the couple had for each other in the beginning. It is easy for a student to let deadlines for papers, reports, books or research projects become the controlling force in his or her life. The marriage relationship, including the sexual dimension, becomes less and less significant.

The same thing can happen in building a career. It takes a great deal of time and energy to become efficient and successful. Generally the worker will be gone for more than eight hours a day. Even if active involvement is limited to forty hours a week, the career will often take much mental and emotional energy, leaving little for the partner.

Building a business can have the same effect. All of us want to be successful. When that success is in its early stages it tends to possess us, taking precedence over some other areas. The marriage relationship is often one of the areas that suffers as a result of such a business push.

Whether the distracting factor is school, career, or business, the effect is the same. When two people do not have a continued, intense sexual involvement, the glue that holds them together begins to weaken. Eventually this weakened relationship will be felt and expressed in terms of having lost the sense of being in love.

Unfaithfulness

Sometimes when things are not going well in a marriage, either in terms of communication or in the sexual dimension, one of the partners begins to look for or incidentally develops a relationship outside the marriage which leads to sexual involvement. Because of its newness and excitement, this sexual involvement will often seem fulfilling and satisfying in its initial stages. When one is unhappy and unfulfilled in one relationship and then experiences fulfillment and satisfaction in another, it is natural to have the feeling of being in love with the new partner. Since it is difficult to maintain an intense passion for two people at the same time, the wandering partner usually feels that he or she is no longer in love with his or her spouse.

Sexual involvement outside one's marriage often forces a choice. If the person chooses to return to the original partner, and the partner is willing to forgive and forget, love may grow again in the marriage.

But if the person chooses to divorce the original partner and marry the new one, the same problems may develop in the second relationship that were present in the first. The pleasure and excitement experienced in a new relationship are deceptive in that they lead the participants to believe that this "love" will last. Time usually alters that. The scriptural directives about faithfulness to one's mate are not there just to make life complicated, but because that pattern works best to bring about long-term fulfillment and happiness for everyone involved.

Never Were in Love

It may come as a surprise to some, but there are some couples who marry for reasons other than love. The reasons always seem logical at the time, but over a period of months and years that "reasonableness" often diminishes. It is not uncommon to hear such explanations as "I thought he was the best I could do," or "He seemed like he would be a good husband and father for our family and would be able to provide well." Some people will confess, "I never really felt I loved her but I thought the love would grow," or "I was taught that love was an action not a feeling, and it seemed as though we had many common interests and that this would work out well." Then there is, "My mother really liked him and he was the first one that she liked, so I thought that would be best for me," and "I knew she was God's choice for me."

Whatever the reason, many couples marry without really loving each other. This almost inevitably gets in the way of their sexual relationship. A sense of passion or love, though hard to define, seems to be a necessary ingredient for total sexual experience. If love was never there to begin with, as times get tough, as love develops with someone else, or as one partner is reminded of past loves, it becomes much more difficult to maintain the relationship or to work toward sexual satisfaction. This is different than the situation in which love was lost.

Instead, love was never there in the first place. In some cultures where divorce is less acceptable, the relationship may be able to survive. But in our society, with all its emphasis on fulfillment, satisfaction and love, and with divorce being accepted even within the church, a relationship not based on love is bound to have difficulty. It is our opinion that couples can learn to love one another if they are willing to commit themselves with all of their beings—spiritually, behaviorally and emotionally. Achieving that commitment, however, is often difficult.

How Do You Fall in Love Again?

How can you build or rebuild love? First, both partners must *want to do it.* If only one is interested in restoring the relationship and works all alone to make the other happy, it will never succeed. It takes commitment from both people. With that commitment, a loving relationship is a possibility. And once you have established that loving relationship, you can resolve your sexual problems. You are extremely unlikely to have a satisfying sex life if you and your partner are uninterested in one another.

Let us say that you and your partner have made that commitment to build or rebuild love. Where do you go from there? Sometimes, especially if the relationship floundered because one or both partners were experiencing it as painful, some counseling will be necessary to help you deal with and heal the pain and the memories. This counseling may come from a pastor or from a professional therapist.

In other cases, a couple will be able to develop love on their own. They do it simply by talking together, sharing their feelings and thoughts, expressing where they have been, where they are now, and where they would like to go in the relationship.

Sometimes love grows again almost spontaneously when a change occurs in the couple's life. The children grow up and leave home, or the career becomes less demanding, and without those external pressures the couple can rediscover their love. The commitment was there all the time, but the corresponding actions were not in evidence.

Specific planning may be required to clear out involvements that interfere with the development of love or to build positive experiences together. Such planning should be directed toward mutually selected nonsexual and sexual events in which the partners are focused on one another for communication, fun, or bodily pleasure.

You may need to examine and deal with old habits. They have a way of hanging around when a couple has been operating apart for a number of years. Examine those habits and decide which ones must be consciously altered. Don't just assume that everything will work out fine—strive to make sure it does!

If one partner has been unfaithful, there is no way that love in the marriage can be established unless that partner will make a firm commitment to the marriage relationship. When one has experienced little satisfaction in the marriage and seemingly so much outside it, making this commitment demands a reliance upon God's strength. Actions of love do not necessarily bring healing to everyone. This means that there may be real struggles with the whole nature of commitment and the development of an understanding of what the marriage contract means for each partner. The spiritual and emotional dimensions must both be faced.

If you are in a one-sided relationship in which all the effort seems to come from your side and your mate does not seem willing to communicate—you are in a tough spot. It is difficult to give general directions about how to proceed but there are several things we recommend as a way of getting some action. Spend some time assessing your contribution to the problem. Are you nagging, withdrawing, demanding, complaining to friends or neighbors or being the "suffering Christian"? Then determine if there are any ways of change offered that you haven't accepted. Be sure your needs and desires have been clearly expressed. Don't wait for your mate's action—you make the first move. If nothing works, seek some help from a professional who has an unbiased perspective.

When the problems are not clear, focusing on the sexual area can sometimes help bring the real problem into the open. The sexual problems are often more of a symptom of a lack of love than the cause of that problem. There are people who have, by their own efforts, built a relationship of love when those feelings were not initially there. For most people outside help is required to achieve this. That support system may be a small group, an empathetic friend, a helpful pastor or a professionally trained counselor. Always remember that people have the capacity to change. God can work in your life as you let him. If you don't have the feelings of "love," you can grow into them in the days ahead. Dennis Guernsey's book *Thoroughly Married* (Word, 1975) is most helpful on this subject.

27

Birth Control Gets in the Way

There is one common complaint that seems to hinder full sexual pleasure. Though it is often not identified as a hindrance, it involves birth control—either the lack of it or the method used. Sometimes this problem is identified only in retrospect; that is, when birth control is no longer an issue, the couple discovers how much relief they feel. For example, if the woman gets a tubal ligation or if the man gets a vasectomy, they suddenly realize that they are not nearly as anxious as they used to be. The woman is much freer to respond, the man is more relaxed. Concern about pregnancy weighs heavily on the minds of many couples. Some are not protected in any way, while others may be unsure of their protection, or the mechanical device used may interrupt the pleasure of the sexual experience. Any one of these may cause low grade anxiety which inhibits the person's freedom to enjoy a full sexual involvement.

Another source of anxiety and concern is that of religious restrictions regarding birth control. This causes conflict for the devout couple. If they go against the church's stand, they feel guilty. If they follow the guidelines of the institution, fear of pregnancy may dominate the sexual scene. Some Roman Catholic couples report that using birth control pills causes them to experience a chronic sense of uneasiness because they feel guilty about "sinning" by making love for the purpose of pleasure with unnatural interruption of the possibility of procreation. Other religious groups also have clear guidelines as to what is acceptable and what is not. When these guidelines are not followed, guilt and anxiety are inevitable for many.

Obviously the issue of birth control causes anxiety because of the concern about pregnancy. The consequences of an unplanned-for act may be with us the rest of our lives together. What can seem like a frivolous, spontaneous, fun event in one moment can have incredibly long-term consequences. When those consequences are weighing on our minds we will not be free to enjoy spontaneity.

Methods of Birth Control

Some couples attempt to prevent pregnancy by withdrawing the penis from the vagina immediately before ejaculation. They believe that this will keep the sperm outside the vagina and hence the woman cannot be impregnated. This is inaccurate information. During extended love play a man will commonly release some seminal sperm even before he withdraws and ejaculates. Hence he may have already released the sperm that could fertilize an egg. Emotionally, regular withdrawal before ejaculation causes frustration. The experience of becoming aroused and building toward a peak of sexual release usually leads a couple to a sense of wanting to be closer and closer. The natural response for both parties is to push and thrust harder. To withdraw or pull away at that time goes against all our natural inclinations. Withdrawal is neither effective in controlling pregnancy nor satisfying in terms of the sexual experience. There is obviously not much to be said in its favor.

Mechanical devices can end up getting in the way. The most obvious ones are the diaphragm for the woman or the condom for the man. The diaphragm is a small device inserted into the vagina to cover the opening to the uterus (the cervix), thus preventing the sperm from traveling into the uterus to fertilize the egg. Some women report that they just automatically insert the diaphragm and never find it to be troublesome. Other women who don't want to put it in until the last minute find that it interrupts the flow of love-making. Condoms ("rubbers") have the same effect. Many men experience diminished sensations, even with a good condom. They find it interrupts the process.

For some, the interruption may be great enough to decrease the erection. Not only is it a bothersome interruption, but it causes further anxiety because the couple must be sure that the seminal fluid all remains in the device. Thus they are not really free to relax even after the ejaculation.

Answers Please

Birth control methods are much discussed right now. The permanent methods—tubal ligation for the woman or vasectomy for the man—are sure ways of avoiding pregnancy. But these are not advisable until the couple has decided not to have any more children. Even then, it is difficult for some couples to make such a decision for various personal reasons.

"The pill" has been used most extensively in recent years. Some of the concerns regarding cancer have been dispelled by the ten-year California study released in the fall of 1980. Other apprehensions about the pill's effects on various body types are still unanswered. Hence for some it may be a less desirable form of control. This takes us back to the mechanical devices and their inherent problems.

We wish we could give clear and simple answers as to the best way to achieve absolutely hassle-free birth control, but currently there are none. Each couple has to continue to struggle out loud with each other as they plan for the future. Having planned and decided, they must behave realistically and in good conscience in line with those decisions.

When birth control decisions push you to the use of some kind of mechanical means, the best thing to do is to learn to incorporate them into the fun of love-making experience rather than seeing them as the enemy or the interrupter. The attitude you bring to the experience is all-important. As you are free to share with your partner how the particular birth control method you have chosen affects you, you will be able to work out details between you. This process can reduce the interruption and distraction to a minimum.

For example, if a woman is using a diaphragm with foam, the couple can learn to insert both of these as an early part of the process, with the husband and wife sharing the responsibility. Or the woman can be actively involved with the condom, helping to get it on so that this step becomes a desirable part of the experience. Granted, it is not as free as it could be without the mechanical devices. But without them there is fear of pregnancy.

If you are determined to control impregnation, a discussion with your physician can determine which methods would be best for you. It is most helpful to get those methods working for you, and you working for them, rather than to continue being at odds with them and letting them interfere with your enjoyment.

This chapter is not intended to be a comprehensive treatment on the whole issue of birth control. Rather, it is designed to focus on the birth control issues that get in the way of satisfying sexual experience. Matters of family size must be decided between the couple. Decisions regarding means of birth control must grow out of discussions between the two of you and your physician.

28

Why Sexual Problems?

Many people ask, "If the sexual drive is so natural, why is it that people have so many technical difficulties? Is this some indication that we are pushing for something not intended to be? If it is all so natural, why don't we just automatically function sexually as we do in other areas?" There are a number of reasons why satisfactory sexual function does not "come naturally."

Lack of Knowledge

There are always those who missed out on getting needed information. They do not know what is normal sexual behavior between two partners. Because of the haphazard nature of most sexual education, we cannot count on everyone growing up with the same information. If we take, for example, the area of mathematics, most of us go through school and learn first of all to add and then to subtract, then to multiply and divide, to do fractions and percentages. Finally, we move on to algebra and geometry. By this time we have most of the basic concepts of arithmetic that we need in order to function in our daily lives. Sexual knowledge, however, is learned mainly in a hit-and-miss way. We learn through what we pick up from books, from what we hear on the streets, or from brothers, sisters and friends. We cannot count on everyone having complete knowledge when their bodies are ready to respond.

Many aspects of the sexual experience are so emotionally charged it is difficult for people to accurately communicate them in a clear or expressive way. Hence, we find many adults, even well-educated adults, reaching the point of readiness for sexual involvement with a dismal lack of knowledge regarding what is normal and natural. Some may not be aware of how to enjoy their partner's body or go after arousal for themselves. Others may not be aware of the acceptability of the feelings in the body. Still others shy away from certain natural bodily responses as if they are abnormal. Often a newly married couple will experience a certain kind of event in their love-making and will wonder whether this is really normal or whether they are odd. Usually the behaviors or bodily responses under question are very natural.

Knowledge about one's self and one's partner is often lacking. Many women particularly come to the marital situation quite unaware of their own sexual feelings, desires, or needs. Every woman is different. There is no way that we can write in a book or declare in a lecture what every woman needs. Some women enjoy rather vigorous physical activity with a lot of clitoral stimulation; others prefer much more general body pleasuring with only light clitoral stimulation at certain times. There is no way for a man to come to the marriage bed with a prescription in his hand that will guarantee a pleasurable response from his partner. If she does not know her own body and what is most satisfying for her, then he may feel the demand to determine what brings her pleasure. They are both likely to find the sexual times less satisfying than they ideally could be.

It can be the same way for the man. He may have learned a way of stimulating himself to the point of ejaculation, but that may be the extent of his knowledge about himself. So it is crucial that the couple's first year or two of love-making be a discovery time. They need to learn as much about themselves and each other as they can.

Another area where many lack knowledge is in an understanding of the sexual process and response. If we do not understand what is happening in our bodies, we often bypass many possibilities for pleasure. For example, if a woman assumes that the woman's desire and response is the same as the man's, then she will wonder why she feels negative when he repeatedly heads for her genital area in his pleasuring. Yet it is a fact that the woman's sexual response tends to be slower than a man's. She normally needs more general touching, caressing, and conversation rather than just the emphasis on genital-clitoral stimulation. But unless both partners understand this as a common need for women, they will likely bypass it.

Similarly, if a woman is hesitant to let her body respond in the way it was designed to, she will inhibit her natural sexual expression. Many women want to stop the intense breathing that occurs when they become aroused. They are embarrassed about this response as if it were abnormal. The body movements, the facial grimaces, the groans that occur naturally, will be cut off because they are "unladylike," even though these responses are arousing to the partner and necessary for her release. For men, there is often the belief that the man should be able to continue to be restimulated after an ejaculation. This may be possible for one or two percent of men in their twenties or early thirties, but most men are physically designed to require at least an hour of rest before they become restimulated.

It is crucial for a couple to understand the normal physical response of the body and to let themselves experience it fully. We are often amazed at the transformation that occurs when a couple gains some basic technical knowledge about sexual response. They experience greater freedom, greater relaxation, and greater enjoyment.

Unconscious Avoidance

Some people cannot allow themselves freedom to enjoy sexual activities even though their heads say that sexual feelings are great! They find themselves cutting off or even sabotaging their sexual response. Sometimes the reason is guilt. Guilt may be genuine, real, and authentic; or it may be false, inauthentic. When we feel guilty about something it does not necessarily mean we have violated any of God's or society's laws. If we have been taught, for example, that the sexual response is evil and is a part of our earthly, fleshly lusts, then regardless of the fact that the Bible endorses sexual activity and society condones sexual involvement within marriage, we may still *feel* guilty. This is a form of inauthentic guilt—that is, guilt over an activity that does not violate any standard.

Sometimes we avoid sexual activity because of *real* guilt. A person may have been raised by parents who taught that sex outside of marriage violated God's law. This person was active sexually before marriage. After marriage this past violation may get in the way of the person's current sexual experience. He or she carries guilt about that past activity. Many times people who make a Christian commitment as adults will feel guilty for premarital sexual behavior even though they did not have a Christian standard when they were involved sexually.

Guilt also arises as a result of extramarital activity after marriage. All of these can inhibit the sexual response. Yet, most of the guilt that gets in the way of sexual freedom is *inauthentic* guilt.

Anger is also a source of unconscious avoidance. Anger has several sources which need to be clearly differentiated. There is anger or bitterness that a person brings into the relationship from his or her past life. And there is anger or hostility that grows out of the current marriage relationship. The old anger or bitterness present in many relationships has its source in pain and deprivation that may have occurred in childhood. If, for example, a man was continually "put down" as a boy by mother or father for his inadequacy or incompetence, or was continually stymied in his growth as an individual, or was continually limited in the expression of his feelings, he may experience bitterness or anger that shows itself in the marriage relationship. The person may not be aware of this old anger or bitterness, but the old scars from his or her early years can affect the present relationship.

Current anger, on the other hand, is often the result of stress between partners. The woman may be trying to be a "submissive" wife. Instead of being mutually submissive, the husband takes on the dominant role in such a way that the woman continually ends up feeling like a doormat. When this is the case, it is likely that anger and resentment will build. This is what the Bible calls "being provoked to wrath." The resentment may not be entirely conscious, but is likely to evidence itself in the most intimate areas of the relationship. The woman who experiences this sort of provocation may become less and less desirous of sexual activity. The bedroom is one more setting in which she feels violated and disregarded. Since she is the "submissive" wife, she will not usually express her anger directly, but she will find ways to avoid sexual activity.

Lack of self-worth, too, can bring about unconscious avoidance. When we do not feel good about ourselves, whether that is in terms of our physical appearance, parental responsibility, or our competency as a provider, we may want to avoid being sexually involved. We will not want to put ourselves in a situation where our lack of worth is pointed out one more time. At times this may manifest itself by unconsciously making oneself unattractive, either by lack of care for the body, by overeating, or by uncleanliness. To be together and responsive sexually requires a significant degree of self-worth. When this is not present, consciously or unconsciously, we are likely to avoid sexual activity.

When guilt, anger, or the lack of self-worth are *unconscious* ways of avoiding sex, we will naturally not be aware of them. The way to determine if these are in operation is to observe our behavior. From that behavior we can determine whether we are needing to avoid sex. It is usually necessary to have some kind of professional help to get at an understanding of anything subconscious or unconscious, since most of us are not equipped to uncover those responses for ourselves.

Sexual Anxiety

Fear of failure is another major source of sexual difficulty. This usually develops after actual experiences of failure. This may be inability to become aroused when stimulated, or it may be failure to be orgasmic after arousal. These tend to be most common for women. Men may experience failure to get an erection or to maintain it; or the fear of ejaculating prematurely; or the fear of not bringing pleasure to the partner. Any time we enter a sexual experience with fear, our responsiveness will be inhibited. This is a physiological fact. Our nervous system is set up so that we cannot experience fear and enjoyable sexual arousal at the same time. Those responses are mutually exclusive. When we fear failure, that failure tends to be perpetuated by the fear itself. The more I fear, the more likely I am to fail; the more I fail, the more I fear, and I'm into a downward spiral. This fear/failure situation is not a major *source* of sexual problems, but is a major way in which sexual problems are perpetuated.

Sexual anxiety grows out of the demand for performance. This demand may come from within one's self or from one's partner. If we enter the sexual experience with pressure to produce desirable experiences for our loved one or a response in ourselves, that demand will cause anxiety. Men tend to place a demand on themselves to bring pleasure to their partner. If that demand becomes predominant, it is likely to reduce the pleasure of the experience. The woman may also feel a demand on herself to respond, to become aroused, to lubricate, to have nipple erection, and to experience intense erotic feelings. As that demand is felt, it is likely to inhibit rather than to help the feelings. The woman may also feel a demand for orgasmic release, to prove to her husband that *he* is a good lover as well as to bring herself pleasure. With this demand the anxiety increases, making any response very unlikely.

The man may also feel a demand for performance. He may "need" to "provide" an orgasm for his wife. While this is a nice by-product of the sexual experience, when the man feels he *must* provide something for the woman, he cannot be relaxed and function in a way that makes it actually happen. Or he may feel he must immediately get an erection and keep it. When this anxiety is present, he certainly will not be relaxed. Yet relaxation is a necessary prerequisite for the erection that he needs for the sexual experience. As with the fear of failure, demand for performance fosters anxiety. When we are anxious, we cannot respond.

The Need to Please

When we have the feeling that our main function in the sexual experience is to please our partner, this may become a source of pressure which can get in the way of sexual freedom. This can take many forms. It may be that the man believes he must get an erection quickly and hold it as long as possible. The woman may feel she has to hurry to get aroused or have an orgasm in order to please. Her thoughts will be, *I can't take this much time.* If there is something she needs for her own satisfaction and arousal, she will think, *I can't ask him for that—he wouldn't like it,* or, *he'd probably be repulsed by that.* These thoughts are present even though she needs his participation in a particular way to experience good feelings for herself.

People with an excessive need to please their partner usually grew up in a situation where they had to work diligently for parental approval. Even with hard work they received little in the way of reward that built their self-worth. These people go through life looking for approval and reinforcement they never received as a child. It is difficult to make the transition from focusing on getting the approval of the partner to taking responsibility for one's own feelings. Once people realize that assuming such responsibility is the most satisfying way to please their partner, they can relax and enjoy their sexual feelings.

In sexual therapy we regularly find that it is most difficult for a couple to change their focus from pleasing one another to pursuing pleasure for themselves. Often each of them will report that they do want the other one to be enjoying himself or herself. This will "turn them on." Yet to make the shift from pleasing the partner to pleasing oneself is most difficult. It is difficult because the conditioning has taken place over a long period. The need to please is hard to overcome.

Blocked Erotic Feelings

When we block off good sexual feelings, we are unable to respond fully. This can happen in two ways. We can stop our feelings by focusing on certain thoughts, or we can get into what is often called the "spectator" role.

What do we mean by stopping our sexual feelings with our thoughts? This is called an "intellectual defense." We stop ourselves from feeling our natural bodily responses by thinking thoughts that get in the way of those feelings. For example, if we have had some negative sexual experiences, we may bring those to mind—they will stop the erotic feelings. Or a woman may think that she is responding in an unladylike, unchristian, or evil way. By thinking those thoughts she stops the good feelings. Many women who have been raised in the church have some sexual barriers connected with their Christian teaching. They will use thoughts about God and his judgment on their sexual activity as a way of stopping themselves from experiencing erotic feelings. Another person may become preoccupied with some of the mundane things in his or her world, such as what to do tomorrow or what didn't get done today. This, too, can stop the feelings that occur naturally.

It is important to make a distinction between the natural concerns which may come to mind without getting in the way and those thoughts which can stop sexual feelings. It is not uncommon, for women particularly, to think about what they need to put on the grocery list, or something they must remember for their children in nursery school the next day, or a matter they must take care of the next day at work. These thoughts can and do commonly occur without intruding on the sexual experience. They only get in the way if they become a preoccupation rather than just passing through her mind.

The "spectator role" is frequently used to block feeling. By this we mean that people stand outside their body and observe what they are doing. "Spectatoring" has the effect of keeping control on what one does and feels. If, as soon as we have a small sexual feeling, we stand outside ourselves to observe it, whether to encourage it or to disapprove of it, spectatoring will interrupt the flow of the feeling.

Perhaps this can best be understood by an analogy. If we are trying to fall asleep, one of the surest ways to stay awake is to think about falling asleep. All of us have had the experience of feeling sleepy, and needing to get to sleep, and then becoming anxious about it. We notice ourself beginning to doze and say, "Oh, at last I'm getting sleepy, I'm about to fall asleep." And by the time we've experienced those thoughts, we have moved into the spectator role. We will be wide awake, because the falling-asleep response is involuntary and requires relaxation, not conscious control. Sexual feelings are likewise automatic responses which must remain free of conscious control. As soon as we stand back and observe what is happening, whether it be arousal, maintaining an erection, maintaining control, or having an orgasm, these thoughts will get in the way of our sexual freedom.

Past Traumatic Experiences

Past traumatic experiences can get in the way of our sexual freedom. These most commonly have to do with those unfortunate children who experienced molestation or rape while growing up. Such experiences leave a child very confused about the sexual dimension of life. Any time an adult plays with a child's genitals, the child usually experiences some good feelings; yet at the same time it is usually a frightening experience. To have good sexual feelings connected with something extremely fear-producing brings conflict and turmoil to the child. An additional confusing factor is that the molestation or rape is usually performed by a person who is close to the child—father, brother, grandfather, cousin, uncle, neighbor, or family friend. In only a small percentage of the cases is it a stranger. Molestation by a family member or friend is much more common than any of us would like to believe. It tends to create in the victims a great deal of turmoil about themselves sexually. This may be carried over into their adult sexual experience. Often they feel an intense sense of guilt, as though they were responsible for what happened, even though they might have been only eight or ten years old.

To break through the barriers created by these experiences, it is essential that the one who experienced them share his or her feelings with someone who can care and understand. A spouse is often the best person. If you fear your spouse's response, you may first want to share with a pastor, an understanding friend, a counselor or physician. Once you have talked about the experiences, their hold on you will often diminish. As long as they are kept secret and the awful feelings of disgust, embarrassment, guilt, and anger are present, you will not have the freedom to respond in a total and enjoyable way to the sexual experience.

Another source of turmoil occurs for men and women who witnessed promiscuous sexual activity while growing up. If their parents were sexually active in their presence, or if they lived in a neighborhood where they observed open sexual activity by the youth of the area, their ideas about sex will be affected. These children may determine that they will never behave in this manner, since it is so repulsive to them. Then as they get older, they find their own sexual responses beginning to stir. They are repulsed by their own natural, God-given feelings, even when those feelings occur in a completely appropriate and acceptable setting. For example, it is not uncommon for a woman who had a rather flirtatious or promiscuous mother to be very inhibited sexually because she does not want to be like her mother.

Another example is the girl whose older sister becomes pregnant out of wedlock. The little sister may, at a young age, determine that *she* will never cause her parents that much stress, so she shuts down her ability to respond sexually. Years later, as an adult, she finds it difficult to be responsive to her husband. If a boy has a mother who behaves seductively with him or overexposes herself to him, this can instill a negative response in him which is difficult to overcome even in adulthood. With this negative set toward appropriate open and free sexuality the man is susceptible to experience sexual problems.

These barriers can be very deep and not easily understood. But as a person works to bring them to the surface and to deal with them, he or she can find release from the limitations the barriers have placed on sexual activity and enjoyment.

Early sexual experiences with peers can also interfere with an adult's sexual life. Often it is not the experience *per se* that causes the trauma but rather the reaction of parents when they discover the children in their play. If, for example, two girls at age six are discovered poking around at each other's genitals, the mother has at least two choices. She can inform the girls that what they are doing is not acceptable behavior and that they can injure themselves by it, thus teaching them about their bodies. Or she can go into a screaming fit, by which she frightens the children as if they have done a dreadful deed, often traumatizing them regarding their own sexuality from that point on. If their natural, sexual and bodily curiosity is labeled deviant and perverted, they will carry this view into adulthood. Sometimes, if there have been many warnings about sexual activity as a child grows up, he or she will develop a guilty attitude that will prevail even in marriage. The warnings need to be accompanied by the positive message about our sexuality.

Young people who engage in *excessive* premarital activity may find that as they enter married life and attempt to develop a normal sexual relationship, thoughts of their early experiences begin flooding in on them. These will cause distraction, sometimes disgust, and often guilt. While this is not true for *all* such people, it is not at all uncommon. When it does occur, it is usually necessary for the person to talk through all of the feelings surrounding the premarital activities before he or she can overcome the difficulties caused by those memories. Frequently those men and women find it difficult to feel forgiven. They *believe* they are forgiven by God and by anyone else they offended in the process, but they do not *feel* that they are forgiven. It is this lack of feeling forgiven that gets in the way of the natural sexual experience.

Finally, any traumatic adult experience, such as rape, can traumatize individuals about their sexual response. The turmoil that is set in motion by the violation has long-lasting effects. The victims usually feel that they somehow brought it on themselves, that they bear some guilt. "If only I had" done this or that—then, they believe, the whole thing could have been avoided. These feelings are natural even though they are usually inaccurate.

Persons who experience rape or other traumas must have the opportunity to talk through all that this has meant to them. They need to give over to God the feelings that continue to be stirred up.

Any traumatic experience that involved sexual activity or a sexual response can be the source of a major barrier for an adult. In all instances, it is essential that the opportunity be provided for communication of these events and the feelings aroused by them. For the traumatized person to find relief, this communication must take place with another committed, caring individual. This is one of the ways in which

Christians can minister to one another. For without healing, the consequences of these violations are often visited on us even to the third and fourth generation.

Relationship Problems

Difficulties in a relationship are bound to show up in bed. This may take many forms. Probably the most obvious is *rejection.* When one of you detests the other, it is not too likely that you are going to function effectively as sexual partners. Detesting, or total disregard for one's partner, usually develops gradually and is the result of both partners' participation. Both parties contribute to the rejection. Sometimes this results from having what Masters and Johnson have called "a second-choice mate." A second-choice mate is one who was chosen on the rebound. If an individual is actively dating someone and then loses that prospective partner through death, rejection, or other circumstances, he or she may quickly marry someone else as a way of soothing the painful emotions. People who do this often find themselves in a state of continual dissatisfaction. Their current mate does not live up to the expectations they had formed regarding the person they lost.

Whatever the cause of rejection, it commonly leads to *discord.* The discord may arise from a wide variety of events, but it usually has to do with one or both individuals feeling they are not being cared for in a way which they experience as loving. This will stimulate anger, hostility, and distance. When these feelings are present, the sexual experience will not be satisfying.

Lack of respect can also be a source of sexual problems. It is difficult to make love with someone you do not respect. Respect may be there at the beginning of the relationship, but then diminishes because your partner does not measure up to your expectations. Lack of respect toward the man will usually have to do with either his competence in his vocation or his integrity and honesty as an individual. Lack of respect to the woman will usually have to do with how she functions in the traditional "women's roles" of cleaning, cooking, and caring.

Discord often shows itself in the "sabotaging behaviors" that couples use to destroy the possibilities of a satisfying sexual experience together. Helen Singer Kaplan, a leading sex therapist and researcher, clearly paints the picture:

He likes her to swing her hips—she lies motionless.

He needs to be made to feel loved and desired—she is tired and "does him a favor."

She likes to move actively—he pins her down.

He is very stimulated by touching her breasts—she feels "ticklish" and cannot bear to have her breasts touched.

She is aroused by having her breasts caressed—he does not want to bother, or implies that her breasts are not attractive.

She likes to talk with him a bit first to relax her before sex—he plunges in wordlessly.

She hates TV—he always watches TV before making love.

She wants and needs clitoral stimulation—he implies his other lovers didn't need that sort of thing.

He likes to experiment—she thinks everything but "straight" missionary position is perverted.

She is very turned on by oral sex—he is disgusted by the odor of women's genitals. . . .

He has his best erection in the morning—she insists on sex at night only.*

These forms of frustrating one's partner are usually subconscious ways of getting back when direct communication of negative feelings has not seemed possible. Obviously, sabotaging expresses a great deal of hostility and communicates much ambivalence about the sexual experience. The hostility and ambivalence need to be dealt with openly. Sometimes couples can do this themselves, but most commonly they need some help in sorting through their feelings without hurting and distancing each other.

It is obvious that distance and lack of communication between partners is going to exaggerate any sexual problem that may be present. Communication is necessary both about general relationship issues and about the sexual dimension of the couple's experience. If partners do not share what they need or are lacking in the sexual experience, they will begin to withdraw from one another. As they withdraw, their frustration increases. If communication does not take place, they withdraw further, and the problem continues to perpetuate itself. As we have said so many times, the starting point for resolving any difficulty

---

*Helen Singer Kaplan, *The New Sex Therapy* (New York: Brunner/Mezel, 1974), p. 165.

is always effective communication. The communication must be gentle, loving and free of negative messages about the other person. Blasting the other person with all your built-up anger will not build the bridge.

The Need for Risk and Guilt

With all of the messages of caution and restriction that we receive about the sexual part of ourselves, it sometimes becomes a source of great pleasure to be involved in the riskiness of "unacceptable" sexual situations. Christian couples who became involved sexually before marriage found themselves to be quite responsive to each other. But after marriage they were much less interested in sexual activity and could not seem to experience the freedom and joy they had felt beforehand. If these people subsequently become involved in an affair, they will again find themselves to be very responsive. These people need to experience risk in a guilt-producing situation before they can become aroused and responsive. Often these are people who have been raised in situations where the direct message was that sex is bad, and yet the indirect message was that sex is good and something to be sought after. (Or it could be the opposite.) This double message created conflict for the person. Where it is acceptable to be responsive, the person cannot respond. Yet in the guilt-producing situation, intense sexual feelings surface naturally. When the person is unaware of the internal struggle, the partner may be blamed for the problem.

Summary

We have examined some of the most common underlying causes for sexual problems. The causes have ranged from internal problems one person brought into the relationship, to relationship stresses, to a need for information. Understanding the source of the problem may provide some relief, but may not correct the problem. To correct sexual problems usually requires specific behavioral changes within a loving, committed relationship.

_____29

Too Soon, Too Fast

An engaged couple anticipating the joy and excitement of life together usually believes that their sexual life will be an unending stream of satisfaction and delight. They experience passion, desire and arousal now and look forward to total enjoyment within marriage. There is no thought that it might not work that way. They assume that the sexual response is a natural one, and that as long as they "do what comes naturally" everything will be just fine. Fortunately, for some couples this expectation is fulfilled. However, for a large percentage this is not the case. At least one-half of the church populations who attend our seminars have significant, serious problems that get in the way of their total sexual freedom and enjoyment.

The single most common problem reported is premature ejaculation (P.E.). The woman might describe it as, "Coming so fast that I am not able to get with the program and then I am left hanging." The most interesting dilemma with P.E. is that many times the man and woman report the problem quite differently. It is not uncommon for a woman to report that the man ejaculates prematurely 80 to 100 percent of the time, whereas the man might report a 10 to 20 percent occurrence. This difference in experience points out the need for clarification of the problem within the relationship.

What do we mean by premature ejaculation? Various definitions have been given. We believe the problem is present when the man does *not have control* of his ejaculation. In other words, if the man ejaculates before he wants to, he is experiencing premature ejaculation. There is great variation in terms of the seriousness of the problem. Some men may experience so little control that they will ejaculate before entry or upon the anticipation of entry. Some will ejaculate as soon as their partner touches them. Others will ejaculate once entry is attempted or within a few seconds after entry. Probably the most common form of premature ejaculation is that which occurs within the first two or three minutes after entry.

It is important to realize that this is a problem which affects both the man and the woman. For the man, lack of control of his body functioning leaves him feeling unsure of himself. His pleasure is often decreased by the abrupt end to his sexual experience. Eventually his preoccupation with trying to postpone ejaculation will hinder his ability to fully lose himself to sexual pleasure. In addition to P.E. interfering with the man's direct enjoyment, he also may feel like an inadequate lover in relation to his wife.

When a man is anxious, feeling inadequate, and ejaculating unexpectedly, the woman will probably be left unsatisfied. Her frustration will only increase the negative pattern. However, P.E. does not have to be a negative experience for the woman. The confident man who really enjoys the pleasure of a woman's body may engage in so much sensuous body play that the woman is well satisfied before entry and/ or ejaculation occur. Unless the man or wife has the need for the woman to be orgasmic with the penis in the vagina, this adaptation may be a successful way of handling P.E. For other women, P.E. is not a problem because they are quickly and easily orgasmic and don't experience as much need for total body pleasure. Whether or not the lack of ejaculatory control hinders the woman's sexual pleasure, gaining control inevitably enhances sexual enjoyment for both the man and the woman.

Premature ejaculation usually gets its start long before marriage. Because of the normal admonitions against self-stimulation, the masturbation that does occur is usually experienced in a most hurried fashion. Most boys (90 to 95 percent) do masturbate. Because of the fear of being discovered, the boy usually tries to hurry through the experience as quickly as possible and learns to bring himself to the point of ejaculation very quickly. Similarly, adolescent sex play and premarital adult sex are also usually hurried events. Often they do not take place in a setting where the couple feels safe. Whether it be manual stimulation or actual intercourse in a car or in the parents' living room, the man continues to learn to rush along through the experience. The woman in these settings may not be oriented toward her own pleasure. She may be highly excited and a little bit frightened, so she rushes along also.

In addition to all the experiences that get the process of premature ejaculation going, the great all-American concept of reaching the goal quickly feeds the problem. Many men feel that the faster they achieve their goal, the more quickly they prove their masculinity. The facts, however, are just the opposite. A man will provide himself and his partner with the greatest pleasure when he is able to slow down, take his time, and have control of the experience.

People assume that once they get married, the problem of timing will work itself out. Sometimes it does. Many times, however, the P.E. continues. The sequence usually goes something like this: After the initial sexual involvement, the couple discovers the problem but are not too concerned about it. After a while the wife begins to feel used and unfulfilled. At the same time she begins to wonder what is wrong with her that is causing this problem.

The husband may be concerned only with his own pleasure, and therefore may not even notice the problem. If he is more sensitive, he may begin to be concerned about his wife's pleasure, but he may not know what to do about it. He may attempt to use some form of distraction to keep himself from ejaculating. He may try to think of something repulsive, start counting from one hundred backwards, imagine himself in unsexual situations, or seek any other mental distraction. These may have short-term benefit, but soon are of no avail.

At about this time, he begins to suspect that maybe there is something his wife is or isn't doing which interferes—so blame enters the relationship. "If she just wouldn't touch me so much, or if she just wouldn't move so vigorously, or if. . . ." The wife, too, becomes involved in the process, both blaming herself for her sexual inadequacy and also blaming him. Many women feel that if he "just tried," or if he "really cared about—," he would be able to control ejaculation. As any premature ejaculator will confirm, it is not a voluntary action on his part, but that fact may be difficult to communicate to his wife.

After a time the couple will begin to withdraw from each other, not wanting to enter an experience that is going to end up frustrating them. The man doubts his masculinity, and the wife often experiences a lessening of confidence in herself along with anger toward her partner. If this continues long enough, the anxiety can lead to impotence for the man. Even if the consequences are not that extreme, there is likely to be hostility and discouragement in the marriage. Some men seek to prove that they are adequate sexually by getting involved with another partner. Thus one disastrous event leads to another.

It is both encouraging and sad to report that the solution to premature ejaculation, when the couple is willing to cooperate, is really quite simple. That's the encouraging part. The sad part is that so many couples go through life without seeking a solution, believing that it is their lot in life to endure the problem. Premature ejaculation can be remedied in a relatively simple way. Some couples have done it without any outside help. Others, where the turmoil is of longer standing, or the pattern is a deeply ingrained habit, need to seek help from a competent professional. The steps to bring about ejaculatory control were first presented to the professional community as the result of research by Masters and Johnson. What we present here basically follows their formula, with our own minor adaptations.

Exercise 15
Learning Ejaculatory Control—The Squeeze

As with any sexual problem, regardless of who owns the problem, the resolution usually requires the active involvement of both husband and wife. It is a "couple" problem, not just an individual problem. Both people are affected by it, the experience of both is limited by it, and both desire the change. Hence, we recommend having both people actively involved in the process. Besides, it's much more fun that way! Willing and loving cooperation from both is usually necessary if change is to occur. If the relationship is fraught with distress and discord, you need to work on that before you can expect to bring about changes in ejaculatory control.

Attitude Changes

There are several attitudes essential to successful treatment. First, the man must desire control and believe that it can occur for him.

Until that happens, there is no point in attempting the procedure. Second, he must be willing to allow his wife to participate with him in the process. As we will see, this requires being able to relax and enjoy receiving pleasure from her. The attitude change for the woman is similar in that she must believe control can be achieved and she must be willing to work toward it. She must also know that her participation in the process is vital. This requires that she see this as a "couple" problem, not just "his" problem. Even more essential is that she be comfortable with his genitals.

Communication Changes

The couple who experiences premature ejaculation may have never talked about it. Until they can do that, no change is going to take place. The man needs to be able to understand what it feels like to the woman. He also needs to be able to explain what his own experience is like, some of the history as he understands it, and perhaps the inadequacy he feels in continually repeating this process. She needs to be able to talk about the thoughts she has had about herself, how the experience makes her feel about him, how she feels about participating in the attempted solution. It is crucial that the couple share very openly all dimensions of their feelings and responses as they relate to this issue before they begin the attempt at learning ejaculatory control.

Learning Control

We want to take you through a series of steps. These will clearly define how you can become aware of the sensations in your body which tell you that you are going to ejaculate. We will be presenting what Masters and Johnson have called "the squeeze technique." Some of you will be able to learn this on your own, others will need help with it. As we talk about the various sessions and experiences, keep in mind that some of you will need to repeat each step several times before you move on to the next. The main task of these experiences is to *become aware* of when you are going to ejaculate and be able to control your body and your activity because of that awareness.

One more guideline: When going through these learning sessions it is important not to attempt intercourse until this procedure suggests it. If you do interrupt the procedure with intercourse and ejaculation, that will tend to get in the way of learning control. Should that happen, it would be best to begin the steps again.

Exercise 16
Procedure One: Body Pleasuring, Excluding Breasts and Genitals

The goal of this experience is to learn to enjoy touching one another without the demand either within yourself or from your partner to become aroused or have intercourse. Many of us have not learned the full satisfaction of pleasure that can be ours. This exercise is designed as a way to refocus on that dimension.

Underlying Principles:

1. *Receiver:* Your only task is to "soak in" pleasure and to redirect the pleasurer when the touch is not pleasing. Check out your concern if at any point you become concerned that the pleasurer is not enjoying himself/herself.

2. *Pleasurer:* Touch your partner in a way that brings you pleasure, trusting that he/she will redirect you when what you are doing is not pleasurable. Check out your concern if at any point you become anxious about your performance rather than enjoying the process.

3. When an experience is felt to be a demand—something you *should* do—stop, share, and either reschedule or shift to an experience desired by both.

No experience is preferable to an experience by demand.

4. Make sure the room temperature and setting are comfortable for being both without clothes or cover.

5. You may or may not use an Allercreme-type lotion. If using lotion, warm it in your hand first.

6. If sexual arousal should occur, this can be seen as an involuntary response but not the intention or purpose of the experience. *Do not become concerned if there is or is not arousal: the purpose of this experience is body pleasure.*

Steps:

Partner #1: Lie on your abdomen in a comfortable position.

Partner #2: Place your hands on your partner's back. With your eyes closed, focus on the sensations of your partner's body: warmth, pulsation, vibrations; begin to move over the entire back with a sensuous touch—then proceed to neck, arms, legs. Inform partner when you are ready for him/her to turn over.

Partner #1: Turn onto your back.

Partner #2: Sitting with your partner's face in your lap, proceed with facial caress, then continue down neck, shoulders, arms, hands and chest (avoid breasts). Move to sitting between the legs of your partner (or to one side of your partner) and enjoy the rest of your partner's body excluding genitals.

Reverse roles and repeat steps.

You may need to repeat Procedure One several times until you can fully experience the joy and delight of pleasuring. It is always important to have a pleasuring session for both of you. Both need to learn to focus on the pleasure of receiving and giving touch.

Exercise 17
*Procedure Two: Body Pleasuring, Including Breasts and Genitals
(Application of Squeeze)*

Once you have become comfortable with the general body pleasuring, you may include the genitals. This is likely to bring an erection. We move closer, then, toward helping the man experience control of his ejaculation. When a man is approaching the point of ejaculation, there are changes in the testicles, sensations in the prostate gland area from the contractions and from the closing of the opening to the bladder, and slight sensations along the tube that carries the semen from the testicles and prostate area to the penis (see Chap. 8). These are the sensations which send the warning to the man that he is about to ejaculate.

When the man is in the receiving role during body pleasuring, it is extremely important that he be able to completely relax and focus on the sensations in his body. He must be able to let himself experience pleasure rather than feeling he has to do something for his wife. The procedure should be something like this:

Step One: Shower or bathe together in a relaxed way so that you can begin the experience of being together in this gentle way and can come to it freshly washed.

Step Two: Pleasure the back of the man's body. Then get into the position as designated by Figure 8 in Chapter 13, where the man is lying on his back and the woman is sitting with her legs stretched out beside him, so that his genitals are within easy reach of her hands.

Step Three: The woman is completely in charge of this part of the experience. After pleasuring the upper part of his body, she gently begins to caress the penis and scrotum with particular attention to those areas that he has let her know are most pleasurable. Some men report that touching the underside of the penis called the frenulum is most stimulating for them. Others enjoy general pleasuring of the shaft of the penis, with particular arousal coming at the ridge around the head—the coronal ridge. This is true whether or not a man is circumcised.

Step Four: After the man experiences a full erection for a few minutes the woman should apply the squeeze. To do this, the woman should grasp the penis with her thumb on the underside of the ridge around the head of the penis and her forefinger and middle finger above and below the ridge of the head on the front side of the penis (see

Figure 10

THE SQUEEZE TECHNIQUE

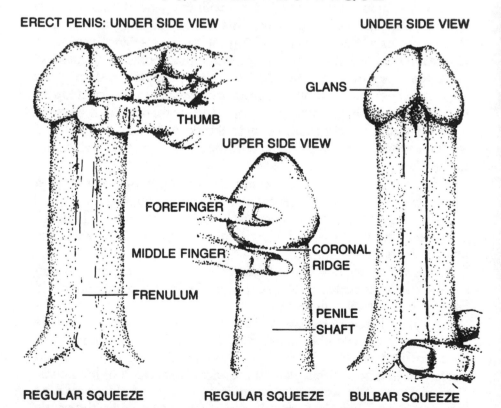

ERECT PENIS: UNDER SIDE VIEW   UNDER SIDE VIEW

THUMB

GLANS

UPPER SIDE VIEW

FOREFINGER

MIDDLE FINGER

CORONAL RIDGE

FRENULUM

PENILE SHAFT

REGULAR SQUEEZE   REGULAR SQUEEZE   BULBAR SQUEEZE

the accompanying diagram). The squeeze should be firm but not hard and should last about ten seconds. Be careful not to use the fingernails in this procedure. When the squeeze has been applied, some men will partially lose their erections; others will not. The squeeze is effective whether the erection diminishes or not. The squeeze is not designed to cause loss of erection, but rather to teach control of ejaculation. So whether or not there is loss of erection, the squeeze can still effectively do what it is intended to do.

Step Five: Whether the squeeze results in the loss of erection or not, move away from the focus on the genitals, pleasuring other parts of the body. After a few minutes or more, move back to caressing and stimulating the penis. Once the full erection returns or the feelings of arousal intensify, again apply the squeeze in the same manner as described above.

Step Six: Repeat the above procedure several different times until you feel you have a good sense of how it works and are allowing longer and longer times of arousal before the squeeze is applied. Note that you do not have to wait to apply the squeeze until the man feels he is about to ejaculate.

Step Seven: Pleasure the woman's body by following Procedure One. Include breasts and genitals in a general sense.

Procedure Three: Total Body Pleasuring Including Ejaculation by Manual Stimulation

Repeat Procedure Two, but this time use a lubricant such as Aller-creme or K-Y Jelly during the genital stimulation for both the man and the woman. The lubricant on the penis will more closely approximate the feeling that the man will have inside the vagina. In these sessions after four or five squeezes and after at least thirty minutes of pleasuring, bring the man to the point of ejaculation by manual stimulation. It is still important not to attempt entry. Again, be sure there is plenty of time for enjoying the total pleasure of each other's bodies.

Procedure Four: Total Body Pleasuring Including Entry without Ejaculation inside the Vagina

Step One: Repeat Procedure Three for two or three squeezes.
Step Two: After a squeeze, even if the penis is slightly flaccid (limp),

Figure 11

FEMALE SUPERIOR POSITION

with the woman in the top position, have her guide the man's penis into her vagina (see Figure 11). If it is somewhat flaccid, she may have to stuff it in.

Step Three: After the woman has inserted the penis lie quietly together for two or three minutes without moving. This step is very important because it helps the man learn to be quiet inside the vagina. This may be very difficult for him because he has always tended to ejaculate quickly and hence move rapidly the moment entry has taken place. Hartman and Fithian have called this period of time "quiet vagina."

Step Four: After several minutes of lying quietly together and enjoying each other's bodies, the woman should begin to gently move her pelvis in a mild thrusting manner. If the man finds himself quickly erect, this gentle thrusting should be very brief, and the woman should move off the man and immediately apply the squeeze.

Step Five: After the squeeze has been applied, move back on top of the man and reinsert the penis, even if it is slightly flaccid.

Step Six: Repeat the above procedure several times, allowing longer and longer times of arousal before withdrawal for the squeeze, unless the man indicates that he is experiencing the sensations that precede ejaculation, in which case the woman should apply the squeeze immediately.

Step Seven: After repeating the above procedure several times, when the man is fully erect and there has been some thrusting by the woman, withdraw the penis and using a lubricant stimulate him to orgasm manually. This will often be a very difficult step to follow because the desire and inclination will be to ejaculate inside the vagina. For the man to be able to learn ejaculatory control, it is important that these steps be followed quite carefully.

At any point in these experiences, should the man ejaculate unintentionally (and we would expect this to happen at least once for anyone learning this control), the couple are encouraged to enjoy the ejaculation, learn as much as you can from any sensations that the man experiences, and move on to pleasuring the woman so that she too may have some joy and satisfaction. If she is able to respond orgasmically from external stimulation, that would certainly be appropriate.

Procedure Five: Total Body Pleasuring Including Ejaculation inside the Vagina

Step One: Begin by experiencing some total body pleasuring, including some genital stimulation and applying the squeeze before entry at least once.

Step Two: Again with the woman in the top position, have her insert the penis, spend some time in quiet vagina, and then begin gentle thrusting. Let the thrusting become more intense as the man can tolerate it, and let the duration of time from the beginning of thrusting to the point of applying the squeeze become longer and longer as the man can tolerate this.

Step Three: After a period of five or ten minutes of thrusting activity, even if the man does not feel near the point of ejaculation, withdraw and apply the squeeze and then re-enter.

Step Four: Continue this procedure until you are able to last up to fifteen minutes between squeezes.

Step Five: When you have repeated the above procedure for two to four squeezes, then decide that you are not going to apply the squeeze on the next wave of arousal. This is intended to allow the woman some opportunity to get with her feelings so that she too can be at an emotional peak when the man ejaculates. Begin with very slow movements and a rhythmically built pace held for as long as possible, and then let yourself fully enjoy the ejaculation inside the vagina. It is important not to be in a hurry but rather to let yourself experience all the sensations so that you are aware of what it feels like as you reach the point of no return.

Step Six: If the woman has not experienced an orgasm as a result of the above processes, and she desires one, focus on her needs so that she, too, can come away with full satisfaction.

Step Seven: Repeat the above procedure on several different days until you feel very confident that you have it mastered.

Procedure Six: Adaptations of the Squeeze

Begin to learn new ways of incorporating the squeeze into your love-making activity regardless of what your position is or where you are in terms of your arousal. Obviously it is not our intention to suggest that love-making should always be a matter of numbered steps. This is a way of learning ejaculatory control. Once you attain control, go on to adapt the squeeze to your own style of free flowing love-making. You will now want to begin to make love in positions other than the woman on top. Various positions have already been discussed, and you may refer to that section of the book for the various possibilities. After you have learned the squeeze in the regular manner you can use the "bulbar squeeze." The bulbar squeeze is used at the base of the penis so that withdrawal from the vagina is not necessary (Figure 10, the diagram on the right).

Outline for Learning Ejaculatory Control

1. Total body pleasuring (Procedure One)
2. Genital caressing until firm erection
3. Squeeze
4. Rest and general body caressing
5. Genital caressing until return of full erection or intensified arousal (but before point of no return)
6. Squeeze
7. Return to general pleasuring
8. Genital stimulation
9. Squeeze (Procedure Two includes Steps 1–9, plus holding each other) (Procedure Three includes steps 1–9, repeat 7 and 8 and bring to ejaculation manually)
10. Entry (stuff it, if there is loss of erection)

11. Quiet vagina
12. Gentle thrusting
13. Withdrawal of penis from vagina
14. Squeeze
15. Reenter
16. Gentle thrusting, gradually increasing intensity and speed for a maximum of five minutes
17. Withdrawal of penis from vagina (Procedure Four includes steps 1–17, and bring to ejaculation manually)
18. Squeeze
19. Reenter
20. Gentle thrusting, gradually increasing to point of ejaculation (Procedure Five includes steps 1–20)
21. Adaptations (Procedure Six)

Some Hitches along the Way

When you are attempting to learn control through this procedure, everything won't proceed according to the book. There may be some individual idiosyncrasies that get in the way of things happening as they are supposed to. One of these might be what we would call "penis hesitancy." If you are a woman who was raised to believe that the touching of your own genitals was evil or dirty, then it would not be surprising that you might have some hesitancy about freely touching the man's genitals. If this is your situation, then before you can begin to learn the squeeze technique you need to condition yourself to become comfortable with the penis in a general way.

Another dilemma that sometimes gets in the way has to do with the man's discomfort at being the total focus of the pleasuring. Some men find it extremely difficult to just lie back and enjoy. They feel they must be doing something for their wife, otherwise she will become disgruntled. Let us reassure you that if this process can bring you ejaculatory control, it is the best thing that can happen for your wife as well as for you. So you can count on it that she is enjoying herself. If she isn't, it is up to her to say so rather than for you to be second-guessing her.

Some men are totally unaware of when they are about to ejaculate, so they may find that the ejaculation will occur without apparent warning. Do not be discouraged by this, but rather proceed more slowly so as to allow yourself the time to become aware of what is happening to your body.

The fourth possible roadblock may be the "top entry" procedure for the woman. This may be new and somewhat uncomfortable emotionally: it may seem dominant since the upper position is traditionally the male's. Not being in the upper position may, also, bring the man emotional discomfort. We encourage you to push yourself beyond this barrier and use the woman-on-top position for these experiences because it has been found to be more effective than any other position. If there are any difficulties with entry in this position, be sure that you follow the position as pictured in Figure 11, and that the woman is in fact straddling across the man's genitals; second, be sure that you are using some lubricant to assist in the entry even if she thinks she is well lubricated. We recommend using lubricant during the time of learning as a way of facilitating the procedure.

Finally, some couples find themselves naturally resistant to the period of quiet vagina. While this period does go against what our bodies naturally want to do, it is important to learn this control. It allows the opportunity for the man to experience the sensation of the penis in the vagina without thrusting and without ejaculation. Since it is crucial for the man to experience these sensations, we encourage you to have those periods of being quiet throughout all your love-making.

Now That There Is Control

Once you have reached the point where you can choose when you will ejaculate, you may find it helpful to continue using the squeeze on various occasions to help lengthen the love-making period. This would be particularly true if it has been some time since the last ejaculation, because then you are more likely to ejaculate more quickly. The use of the squeeze should be incorporated into love-making and used at any point along the way for the rest of your life.

Some of you may have heard or read about the stop-start method of ejaculatory control. This procedure is identical to what we have described, but without the squeeze. Our own finding is that the squeeze is very effective since it involves both partners, gives the wife some sense of having control of when ejaculation occurs, often functions as a distraction, and is regularly found to be an effective means of gaining control. Some men prefer to stop the thrusting without applying the squeeze after they have achieved control, and this would certainly be a healthy and adequate adaptation.

If your premature ejaculation has evolved into impotence, then that should have your first attention. The impotence must be dealt with before the P.E.—usually with professional help. In Chapter 30 we address this subject.

30

Not Enough When You Need It—
Impotence

Everyone knows that all men are "supposed" to be ready and raring for sexual action at any time of the day or night. This myth gets perpetuated from youth, and is accepted as a fact. The myth says that from adolescence on, a man is so charged sexually he is always waiting and ready for a sexual experience. According to this theory, the woman is the one who is hesitant, unsure, and in need of extensive build-up. The symbol for this "masculinity" is the erect penis. It represents manhood and is expected to be ready to perform at a moment's notice.

We have been surprised at how early this concept is developed. One night when our son was five years old we asked him to get into his pajamas during a TV commercial. His older sister was also in the room. During his changing process he covered his genitals with his hand. When we asked him about this unusual behavior, since he had never demonstrated modesty before, he replied, "Well, it pops up if it sees a girl." There must be some truth in there somewhere.

For men it comes as a major shock when suddenly the symbol of their masculinity does not respond on cue. It usually means much more to the man than the simple fact that he is not responding sexually at that moment. It causes him to question his status as an adequate male. Obviously, when we put so much pressure or expectation on one dimension of a physical response, and that response fails, we will panic.

Impotence refers to the man's inability to *achieve* an erection or his difficulty in *maintaining* an erection. Impotence does not refer to the inability to impregnate (this is sterility). Nor does impotence refer to the inability to ejaculate. This is called retarded ejaculation.

Impotence can take on many forms. Some men achieve no erection at all. The usual kind of stimulation may occur, but the penis remains flaccid. For others, an erection may occur in the regular manner, but as the love play continues anxiety sets in and the erection is lost. For still others, the erection may be maintained very adequately up to the point of entry. As soon as entry is either contemplated or attempted, the erection dissipates. For some, erection may be maintained beyond the point of entry, and then wane after a period of activity inside the vagina. No matter when the erection goes away, its loss is always troublesome. It is always called impotence if the man does not have the confidence or relaxation to be able to let the erection return.

In any extended love-making time it is normal for the intensity of the erection to wax and wane. For many men an erection may disappear almost completely and then return again. This is not impotence but rather a normal part of the process. The only time the loss of an erection is considered impotence is when the man is unable to relax enough to regain the erection.

How do you know whether your impotence is the result of a physical problem or emotional distress? The simplest rule of thumb to follow is to observe whether or not you experience erections at any time during the day or night. If this is the case, then it is very unlikely that the impotence you experience is due to any physical cause. If you are never aware of erections occurring at any time, day or night, during love-making or away from the love-making experience, then we would advise a physical and urological examination to rule out any physical causes. Only a small percentage of impotence is the result of any physical condition. The majority (97 percent) can be attributed to emotional factors that may have started in many different ways and then have been perpetuated by a pattern of anxiety.

The Anxiety Pattern

For the sexual experience to be delightful, satisfying, and complete, you need emotional abandonment. By that we mean that you (man or woman) cannot be focusing your attention on how your body is responding, but rather must focus on the joy and delight of the physical sensations, the emotional satisfaction, and the experience of loving and being loved. This usually happens quite naturally until for some reason (which will be discussed shortly) your body does not respond the way you expect it to. When the natural bodily response of an erection does not occur or is not maintained, then the man is likely to become preoccupied with his physical response. This preoccupation or self-consciousness usually moves the man into what has been called the "spectator role." When the man is the spectator of his physical response, he is observing what should be happening automatically and then attempting to take control of that happening.

Any time you try to force your body to do something it can do only without demand, you will most likely keep yourself from doing the very thing you are trying to do. The falling asleep example that we used in Chapter 28 fits here as well. You can probably recall the times when you have needed to get a good night's sleep but you were keyed up or anxious for some reason. You went to bed and thought about falling asleep, or tried to get to sleep. In this process you moved into the spectator role and observed how you were doing in your falling-asleep process. And so you kept yourself awake. Finally you began to count sheep. "Counting sheep" is a way to distract yourself from thinking about falling asleep. Distraction is also needed when you are attempting to overcome impotence.

The pattern thus begins with an experience in which an erection does not occur automatically. The man becomes a spectator, attempting to bring about the desired response. During this time, anxiety is building about his competence to function sexually. There are several directions that it could go from this point. Some men try even harder by frequently initiating sexual activity in the attempt to get past the dilemma and to "prove" themselves as men. Others respond in just the opposite way. They begin to lose interest in regular sexual activity and initiate it less and less frequently.

Many men report that as the impotence perseveres they are continually conscious of the state of their penis, watching to see whether it is responding at all. In some ways this has the function of isolating the penis from the total body and the bodily responses. It may reach the point of feeling anesthetized, losing feeling, because of the anxiety that surrounds the problem. As the pattern progresses, it can bring about extreme depression and discouragement because the man feels that he will never regain his ability to have and maintain an erection.

A similar pattern is happening to the wife. She might respond in a number of different ways. The initial response is usually not one of great concern. She assumes that this is a temporary situation and the man will soon function adequately again. However, if it happens early in marriage, the wife may be immediately concerned because she has not had enough experience to give her some kind of security. If the impotence persists, the wife may begin to feel rejected by the husband's lack of response, feeling that she is no longer attractive to him. Most women cannot help wondering if it is their fault that the husband is not able to respond as he used to.

If the woman is a highly responsive sexual partner, she may experience some anger in response to the husband's impotence—anger that the man is not providing her with the kind of sexual experience which brings her satisfaction. This anger, whether expressed or only felt, will often increase the pressure on the man and further inhibit his sexual freedom, thus increasing his preoccupation with his sexual response. You can see how the downward spiral is perpetuated by the natural reactions of both the man and the woman.

Over a period of time, the woman will feel decreased worth as a love partner. To protect herself from these feelings, she may also begin to show less interest in sexual activity, establishing a distance between them that helps them both avoid the failure experience.

Some women attempt to take on the responsibility of trying to reverse the problem. They become very provocative or seductive toward their husbands, either in the type of love-making scenes they set up or how they behave or talk. If the impotence is relatively new, this may be just the distraction that the man needs. But if the problem has been there for some time and has become an ingrained pattern, this seductive behavior may be experienced as added pressure for the man to perform.

How Impotence Gets Started

In times past, it was thought that impotence was the result of some hidden emotional conflict and could only be resolved by psychoanalysis. While analysis may sometimes be helpful in understanding why one has responded this way, it will seldom bring about a change in the conditioned response of impotence. But there are some general background issues that are common to a large number of men who do experience impotence.

Premature Ejaculation

Probably one of the most common sources of the problem is premature ejaculation. We have already discussed how premature ejaculation causes a man to focus more and more on his own sexual response pattern, thus getting away from the freedom and naturalness of allowing the response to occur by itself. As he concentrates on controlling his ejaculation, this concentration may begin to get in the way of maintaining the erection. This then can bring about the loss of the erection. In time this may even completely inhibit the erection from occurring. Often a problem that might begin with premature ejaculation gets joined to a problem of impotence, and then both issues have to be dealt with. We should emphasize that even here, impotence is a result of focusing on the physical response, the anxiety about performing, and the tendency to move into the spectator role and watch how one is doing.

Drinking and Drugs

Any use of a substance that inhibits the natural bodily responses can be a cause of impotence. While it is true that a slight amount of alcohol may often reduce inhibitions and thus enhance the sexual experience, the actual physical effect of alcohol is to function as a relaxant and to inhibit the sexual response. Again, once this pattern gets started, anxiety will keep it going. Often men will drink more to bolster themselves in the face of the anxiety, which in reality only makes the problem worse. Many drugs have the same effect. If you are taking prescribed medication and experiencing impotence, consult your physician and determine if reduced sexual responsiveness happens to be one of the side effects of the specific medication. Many of the illegal street drugs also have the effect of reducing sexual responsiveness—one more reason to avoid them.

Dominant Parents

In checking into the history of men who experience impotence, it is quite common to find that they have had rather dominant parents, particularly dominating mothers. This may have been manifested in the form of emotional or verbal dominance. As a boy, this person did not experience being in control of his own life with the freedom to make choices or respond in a natural way. One married man lived within a short distance of his parents. He was expected to visit them every day, or at least make contact by telephone. Though he was a highly successful attorney who managed large corporate accounts, he was controlled in his behavior by his parents' expectations. He also had great difficulty being responsive sexually, experiencing almost complete impotence. It is interesting to note that men who have had a dominant mother will often also select a wife who is dominant. Then they feel the familiar sense of being under a woman's control.

Rigid Training

In about 25 percent of the cases of impotence, we usually find some form of rigid moral or religious training with a strong anti-sex bias. This often took the form of viewing sex as evil or as the source of all evil. Any behavior or conversation that had sexual overtones was promptly and severely squelched. We do not imply that moral and religious training are harmful to sexual development, but only that unbending, rigid, moralistic training inhibits a free sexual response.

Emotional Depression or Anxiety

If a man is experiencing some form of clinical depression or anxiety that has nothing to do with his sexual functioning, it may begin to affect how he responds sexually. He may become impotent. This is a secondary problem that will need to be dealt with after the clinical depression or anxiety has been treated. Depression can come about as a result of long-term problems in one's life—loss, pain, or various other emotional traumas. Once the depression or anxiety has been treated, sexual functioning will often return. If it does not, it should then be dealt with directly and behaviorally.

Fatigue

Impotence can get its start if a man attempts to make love when he is physically exhausted. It may well be that his responses have always been quick and natural without any forethought. Then if on some occasion he feels he should make love to satisfy his wife, even though he is exhausted from work, travel or stress, he may find he has no energy for a good sexual experience. The best thing to do would be to tell his wife that he is too exhausted, and to make plans for another time. But if he does not have this kind of freedom or if he feels a demand from his spouse, he may attempt to go ahead anyway, with the ensuing result of no erection. If this becomes a matter of concern or if he continues to find himself in a fatigued state, this may mark the beginning of an ongoing impotent response. We encourage wives to understand that even as you sometimes feel "too tired," your husband, too, may experience fatigue. It is more difficult for a man to admit he is tired since, as we said earlier, the man is "supposed" to be ready for sex at any and all times, day or night, tired or rested.

Aging and Impotence

All too frequently we hear of situations in which the man has had a few experiences of impotence, has consulted his physician and has been told, "What do you expect, you're over fifty, aren't you?" This pronouncement by the authority has the effect of sealing the impotent response as a pattern forever. We should quickly say that there are many physicians who are well informed regarding the natural sexual response patterns, but only recently has sexual education been included in medical or psychological training. So unless a physician, psychologist, or minister has kept up with current information, he may still be perpetuating these concepts that we now know to be untrue.

How does aging affect the sexual response? As with all other physical responses, we begin to slow down as we grow older. Most fifty-five-year-old men cannot get by with as little sleep, work as many days with long hours, travel as hard, play as hard or put their body through the same kind of stress over a long period of time as they could when they were twenty-one. In all other areas of our life, this doesn't surprise us. But when we begin to sense it sexually, we feel we are being threatened at the most vulnerable part of our masculinity.

As we grow older, there are three response changes that we may notice. The first effect of aging may be that we will find ourselves somewhat *slower* to get an erection than we used to be. We may also find that the erections are *less firm* than they once were, and finally it may be that we will *not need* to ejaculate with each experience of sexual arousal and may even need fewer sexual experiences. None of these changes, which usually happen gradually, need get in the way of our sexual experience unless we become anxious about them. In fact, many couples report that as the man begins to slow down, he is free to enjoy some of the more pleasurable dimensions of the sexual experience rather than just being focused on the excitement dimension. This brings more pleasure for the wife. For years she may have been feeling that he always moved through the experience too quickly, without giving her the chance to keep up with him. Women often consider the slowing-down effect of aging as a blessing rather than a loss. Let it be clearly heard: the normal aging process does not cause impotence at any age; but anxiety and concern about aging can bring impotence. God has designed us to function sexually throughout our whole lives.

Immediate Causes of Impotence

We have looked at some of the life patterns that may bring about impotence, and we know that aging is not one of them. What can cause impotence in the immediate sexual experience?

Sexual Anxiety

If a man comes to the sexual experience anxious about his adequacy, the size of his penis, the relative attractiveness of his body, his body weight, or his ability to be an adequate sexual partner, this anxiety may be the precondition to impotence.

Fearing Rejection

When a man generally fears rejection or fears it only in bed, the fear may well show itself in impotence. Rejection may take many forms.

It may be connected with a general lack of respect that the woman may feel for him, or it may be that she is specifically rejecting him sexually. In many instances, she may not be rejecting at all, but for various reasons the man fears being rejected and then the fear itself brings on the impotence. Often the fear is connected with overconcern about satisfying the woman. This can easily lead the man to being a physical fumbler, and in all his bumbling he may provide such an uncomfortable experience for his partner that she does become rejecting.

Any time the man is so preoccupied with bringing the woman satisfaction that he is unable to function, it is not surprising for him to have some difficulty with getting or keeping an erection. This pattern would become even more exaggerated with a demanding partner. The wife who demands certain kinds of behavior in response, rather than encouraging those responses by love, is likely only to perpetuate the man's ineptness and set up the possibility of an impotent response. This then diminishes the likelihood that she will be satisfied. Fears, overconcern, or experiencing demand are frequently ingredients found in the impotent pattern.

Guilt

When there is guilt in relation to the partner, this too can cause the anxiety which brings about impotence. Guilt may be caused by not living up to the contract, by unloving behaviors, by unfaithfulness, or even by enjoying the sexual experience when the partner is not as desirous or responsive. For liberty and abandonment to be present, the man needs to be free from the intrusions of guilt, or else the guilt will be translated into anxiety which will stop him from functioning.

The Unconsummated Marriage

There are always stories floating around about some couple who lived together for fifteen years and never consummated the marriage because they did not know what to do. This may seem humorous until we actually encounter some real live people who are functioning normally in every other area of life but have been unable to come together sexually, even though they "know how" and have been trying. Usually some event in the history of one of the individuals is the source of this problem. Whether that event took place for the man or the woman, as the couple fails in their attempts to make entry during the initial days of their marriage, the man becomes anxious about his sexual performances and becomes impotent.

The sequence often goes like this. Most couples go into their first sexual experience without any fear that they will not be able to consummate it. They may be a bit anxious about how they will perform, but seldom do they think that they will not be able to perform at all. Then, in the awkward and anxious attempts to make entry, the man will find himself seemingly pushing against what seems to be a solid wall that he cannot penetrate. This solid wall is the rigid tightening of the lower one third of the vagina due to past trauma or severe anxiety (vaginismus). As he tries over and over, he finds himself beginning to lose his erection even as he thinks about entry. Eventually he will be impotent before the attempt. By this time the pattern has been established and we now have two problems—an unconsummated marriage with secondary impotence.

The discouragement at this level is obviously overwhelming, and this tends to push people even further apart. Some couples are able to resolve the problem by themselves, but often it is best to seek competent help. If you are in this situation and want to begin by taking some steps for yourself, follow the guidelines in this chapter for dealing with impotence and the suggestions in Chapter 32 for correcting vaginismus.

What Keeps the Pattern of Impotence Going?

Whatever the source of the impotence, whether it is related to something of long standing that happened in childhood, a relatively new drinking or overworking pattern, or an immediate problem that arises out of the sexual experience, once impotence with anxiety has occurred several times, it perpetuates itself. This is true even if the original source of the problem is removed. It is the anxiety caused by anticipating impotence that keeps it going—it is a cycle. First there is the initial failure with some anxiety following. Then if there are subsequent failures, the anxiety increases. As the anxiety increases, there is more preoccupation with the problem, which only makes the impotence more likely to occur. Finally, it is a response so conditioned that it takes over as the dominating emotional force every time the couple tries to have a sexual encounter, and so they begin to avoid such attempts.

Reversing Impotence

A man said to us, "I have been plagued with this problem so long that all I can do is think about whether or not I am *going* to have an erection or whether I *am* having an erection." This vividly portrays the feelings both for the man and the woman. All of the focus around the sexual experience gets centered in on the state of a man's penis, rather than on the total experience of love. To reverse this pattern, the focus has to shift. There are two basic ingredients necessary for that to occur. First, the man must experience some distraction and do some refocusing. Second, he must have a partner who can positively enjoy his body. What then can be done to bring this about?

The changes begin with some *new attitudes* that grow out of new understandings. The man obviously needs to regain his confidence. To do that he must be convinced he does not have to try to do anything. You will recall that the erection is a natural physiological response which happens when the man is relaxed enough to allow himself to be sexually aroused. Trying to change the pattern only gets in the way. The wife, too, has to stop trying to bring about an erection. Both must refocus. The refocus is onto the man's sensual and bodily pleasure without any demand for erectile response.

Part of the change necessary will also be a new kind of *sharing*. As a way of cleansing the couple of all of the hurts and disillusionment, a time of talking, confessing, crying, and forgiving will be a crucial start to a new beginning. This kind of communication is crucial because by the time the impotent pattern has become ingrained, there has usually been so much self-doubt, blame, anger, resentment, frustration and disillusionment that it is not possible to dive into a new format without communicating about all of the past hurts.

There are four major problems to overcome, two for the man and two for the woman. The man has to rid himself of his fears of performance, that is, his *performance anxiety*. He also has to stop watching himself, or, get out of the *spectator role*. The woman has to have her *fears or other negative feelings relieved* so that she can become a caring and loving participant. She also has to become comfortable *fondling the man's penis* for her pleasure, not for his response.

To get the focus off of erection and on the enjoyment of pleasure, begin with some pleasuring experiences as outlined in our chapter on pleasuring (Chap. 13). These experiences should not include the possibility of intercourse. To have intercourse there has to be an erection, which immediately brings demand. Spend a number of sessions focused on caressing hands and feet and on facial and bodily pleasuring without any focus on the genitals. As there is response, gradually begin to move toward including the genitals in the pleasuring. If there is anxiety, back off. One man reported how he could enjoy all the body pleasuring until his wife touched his penis. Her hand on his penis felt like a demand for a response. Whenever he felt her touch, anxiety was the automatic response. If this is the case, then the touching needs to be very gentle, brief and indirect (not with the hands), until the man becomes deconditioned.

Even in the initial touching, there should be no expectation for an erection, only pleasure. As erections do occur, there should be no attempt to bring the man to the point of orgasm. This should extend over as many sessions as are needed. It is essential to proceed at a pace the man can enjoy without feeling demand.

As soon as there is any self-consciousness about how the erection is coming along, any getting into the spectator role, any performance anxiety, it is absolutely vital for the *man to inform* his wife that he is having those kinds of thoughts. They should then move away from any direct attention on the penis to pleasuring other parts of the body. Gradually as the demand subsides, she can move back to some touch, but if the self-consciousness returns, then he must again inform her.

This communication about the anxiety is one of the most difficult aspects of this experience to learn, and yet it is most crucial in getting past the response of impotence. Many men will say, "But why should I talk about it? If I just think about it maybe it will go away." Others will say, "That's going to get in the way of my wife's response." Those are all understandable fears. However, if the anxiety is not expressed it will become larger and interfere with response. This is the same as with any other fear. When you talk about it, it is often reduced. So wives, encourage your husbands in this, and husbands be willing to experiment with the sharing of this reaction. It is absolutely vital.

As the pleasuring experiences continue and erections come and go, the man begins to build up some security about getting and maintaining them. This is the purpose of these experiences. The man has had a period of impotence, has been concerned about erections, so now he needs to learn that he *will* experience erections. There may be a dip in the arousal and they will go away, but they can be regained. After a period of time like this, the woman can gradually move to where she stimulates him to the point of orgasm without entry.

Before any attempts at entry, the penis and vagina need to become reacquainted. They need to be gently and gradually reintroduced to each other as friends, not feared objects. To help the penis become familiar with the vagina without performance anxiety, we encourage both the man and the woman to use the penis, whether flaccid or erect, as a paint brush across the clitoris and opening of the vagina. Through this activity, the man gains new confidence in the use of his penis to pleasure his wife without demand for an erection or for entry. After a number of sexual experiences that include positive responses to paint brushing, the woman can teasingly insert the tip of the penis into the opening of the vagina for a few moments. After several positive responses (no anxiety about the erection) to playful insertion of the tip of the penis in the vagina, she can insert it a little further, maybe only half an inch more. This playfulness can continue until, eventually, the penis is fully in the vagina. The woman should take charge of this process without drawing attention to her activity. The more distraction the man has from the actual entry event, the less likely will be the occurrence of anxiety and loss of erection. She can be as creative as her own freedom and his response allow. Distractions during the playful process of moving toward entry might include verbalizing fantasies, pleasuring the rest of his body, or cooing love messages.

The next steps would be comparable to those of working on the problem of premature ejaculation. You move to the point of entry but without orgasm, just entering and being together, letting the erection diminish while inside the vagina. Then you begin to experience a small amount of movement, gradually increasing it. Finally you withdraw and experience orgasm outside the vagina. When you have done this several times and feel quite secure, decide at some point while inside the vagina that this would be a comfortable time to go ahead to the point of ejaculation.

At many points along the way, it may be necessary to back up as anxiety grows. Keep in mind that it is crucial always to have the focus off the erection and on the pleasure. Any barriers that prevent this focus will perpetuate the impotence. Any time during the sexual experience that you begin thinking about the erection, share the thoughts. At all times you should move slowly and gradually to the next step without any major jumps.

What about the woman in all of this? Every pleasuring experience for the man should be accompanied by one for the woman. If she is not having difficulty with orgasmic response, feel comfortable to stimulate her to orgasm manually if she wishes. If some barriers show up along the way for her in terms of freedom to touch or comfortableness with communication, these should be shared to maintain an openness between the two of you. It is asking a lot of the woman to go through this whole experience with the man, and yet it is important to bear in mind that the benefits for her are equal to those that will come to the man. As he becomes relaxed enough to enjoy an erection and a release with her she finds new fulfillment. This is one of those times when the deep love that two people share will be tested. Love is patient, bears all things, and hopes for all things, even when struggling with the problem of impotence.

Professional Help

If you are one of those couples who have been experiencing years and years of impotence and avoidance, with all the ensuing frustrations, you may not be able to reverse the problem on your own. You may need some professional help. In a later chapter we will talk about the various professionals who can help. The majority of people who seek help for impotence can be aided by a qualified counselor. There is hope regardless of how long your problem has gone on.

After nineteen years of marriage, one woman finally reached the point of frustration where she said, "We either need to do something about this or I am getting out." With fear and trembling she and her husband sought help. Their history was one of difficulty right from the start. It had been several months after their marriage before they even consummated it, and when they did, it was to the satisfaction of neither of them. Over the years they had made enough awkward love-making attempts to produce two children, but intercourse never brought them pleasure. As time went on, the man felt more and more inadequate, and more frequently experienced impotence. By the time they came for help, he was impotent in virtually every attempt at a sexual experience. The woman was incredibly angry, and the man's self-worth was radically deflated. They did share a deep commitment to their marriage and family. By working diligently over a number of months, they moved past one barrier after another to the point where they now regularly enjoy total sexual fulfillment with each other. The hurt and defeat that used to be the inevitable part of every experience is no longer there. We tell this story only to encourage those of you whose lives fit this same pattern. You do not have to stay in the rut where you find yourself but can move on to a satisfying experience.

31

No Arousal or No Release—
Some Women's Frustrations

As far as I am concerned, sex can go away forever. I never feel anything anyway. I have never been aware of a single sexual feeling in my body. I never get aroused, and I wouldn't even know what an orgasm was if I had one.

This statement is representative of the feelings expressed by women who go through the sexual experience with little arousal and hence no response.

Every woman is born with a capacity for sexual response. Even as we are born with physical appetites, we are born with sexual appetites. As we have mentioned, a boy has his first erection within moments after birth and a girl lubricates vaginally within the first twenty-four hours. Even as we are born with emotions, we are designed to have sexual feelings. Naturally there are some variations from one woman to another in terms of the intensity of the appetite. But unless there is some physical abnormality, all have the capacity for response.

Women who experience little arousal and are still preorgasmic do not need to learn some new skill; rather, they need to uncover what is already inside them. They were made with that special apparatus to receive and transmit sexual feelings—the clitoris. They were given ability to feel with a great deal of intensity. And they were given bodies

301

that respond in many more ways than men's bodies do. So with the unresponsive woman, the task is to strip away the layers of problems and past experiences which have gathered over and obscured the sexual response potential that lies within her.

Causes from the Past

While the definition of the task may be simple, for some women it is a life-long struggle. What are some of these layers that cover up the sexual response and block it from happening? They are formed by life experiences. The input from experiences that causes blocks for women is the same as those for the men who experience difficulty with impotence or premature ejaculation. The first input may have come from the home atmosphere. Those who have been raised in homes where intense emotions were not expressed will also tend to stifle the expression of their sexual intensity. If the antisexual teachings have been clear-cut, particularly if they have been connected with a rigid religious training, then this too will add to the factors that keep the response from happening. We also commented in an earlier chapter on the problems of lack of interest, where the woman has never really developed an interest in sexual activity. When this is the case, she has little arousal and no release and is not likely to desire the sexual experience.

For other women, the lack of response may be more directly related to their husbands. Many women are able to become aroused but have husbands who ejaculate within seconds after entry. If these women have never learned to reach the point of orgasm by manual stimulation, they are left frustrated. Because of various life circumstances, a woman may be married to her second-choice mate. If a woman lost her anticipated partner either through death or through desertion, she may have quickly married someone else, thus finding herself married to a man whom she does not deeply love. There may be other reasons why she dislikes her husband. She may have difficulty trusting men. Sometimes the commitment of marriage raises a woman's anxiety and interferes with her ability to enjoy herself sexually with her husband.

Many such barriers may creep into a woman's being and prevent her from experiencing the positive sexual responsiveness that is part of her nature by creation.

Current Situations That Lead to Difficulty

Just as circumstances in a woman's past may inhibit her sexual response, some current thinking may also set up a lack of response. One of the most common problems is the feeling that she does not have a right to sexual pleasure. We cannot emphasize enough that women are created to enjoy sexual pleasure, even as men are. Their bodies need sexual release, even as men need release. They have an incredible capacity for sexual arousal and release. For the concerned Christian woman, all of this sexual activity is heartily endorsed by the inspired writers of the Old and New Testaments. The clarity of this writing is most obvious in 1 Corinthians 7:3–5. Mutuality is spelled out in vivid terms: the man has sexual rights and the woman has sexual rights. Knowing this in one's head is one thing, but to be convinced so that it can happen is another.

Related to the uncertainty about the right to pleasure is the *fear of orgasm*. For a woman to have an orgasm, she must allow her body to let go, to be out of control. She has to trust that nothing destructive or harmful will happen to her if she lets the forces in her body take over. Some women, as they approach the point of orgasm, get the same sensation that they might get if they were in a high place and were afraid of falling. Others have a sensation similar to the fear of dying. Still others report that they are afraid of "going out of their minds." Another fear connected with orgasm has to do with a hesitancy to allow themselves to experience and express all the things that happen to their bodies—the movements, the sounds, the changed appearance. They are embarrassed in front of their partners. Whatever the cause, if a woman fears orgasm, she is likely to inhibit any movement toward climax and will often even block the process of arousal.

Finally, if a woman comes to the sexual experience with the idea that it is her *duty to please* her husband, and if she is not expecting anything for herself, it is likely that she will not receive anything for herself. Many girls have been told that the sexual dimension of marriage is "a drag." It's something that a woman has to put up with; it is her responsibility or her lot in life. It is a way to compensate a man since he is taking care of her. Anything that involves all of your being, your body, your emotions, your spirit, cannot be done out of duty or responsibility. You must desire the enjoyment and expect to get something out of it for yourself. When a woman has been conditioned to believe that sex is something she must do for the man, then the likelihood of a free and easy flow of sexual arousal and release is greatly diminished.

Learning to Let It Happen

To learn to be sexual and to allow spontaneous sexual feelings often seems like a contradiction. It seems that you ought to try to feel, and yet we are saying that you cannot try. Response will only happen if you do not try. This is a first principle to help you move to greater excitement and release through orgasm: *stop trying!* The focus has to move away from striving for arousal. You must get away from seeing arousal as the goal, and focus on the process of enjoying your body. Performance anxiety, as we discussed earlier, is an inhibiting force (see the section on Sexual Anxiety in chap. 28). This anxiety interferes when a woman tries to get aroused.

The second principle promotes a positive *re-focus.* The emphasis should shift from *trying,* to focus on the *pleasurable sensations* and the *communication* of these sensations to your partner. If you are going to be free to respond sexually, your response will not begin by having a cataclysmic orgasm but rather by allowing yourself the privilege of enjoying any small bodily sensations that come your way. Each small twinge can be an encouragement. It is vital to share with your husband any enjoyable bodily sensations that you experience. If your lack of arousal and release has been a long-term struggle, he will need the boost of sharing in your sense of moving toward fuller bodily pleasure.

The performance anxiety must be reduced, there must be a re-focus on and communication of the enjoyable sensations, and then there must be a *reduction* of *self-consciousness.* The *natural noises and behaviors* typical of the sexual response cause in some women an inhibiting embarrassment that must be corrected. If you recall from our earlier discussion, as we—men or women—get aroused, we respond. Our heart beat increases, we breathe faster and louder, we may experience slight muscular contractions, our bodies may feel like moving in thrusting or pushing motions, and we may have the urge to make gasping noises. Women who have difficulty allowing themselves to experience arousal or release are often unable to let themselves exhibit any or all of these behaviors. They are embarrassed and uncomfortable, and, as with any other discomfort, they tend to avoid that which causes these negative feelings. Thus they will hold back their natural sexual responses.

If you are going to change your response pattern you must make a conscious attempt to become comfortable with your natural bodily responses. First notice what responses you are avoiding, then push yourself to experience and exhibit those responses. Throw in a little humor about them if that helps relieve the tension. For example, heavy breathing is a natural body response. If you notice that you back off from this response by stopping your breathing, reverse the trend by breathing even harder. Exaggerate the breathing to the point of absurdity. Pelvic thrusting is another natural body response. If you find yourself pulling your pelvis away from the thrusting, push it the other way all the more emphatically. *Decide* to *behave* and *sound* sexually aroused.

The last principle is that you must *take responsibility* for and control of what you need. Your partner cannot give you arousal or release. He can participate in your having it, but only *you* can allow it to happen as you free yourself to experience it. This may seem obvious, and yet it is one of the most difficult mental shifts to make, because for so long the subtle teaching has been that it is the man's responsibility to bring the woman sexual pleasure. On the contrary, sexual pleasure begins with your taking responsibility for yourself and being ready to go after what you need.

Pinpointing Your Dilemma

If you are going to work directly at moving past your point of blockage, it is crucial that you understand exactly where you are stuck. It is important for you to identify whether your problem is a lack of excitement and arousal or whether you experience a great deal of arousal but have difficulty letting that arousal reach the point of orgasm. For some this will be very clear. For others it may take some sorting out to define your situation. You will recall that as you enter the sexual experience, arousal begins with vaginal lubrication and nipple erection. Then other changes begin to take place, both physically and emotionally. From a physical standpoint there is the formation of the orgasmic platform in the outer third of the vagina. The inner two-thirds of the vagina balloons out, the uterus tends to pull slightly up and away, there may be the sexual flush in the upper third of your body, and those whole-body sensations of heightened arousal.

Many women report that they reach a certain peak and feel as if they are about to go over the mountain, and then something dies or levels out. Often that something is exactly the same every time. We encourage you to identify what that point is. Perhaps you would even want to use the graph in Chapter 8 that pictures the four phases of the sexual response. You need to be able to identify where on this graph your feelings cut off and what is happening right at that precise moment.

It may be that your feelings are cut off at the very moment you begin to wonder whether this will be the time when you have an orgasm. The feelings are blocked as soon as you get out of your body and into your head. Or you may stop the feelings as soon as you begin to breathe intensely or begin to feel like pushing harder against the clitoris. Perhaps some behavior in your partner such as vigorous movement is your cue to stop responding. Pinpoint this event as precisely as you can and share it. Your partner needs to know what is happening to you and may even be able to bring some added insight to your understanding. Keep in mind that any discussion about what will move you toward greater pleasure is likely also to heighten his interest and arousal. Normally, he will not be turned off by this kind of talk but rather will find it encouraging.

Getting Comfortable with Your Body

Before you attempt to be comfortable with your husband, it is essential that you be comfortable with yourself. Many women have been taught to think of their bodies as unpleasant or distasteful, particularly the genitals. They have learned that this is the doctor's area, the "messy" part of them, the bloody part, and certainly a complicated part. To overcome these teachings, begin with a time of self-discovery. Wash well, then take out a mirror and get to know yourself in specific detail. Look at a diagram of the internal and external genitalia and identify the various parts, touching them as you explore. It may be necessary for you to do this several times before you feel comfortable enough to share such an experience with your partner. For a full discussion of this experience, follow the details as outlined in Exercise 2 in Chapter 6.

When you have reached the point where you are familiar and comfortable with yourself, then plan a time when you and your husband can share this discovery time together. This should not be seen as a time for sexual arousal but rather as a time of education. You can best teach him about you and he can teach you about himself. Go into complete detail even if this feels a little awkward. Talk about your discomfort as you go along. It may take several experiences of this sort before you really feel comfortable sharing your genitals with each other, but this is vital in terms of moving on to experiencing greater pleasure (see Exercise 5 in Chap. 6).

Some people ask, doesn't this take the mystery out of love-making? It is our experience that mystery based on ignorance only causes problems, not joy. After we know all we can about each other's bodies and have shared all we can about our feelings, mystery is still left. The mystery does not have to do with our various bodily parts but rather with all the sensations and feelings that come to us in the loving experience. Mystery about the body is better labeled "ignorance." Ignorance does not lead to fulfillment.

After you have discovered yourself genitally and shared this with your partner, spend some time in becoming aware of where you feel the most enjoyable sensations. The setting for this should be very secure and relaxed. It might be while you are in the bathtub, or it may be in your bedroom when everyone else is out of the house or the door is locked. Be sure the kids are napping or away and you have some time to yourself. You should be confident that you will not be interrupted and that you need not be rushed.

Every woman enjoys different kinds of genital touch. There is no right or wrong way. For you there is only your way. Some women like to have the head or glans of the clitoris stimulated directly, but for most that is too painful. That is why the majority of women enjoy the touch around the clitoris rather than directly on it. The main part of the clitoris—the clitoral shaft—is directly above the head of the clitoris. Thus, the skin that covers the shaft and extends to both sides may be the area that you most enjoy having touched. (Likewise, most men enjoy having the shaft of the penis stimulated rather than the head.) The opening to the vagina may also bring special pleasure. For most women the deep insertion of fingers into the vagina does not bring much pleasurable sensation. Discover for yourself not only where you like to be touched, but how—directly or generally, pointedly or broadly, with much pressure or light pressure. Keep in mind that there is no normal or right way, only your way, and even that way may change from day to day.

While you are in a relaxed state test your pubococcygeus (PC) muscle to see whether you can feel it tightening. If you need to review how to do so, refer to Chapter 20, page 191. If you cannot feel the tightening against your fingers, then either you're not tightening the right muscle or the muscle is loose. For a vigorous sexual response this muscle needs to be in good tone. Begin doing the exercises as outlined in Chapter 20.

This would also be a good time to identify any point in the outer third of the vagina that has positive sensations for you. Some women report that the lower right hand and lower left hand areas of the vagina bring them the most positive sensations. This may or may not be true for you. If it is, enjoy it and share it. If it is not, there is no need for concern.

Whatever you learn from self-exploration, self-stimulation, tightening the PC muscle and identifying the responsive parts of the vagina should be shared with your partner as a way of keeping him up-to-date with your own discoveries. Then he can incorporate this new information into his love-making pattern.

You need to be comfortable not only with the specifically sexual parts of your body but with your body as a whole. This would be a good time, therefore, for you and your partner to share with each other how you feel about your bodies from head to toe. This should include how your body looks, how it feels, how you think about it and how you sense others respond to it. Take turns standing in front of the mirror without any clothes and describe what you see and feel (see Exercise 1, Chap. 5). All of these experiences are designed to help you be more comfortable together. They need not be experienced as arousing. Let yourself enjoy them without any kind of demand that there be sexual feelings. But if you find that in fact they are arousing, let yourselves enjoy the stimulated sensations without feeling you have to act on them.

Pleasure without Demand

The previous experiences were designed mainly for educational purposes as a way of teaching you and your husband about your body, and also to learn the specific kind of genital touch you most enjoy.

We move now to some experiences that are more for pleasure. Begin by knowing that in these experiences there is no expectation for intercourse. Rule intercourse out for the time being. Also know that there is no way you can fail in these experiences because there is nothing you have to achieve. The goal is to let yourself experience and enjoy as much of the pleasure as you can take in. Begin by getting clean together. Bathe or take a shower and if it is comfortable even wash each other's bodies. For some of you this will be a familiar experience, for others it may seem strange or awkward. Talk about those uncomfortable feelings, but push yourself to complete the bathing in spite of the discomfort.

After you are clean get into a quiet comfortable place—perhaps on the bed—and take turns learning to pleasure each other through touch by a *foot and hand caress*. The idea is to receive pleasure through touch without feeling any demand for a response. As the receiver your only task is to enjoy the sensations and to communicate anything to your partner that is not enjoyable for you. He has to be able to count on this, otherwise he cannot relax in the giving. His task is to pleasure you in a way that brings him pleasure. We enjoy ourselves most when we can relax in the assurance that the other one will let us know if anything we do is not pleasurable. Limit your touching to the hands and the feet as outlined in Exercise 8 in Chapter 13. It may take several sessions of foot and hand caressing before you can really relax with it and enjoy yourselves.

In the next experience move on to the *facial* caress (Chap. 13, Exercise 9). This is obviously more personal and has more sensuous areas. The lips, the neck, the ears can be sexually responsive and are certainly more personal than the hands and the feet. So, focus on receiving and giving facial pleasure. Take your time, sink into it, soak it up and enjoy it. Couples are often amazed at what they learn about each other by slowly, carefully, and pleasurably touching each other's faces. Keep in mind that this is not a massage designed to get the "kinks" out, but rather a form of sensuous communication which brings familiarity and pleasure. After each experience, talk about what it felt like both to be the giver and the receiver. Alternate who pleasures first. Apply the same principles for both the pleasurer and the receiver.

Having learned to let yourself enjoy the pleasure of feet, hands, and face, move on to the *pleasuring of the whole body, excluding breasts and genitals*. In this body caress take your time. Let the pleasurer and the receiver enjoy the experience. Again, keep in mind that there is no demand for a sexual response of arousal. Your only task is to let yourself receive the touching. If there is arousal, welcome it and enjoy it but do not feel that you have to pursue it or extend it. Again, for details on this pleasuring refer back to the guidelines as set forth in Chapter 29, Exercise 16.

It is most common that with the total body pleasuring, some demand or pressure may set in. This may be due to conditioning or to impatience. If you have always been a woman who felt that as soon as your husband got near your genitals you needed to respond, this would be a good time to reverse that pattern. If you find yourself making demands on yourself to become aroused, share these thoughts with your husband as you notice them. Stick with this experience enough times to learn to receive, share and enjoy total body pleasure, realizing that many experiences can be fully satisfying without even touching the genitals. Both of you can come away knowing that you have given and received.

Once you are comfortable giving and receiving sensuous touch on the rest of the body, move on to *include the genitals in the total body pleasuring.* Having finally come to this point it is natural to become somewhat eager and to quickly focus in on the genitals. Usually this will bring immediate demand and hinder the relaxation and pleasure. Therefore, in these experiences it is particularly important to begin with hands, feet, face, and back and then gradually move in closer to the genitals. Let the first genital touches be light and whispery; move away to some other part of the body and then move to the breasts and then down the torso, down the stomach to the thighs and then the opening of the vagina and the clitoris without a major focus on just the clitoral area.

Let the touches be light and of short duration, gradually increasing both of these. If any anxiety, spectatoring or demand creeps in, share this with your partner and have him move away from the genitals until that demand subsides and you are able to relax back into the total pleasure. Do not be concerned about the extent of the arousal. The focus here is for pleasure. If you desire more genital touch because it feels good, communicate this and let your body go after it but let the desire come from deep inside you rather than from your head. Have a similar time of reversing roles while you pleasure your husband's total body, including genitals in a playful way.

We end this section of mutual discovery with an exercise that is designed first of all to teach and then to bring pleasure. Masters and Johnson have called it the *nondemand* pleasuring (see Figure 8 in Chap. 13). The man leans against something solid like the headboard; the woman sits on the bed between his legs in front of him, leaning back against his chest. The woman takes his hands and guides them all over her body. She starts with the face and moves on down the front of her body, communicating to him with her hands on his how, where, and how long she likes to be touched. Through the touch and description, he can learn what gives her the greatest pleasure. Sometimes it is difficult for a man to relax enough to let the woman take over, but there are dimensions to pleasuring that are difficult to communicate in any other way. Recall our earlier analogy of the individual knowing just how he or she wants the itchy spots scratched; even so a woman or a man can, through demonstration, best communicate the kind of touch that he or she enjoys.

Once you have covered all of the body including genitals that can be reached in the nondemand position, the woman can gradually let the man take over without her guidance. As you let him take charge, let yourself sink back into freely enjoying the pleasuring without demand for any response. If there are pleasurable sensations that move you to arousal, communicate this and go after those feelings. As your body feels like moving toward the heightened sensations, let it. Exaggerate the aroused feelings. This may mean that you will feel like breathing more deeply, pushing your thighs toward your partner's hands and squeezing your legs together or many other responses that are hard to specify. Take those good sensations as far as they go, then back off, pleasure in some other area and then move toward them again.

It is important to keep this wavelike motion in mind. Sexual arousal will be heightened most as we move toward it and then move away from its source as we feel the excitement lessen. This teasing kind of response is less demanding and more tantalizing. Flowing with one's level of arousal has to be learned and can only be learned through communication. If something is feeling particularly good and your husband moves away from it, bring his hand back to it and show him what you would like.

If you are a woman who inhibits a *specific* body response, *practice* on that dimension separately. Let us say, for example, it is difficult to let yourself breathe with excitement and intensity. In one of your teaching times plan that the two of you will just lie together in bed and experiment with different kinds of breathing. This should not happen when you are aroused or when you are pleasuring each other, but just breathing out loud with each other. It may turn into a hilariously comical experience as you let yourself be somewhat melodramatic. Even though you are acting out the response, this exposure to the sensations and noises will allow the natural breathing to feel more familiar. This fake practicing could also be utilized to become comfortable with making loud noises, thrusting, pushing, or any other behavior that seems unladylike or unacceptable to you. Practice these behaviors with clothes on and in an unaroused state. This rehearsing can help you break down the inhibitions and let out the natural you!

Exercise 18
Mutual Pleasuring

Now incorporating all you have learned, move into experiences that bring both of you a kind of touching joy that is most satisfying. Remember to begin slowly. Start on the outside edges of the body—face, feet and hands—and gradually move in to breasts and genitals, then back out to the rest of the body. Never stick with any one bit of anatomy for too long. Enjoy the excitement together and learn ways to heighten the good feelings. Instructions for increasing aroused feelings are outlined in the chapter on stimulation (Chap. 15). By now you should be able to count on each other to take responsibility to inform the other if anything occurs that is not positive. Don't rush into intercourse. Rather, continue to go after all the positive feelings.

In all of your pleasuring experiences follow these guidelines: be sure not to fake a response; stop and rest any time you need to; communicate when you feel pressured; and remember that the goal is to increase the frequency, the intensity and the duration of the positive feelings. If the woman should happen to become intensely aroused and wants to continue the stimulation, *she* (not *he*) may pursue her desires even to the point of orgasm. It is critical that this be a possibility, not a goal! If the man desires further stimulation and that is comfortable for the woman, she may stimulate him to the point of orgasm, though this should be saved until they are near the end of the experience.

A word to the wives here may be important. Many a wife becomes anxious about what is happening to her husband during these periods of time when there is no intercourse. Manual stimulation to orgasm brings adequate physical release. A committed, loving husband understands that experiences without the possibility and demand of intercourse are necessary to allow you to realize your sexual potential. He will be willing to do without intercourse until you are ready. Do not let your fantasies about what he is needing or wanting get in the way.

As you feel comfortable, lie together with either one of you on top, having the erect penis in contact with the clitoral area. Many women enjoy using the penis, erect or flaccid, as a paint brush over the clitoris and vaginal opening. This brings extra stimulation. Use the penis in any way that brings you pleasure. Put the end of the penis at the opening of the vagina without entry. All the time be assured that finding ways to use his body to arouse you will bring pleasure for him.

Finally

As the previous experiences become free of demand, you may move ahead to entry when the woman wants and initiates it. Entry would only be an option after extended time of total body pleasuring with arousal. With the woman in the top position as pictured in Figure 11, guide the husband's penis slowly into the vagina, perhaps using a lubricant to make entry easier. After entry rest together and focus on the good feelings of the penis in the vagina. While lying together you may want to caress or stimulate other pleasurable areas or you may choose just to lie quietly together. After a few minutes of "rest," contract the pubococcygeus muscles around the penis both so that he can feel the tightening and so that you can be aware of the feelings in the vagina. When you feel ready, begin a slow thrusting motion up and down on the man's penis. The man's only task during this time is to let you know when he needs you to slow down or stop thrusting in order to avoid ejaculation. Other than that, you as the woman should take charge of the experience, going after those movements and sensations that bring you the greatest delight.

It is important to be free to experiment so that you can learn what is most satisfying. Take good feelings as high as they will go without pushing or demanding more of yourself, then back off, rest, and move into them again. As you are going after a "high" and realize you do not have energy left for much more, signal your husband that he may go after his ejaculation. It would be helpful to have a prearranged signal. Don't expect an orgasm for yourself during this first coital experience.

If at any point in this progression the experience becomes negative for you, *stop* everything, *rest, affirm* each other. If relaxation and refocusing is not possible, back up a session or two and stay at that level until comfortable. Always keep in mind that your body was built for response. You will not get stuck at a halfway point as long as you can allow the security, the relaxation and the pleasure to build.

As arousal becomes more common and natural for you, pursue the turned-on feelings by exaggerating the responses intentionally. This is not designed as a fake, but rather as a way to push past the barriers that block your response. If you feel like moving, move more vigorously. If you experience feelings of arousal, move toward them. Always bear in mind that the overall goal in this experience is to actively go after greater and greater arousal and pleasure. We are so made that when we allow this to happen, the orgasm will naturally follow. It is a reflex response that will be triggered as the intensity of arousal builds.

In Summary

As the woman you must be in control and take responsibility for what you need. Keep moving toward the good feelings. Inform your partner as soon as the good feelings are turned off, then back away from that particular form of stimulation. Rest for a period of time until you are wanting more and then go after it again. Stop at a point when the feelings are good, and rest together, holding each other. Ideally these segments of pleasuring will grow in duration. Practice this pleasuring every day or every other day. After several sessions of comfort at each level move on to the next step, but always at the woman's initiation. Be sure to attempt the insertion with the woman in the top position guiding the penis. When you are aware of vaginal feelings, initiate the thrusting and the swiveling of the pelvis. With each thrust, attempt to tighten the PC muscle. Continue this activity with the concept that the penis is yours to play with in order to achieve your greatest pleasure. You can count on it that it will bring pleasure to your husband. This is sound thinking in every way: physically, emotionally, and biblically (1 Cor. 7:3–5).

Moving toward Post-entry Release

One other dilemma should be touched on briefly. What if an orgasm can only be achieved by external stimulation before entering? As we outlined earlier, all orgasms are the same and one should not be held up as superior to the other. It is not uncommon, however, for a woman to want to be able to respond orgasmically during intercourse. What can be done? To learn to experience orgasm during intercourse, you need direct clitoral stimulation while the penis is in the vagina. You can reach down and stimulate yourself, your husband can do it (particularly when using the rear entry position), or a vibrator may be used. Some women might object that they want to be orgasmic without any extra manipulation of the clitoral area. Eventually this may be possible, but to learn the response you need to connect intercourse with the more direct, arousing activity. When this pattern becomes ingrained, arousal and release may occur without extra manual manipulation. This pairing of clitoral manipulation with intercourse has been found to be quite effective for many couples.

Whatever the causes for your difficulty with arousal or release, we hope that you will be able to create an atmosphere that allows your sexual response to surface. As you feel affirmed, free of demands, comfortable with your own body, and able to soak in and go after bodily pleasure, sexual response will inevitably follow.

_____32

Pain Reduces Pleasure

After my children were born (which was an awful experience) I have not enjoyed sex at all. I am protected against getting pregnant again so I feel that's not a problem. Also, I enjoyed sex a lot before children. Sometimes I think it's all in my head, that if I could let myself enjoy it I wouldn't feel any pain; yet I know there's something wrong down there. My gynecologist hasn't been able to figure anything out.

This kind of report typifies a woman who is eager for a sexual experience but is finding each encounter to be more and more negative because of the intense pain she experiences during each sexual act. Pain during intercourse is technically called *dyspareunia*. It has a number of different sources. Whatever the source, when pain is experienced sexual enjoyment will be greatly reduced if not eliminated altogether.

Pain and the New Bride

For the new bride who is a virgin it is not surprising if there is a small amount of pain. Most women experience at least a little. This can be due to the opening in the hymen being tight and small. In the great majority of situations it is due to a combination of newness, excitement and anxiety which prevents the woman from relaxing. When the necessary physical changes do not take place (the opening up and laying flat of the majora lips, plus lubrication), then entry is going to be more difficult and pain more intense. Entry under these conditions increases the pain and reduces the possibility of pleasure. Once the woman feels pain, tension is likely to set in. This tension will inhibit arousal and block any kind of release. While many couples begin in this way they usually get past the sequence quite quickly. But the sequence can be avoided to begin with.

If you are an engaged couple or if you counsel engaged couples, attending to a few small details will reduce much of the anxiety and potential for pain. First, six weeks to two months before the wedding date the woman should be *examined by a gynecologist* or qualified general practitioner. In this experience the doctor should be able to communicate to her whether her physical anatomy is normal and whether there are any particular barriers of which she should be aware. The couple and the physician should discuss birth control methods.

In the weeks before the marriage, every time the bride-to-be takes a bath she should use her fingers to *stretch the hymen* until she can insert three fingers into the vagina and pull it apart slightly. This stretching procedure will prepare the vagina for entry and will also help the woman become familiar with some of the sensations of having the vagina stretched. As the wedding comes closer this might be done several times a day.

The couple should be encouraged to *take along a lubricant* that is not sticky (not Vaseline). K-Y jelly or Lubrifax are recommended for genital use. For use over the whole body as well as genitally, a nonallergic lotion without lanolin such as Allercreme is good. The couple should plan to use the lubricant for all entry experiences, whether they think they need it or not. The lubricant protects the woman in case she dries up during the excitement. It also provides a distraction from the focus on the entry. A small amount of lubricant should be applied to the head and ridge of the penis and to the opening of the vagina.

A final word of instruction to the new bride and groom is to move *slowly*. No matter how many times they tell themselves to proceed slowly they will still most likely move ahead too quickly. If a couple can plan to move into their first experience with a great deal of gentleness, patience, ease, and relaxation, they are most likely to create a positive beginning to a life of loving.

Stress Brings Pain

All of us show our tension in our own unique way. Some women, as they experience tension surrounding the sexual experience, will tend to tighten up their genital muscles involuntarily. In fact, they may not even be aware that the tensing is happening. Since this is counterproductive to a fulfilling and releasing sexual experience, it is not surprising that these women end up frustrated. But even more than the frustration as a result of the tension, they may experience pain. For example, if the tightening occurs before entry it may cause pain upon entry. Sharp, spasmodic contractions after entry may also cause pain. The extreme form of this tension is called vaginismus.

Vaginismus is the involuntary tightening of the muscles in the outer third of the vagina which prevents the insertion of the penis. This contraction can be so severe that it is impossible to insert even your small finger. It can become a permanent state rather than just occurring as a result of the initiation of sex play. Because it is impossible for the man to enter, vaginismus is easily identified. Should this be your situation, consult a gynecologist immediately and specifically explain your situation. If he or she is not familiar with the usual treatment procedures ask for a referral either to another physician or to a sex therapist. This professional must be competent to guide you in the use of a series of dilators which are graduated in size and designed to eliminate these involuntary spasms. Be encouraged that this condition is extremely responsive to treatment in a relatively brief period of time. However, there should be some attempt also to understand the events leading to the vaginismus so that this pattern will not be repeated.

Another source of pain due to tension occurs with lack of release. When a woman does not experience an orgasm, she may sense some painful sensations in the lower abdominal area and the lower back. As she has become aroused the whole reproductive system, including the vaginal area and the uterus, has become congested with blood in preparation for the orgasmic release. The contractions of the orgasm are designed to release the congestion so that the blood which has filled the cavities can be drained. When there is an orgasm this process provides a great deal of pleasure. When the woman does not experience release, the whole pelvic area remains engorged, which may cause chronic pain. This pain is usually not intense, but is a dull, throbbing ache similar to lower back pain. The difference is that it feels like it is further inside the body. Obviously the best remedy for this pain is for a woman to allow herself to experience orgasm. In consulting a physician or therapist, it is crucial to identify when the pain occurs and thus determine if it is the result of lack of orgasmic release. In the previous chapter specific steps were given to help the woman toward orgasm.

Physically Based Pain

Infections and irritations will obviously reduce pleasure. Whether the infection is in the external genitalia, causing pain during clitoral stimulation, or is inside the vagina, causing pain during intercourse, it will hinder freedom and enjoyment. Any kind of infection should immediately be dealt with by a physician. Sexual activity should be limited according to the instruction of the physician. Sometimes an infection provides the opportunity for the couple to focus on the rest of the body for those often bypassed, special pleasures. Just because there is an infection does not mean the couple should abstain from all sexual activity. If it is comfortable for both, the man can be stimulated to orgasm at the end of a total body experience without ever having contact with the woman's genitals.

Irritations are troublesome because there is no specific identifiable disease present. Yet an irritated vaginal opening or vaginal barrel can cause as much distress and pain during love-making as an infection. The best antidote to irritation is the generous use of a lubricant. Some women experience a thinning of the vaginal walls. Sometimes this happens with age, particularly around the time of menopause because of a reduction of estrogen. If the walls of your vagina are thinning, again consult a physician to determine the cause and then always use a lubricant to reduce friction. Even if the walls of the vagina are becoming thin, pleasurable activity need not cease.

Pain can also be the result of *tears* either in the opening of the vagina or *small cuts* (fissures) *inside the vagina* itself. Tears in the hymen usually cause pain on entry. Some women can identify pain at a very specific spot inside the vagina. Their report usually goes something like this: "It feels as if it is in the lower left-hand corner about an inch inside the vagina and it hurts exactly the same way every time. I feel I can even reach in and put my finger on it." When the pain is this specific, it is usually not the result of tension or the thinning of the vaginal walls but rather the result of a small tear inside the vagina. Because of continued sexual activity and the moist environment, healing is slow. When consulting a physician be sure to identify the exact location of the pain. Show the doctor so that he can carefully examine it and determine the nature of the problem. As a rule these tears can be treated with an ointment, but even if they have to be dealt with in a minor surgical procedure the treatment is relatively simple.

Some women report pain only during *deep thrusting*. There are three main sources of this kind of pain. The most commonly reported discomfort is the result of a *tipped or retroverted uterus*. When the muscles that suspend the uterus are weakened, the uterus drops so that the cervix, the opening to the uterus, falls into the upper end of the vagina. As deep thrusting occurs the penis strikes the cervix, causing sharp, stabbing pain. It may cause a woman to cry out. Relief can be found immediately by a slight shift in position. For many women a small pillow or folded towel under the lower back (if she is under the man) will shift the uterus enough so that deep thrusting can be enjoyed.

Other internal pathologies such as endemetriosis or a misplaced IUD can also cause pain upon deep thrusting.

Finally, there may be pain as an outgrowth of trauma from childbirth. One such pain occurs in the sensitive scars from the episiotomy, the incision that is made between the vagina and the rectum to assist the birth process. There also may be tears in the ligaments that hold the uterus in place, in the vaginal wall, or around the opening of the vagina. Tears are more likely to occur with a difficult birth. This was true for us after the breech (feet first) delivery of our first child. For those resuming sexual activity after the birth of a child we would issue the same encouragement given to the newly married couple: move carefully and slowly; haste will only hurt; be generous with the lubricant.

Managing Pain

Whenever you experience pain, the first thing you should do is talk about it with your husband. Never grit your teeth and bear it. Define exactly where the pain is located and when in the love-making process it occurs. Even before you get to the physician you may be able to avoid the situations that cause the pain if you guide the penis for entry and shift positions to make adjustments. Except for pain from deep thrusting, lubrication will almost always reduce some of the intensity, even if it is from an infection. Then, discover what is pleasurable and focus on that for the time being. Avoiding entry for a few love-making sessions may be necessary. It is important not to continue the activity that triggers the pain. Whenever a negative sensation like pain is associated with a pleasurable activity like sexual play or intercourse, the pleasurable event will begin to take on the negative feelings. Even after the physical reason for the pain has healed, a woman may continue to tense up or avoid the sexual activity that was linked with the pain. Her pulling away and tightening up has become a conditioned response. Sometimes the pain will continue because of the tension. In dealing with this, use the same approach as you would for any emotional hesitancy or avoidance. Begin gradually, letting the woman take the lead until the tension concerning the pain has been reduced.

An increasing number of women, particularly young women, are reporting pain during intercourse. If you are among these, seek help after talking about it with your partner. Pain does not have to be tolerated. In fact, pain *cannot* be allowed to continue if you are going to enjoy sexual pleasure.

_____33

Getting Ourselves Together

After ten years of a woman's "shelving" her sexual needs and entering the "avoidance" stage, can a couple pull out of this pattern without professional help (i.e., self-help books, etc.)? If so, can you recommend literature and/or a basic generalized plan of action for revitalizing their sexual relationship—how do you make it fun again? Perhaps this is too much to cover.

So you want to do something about your sexual dissatisfaction but you don't know where to start. The unsatisfactory behavior has been going on for so long and is so natural, it seems to be the only way the two of you can function together. Sometimes you think it would be easier to start over with someone else than to try to resolve all the bad habits and uncomfortable feelings that have grown up between the two of you. But you can be encouraged. Many couples have changed for the better after long, unrewarding years. This is true whatever the source of the problem—but it takes work. This chapter gives you guidelines for doing that work.

Defining Your Experience

How do you start? Begin with a period of individual reflection in writing. (Much of what we will suggest in this chapter is taken from

In Touch with Each Other, a self-help book that we wrote a few years ago with H. Norman Wright.) This writing should be done separately, when you are not in the middle of some intense stress. Take your paper and describe as best you can your total sexual experience. Begin with the desire phase. Write about various ways you *feel desire* throughout the day. What sets off that desire, how long does it last, what do you do with it, and what is it that you are desiring? If you are one of those people who experience little desire, write about your understanding of that situation. What kind of feelings do you have about the sexual area? When some kind of sexual stimulus or input comes your way, what does it feel like to you? If you are aware that other people get "turned on" by music or exercise or reading or seeing certain things or thinking certain thoughts, and this does not happen to you, attempt as best you can to understand why. Be aware that this is not a composition to be published or a term paper to be handed in. You need not write in full sentences or paragraphs. Just get your thoughts down on paper while you are thinking them.

When you have written all you can about your understanding of your own sexual desire, move on to the next page and write about how *initiation* takes place as you understand it. Write about who does the initiating, how it is done, how you feel about it. Is it a demand or a burden to always initiate? Describe in detail what you would think of as a typical scene when the two of you get together. Who does what and how does each respond? Finally, note any areas of change that you would like to see, both in yourself and in your partner. If you are the one who always initiates, would you enjoy having your spouse assume that role on some occasions? Communicate this. Be as specific as you can about ways that you would like to see things changed between you. This could include not only the "how" but also the "where" and "when" of your love-making.

On the next page write about the *pleasuring* part of your experience. Begin with a description of your understanding of what takes place. Again, be very specific as to who does what as you see it. Write about that pleasuring in terms of how much demand it brings to you or any demand that you sense your partner feels. Describe the kind of touch that takes place and what you enjoy most. Describe the places that you enjoy being touched and where you would prefer not to be touched. Many couples are not aware of the location of each other's

---

* (Elgin, IL: David C. Cook Publishing Co., 1976).

sexual feelings. Describe any part of your body that is erogenous or highly susceptible to stimulation. If you happen to particularly enjoy being kissed and caressed around the neck and ears, your partner needs to know that. On the other hand, if this turns you off, he or she also needs to know that. Point out not only the general areas where you feel stimulation but also the most intense pleasure areas that bring you satisfaction. Finally, discuss the emotions that you experience during the pleasuring phase. Do you feel rushed, pressured, or bored, is this really a meshing of your two worlds or do you sense some real lack? If you do, point it out.

Stimulation is the topic of your next page. Focus on those behaviors and activities that you find most arousing and which bring you to the point of orgasm. If there are some things that happen which are negative for you, describe them. Share any changes that you desire in stimulation, even if you have been uncomfortable sharing these in the past. Some women, for example, when they become aroused, feel closed in if the husband is too close to their face. Others want to be smothered with kisses. Some men enjoy a great deal of vigorous activity on the part of the woman as they get near their point of orgasm, others do not. These individual preferences need to be shared.

As you move into the next section, describe your *orgasmic release,* if you have one. Be very clear about what your favorite positions are for this, what brings you the most sensation and what kind of love-making usually precedes your most intense arousal. If you do not experience an orgasm, describe in detail what it feels like to you at the peak of your sexual experience. What it is that reverses your arousal? What happens to you during your partner's release?

Finally, write about the *affirming-relaxing time.* First describe what normally happens. Compare this to what you desire. If the experience is perfect, say so. If there are some changes you would like to see, write about them. Note also what you experience from your partner during this time. It is important to know that there are many different desires during this affirming phase. For some couples this is the most pleasurable and "together" part of love-making. Others feel exhausted and both partners drift quickly off to sleep. In times past it was suggested that the woman needed more affirmation than the man. This is not necessarily so if the woman has had an orgasmic release. There is no right or wrong way to be during this time, only how you need to be for yourselves and each other.

As you come to the end of your writing, in this last section include any issues that did not seem to fit anywhere else. Note special positive things that you are aware of or areas of change that you desire. This may have to do with room temperature, new kinds of stimulation, body odors, experimentation, or some kind of clarification that is necessary. This is a perfect opportunity to share any issue that you may never have mentioned before. If you have faked responses this is a natural time to let it be known.

Sharing and Clarifying

Having set your thoughts down on paper, plan an hour to two in which you can sit down and discuss what you have written. It usually works best if you take one point at a time, one person sharing first and then the other. Begin, for example, with one of you reading to the other what you have written about your sexual desire. When you have finished reading, amplify anything that you did not write. The listening partner should then attempt to feed back what he or she has understood you to say about desire. Keep working at this until the communicating partner is convinced the listening partner really understands what has been shared. Then welcome any reactions or different viewpoints. Finally, the listening partner becomes the communicating partner and reads his or her statements about sexual desire. The other partner feeds back, then gives reactions and so on.

Proceed in this way throughout the whole experience, always being sure that what has been shared is completely clarified before the listener gives any reactions. It is amazing what a difference it makes when you feel understood. It is natural to become defensive toward criticism. Fight that impulse by trying to understand what is being said. So the pattern is: share, listener reflect, and sharer clarify. Reflect not only the words and details that were said but also the emotional dimensions. At that point you are ready for the listener to either share his reaction or to share his own view from what he or she has written.

Defining Your Dilemma

All of us have some area in our sexual lives that could be improved. For some that desire is intense because the problem is severe. For others the desired change would lead to enhancement. Whatever the case, spend some time clarifying what the two of you most desire to work on. Determine your greatest area of concern. Is it frequency of intercourse, variety within love-making, or the amount of pleasuring that takes place? Do you particularly lack desire or wish for a new style of initiation? Perhaps you need for your partner to respond more quickly or to slow down. You may need more active or verbal responsiveness, or want to attempt some new activity that you have been hesitant to experiment with before. For some there will be several problem areas. Do not take on the largest problem as the first step. Choose a small problem and work up. For example, you might begin by becoming comfortable pleasuring one another before you attempt oral stimulation.

Once you have specified the problem you want to focus on, then be very clear about the changes that you desire. Let us say that you want to change your initiation pattern. If the man has initiated 90 percent of the time and you would like to make it 50/50, then be very clear what you are moving toward: "I want to initiate about as often as you do." Or if the problem has been that the woman has been very immobile and unexpressive during love-making, identify exactly what it is that both of you would like to see changed.

Factors That Influence the Dilemma

Together look at your individual histories and your history as a couple to see what has influenced you in the direction of the current problem. Some factors in your home background may have set you up for it. Some early experiences during dating or a traumatic experience either before of after marriage may have pushed you in this direction. Or you may have certain beliefs, either social, moral or religious, that influence you. Be as clear as you can in defining what you see from your past that affects this problem. Then talk about what perpetuates it now. What keeps it going? Is it fear, anxiety, old habit? What behaviors happen between you that make it continue? Include as many factors as possible.

If there have been times in your history in which the problem did not exist, pay special attention to those periods. Attempt to understand what made a difference then. If there were any periods of time that were notably low times for you in regard to your dilemma, be clear about that. Some of you will find that your emotional or spiritual state is closely related to how you have been functioning sexually.

Share as much of your understanding of this as you have available to you.

Goals toward Enhancement

Once you have defined the problem, identify the desired changes and clarify the influencing factors. Develop some specific goals that you want to work toward. Often it is good to write these down almost like a contract. For example: "We have decided that we would like to improve our sexual relationship and enhance our marriage by focusing on the following area . . ." and then outline the specific problem or problems you have decided to work on. Keeping in mind what you have identified as the influential factors for your good times and for your not-so-good, write out what you think needs to happen to improve this precise area of your sexual life. It may be helpful to determine together exactly what your ideal experience would be. Note any ideas from all of your writings that may be of help in the task ahead.

A Clear Plan

It is easy to talk about the kind of change you desire and how you wish your partner would bring it about. It is a different matter to sit down and determine together specifically how and when you are going to work on a problem. We would encourage this to be part of the written contract also. Write out as many steps as are necessary to bring you to your goal. *Be careful to keep the steps small and manageable.* Both of you need to be in agreement about these steps. Plan to set aside adequate time for the accomplishment of them. The most common error when setting out a plan is that you expect change too quickly. Keep in mind that you have years of experiencing in the old way. It will take some time for these patterns to be reversed. You have a whole lifetime to learn together, so give yourself a generous amount of time for the changes to take place. Some of you will naturally make this a matter of concern in your prayers. Try not to push that on each other. If you can comfortably pray together, this can be most constructive and encouraging. The Lord does want and expect you to have a fulfilled and happy sexual life, and he is there to help.

After you have begun to put the plan into practice, keep it fluid.

Talk about it as you go along. Make adjustments as necessary, bearing in mind that the plan is only there to bring you toward your goal. If it is not doing that, then it must be readjusted. To get yourselves together you have to know yourselves, be ready to share, and agree on what needs to change. Understand what has caused the problem, and how you are going to go about changing it. Finally work together lovingly, with commitment and diligence, to bring the change about.

34

Going for Help

Couples can work out many sexual difficulties together. Success requires commitment to each other plus diligence and perseverance to work through the problems. Certain situations, however, demand assistance from a competent professional. This is particularly true if a man's premature ejaculation is severe or if his impotence is continuous. It would also be the case if he happens to be one of those individuals who are unable to ejaculate at all (retarded ejaculation). For the woman, professional help is necessary if she has difficulty getting aroused, or if after much practice she is still unable to experience orgasm. If either of the partners is unable to feel desire for sexual activity, this too would suggest the necessity for professional help. In some situations the main barrier has to do with coordinating religious beliefs and sexual responses that a person finds incongruent. Here a Christian helper would be needed.

Who Can Help?

There is much confusion as to the difference in qualifications and competence of the various helpers in the community. Let us briefly state their backgrounds and qualifications. All of the professions listed here *could* be helpful with a sexual difficulty, but would not necessarily *be* so. Let us begin by talking about physicians. There are several medical specialties that tend to be helpful in dealing with sexual difficulties. Psychiatrists, who have an M.D. and then have specialized in psychiatry, would be one obvious source of help. Yet many psychiatrists have neither the specialized training nor the interest to work specifically in sexual therapy. Their focus may be more on a hospitalized population or on long-term, psychoanalytically oriented therapy. More and more gynecologists and general and family practitioners are being trained in the treatment of sexual dysfunction. These are the main specialties among physicians who would be able to provide sexual treatment.

Psychologists are trained in many different areas. There are educational psychologists, social psychologists, industrial psychologists, and clinical psychologists. Those who provide sexual therapy are usually designated as clinical or counseling psychologists, depending on where they practice. All clinical psychologists are now required to receive a minimal amount of training in human sexuality, but this does not necessarily qualify them to work with a major sexual problem. Further specific training would be necessary. Psychologists normally have a Ph.D. degree.

Psychiatric social workers (M.S.W.), marriage and family counselors (M.A), and nurse therapists (R.N. plus M.N. or M.Sc.) may also be of assistance with a sexual dilemma if their background and training meet the qualifications.

Finally, ministers (B.D., M.Div., D.Min., Th.D., or Ph.D.) may all function as pastoral counselors. Some have been trained to work with sexual problems. One sign of a competent counselor is that he or she knows his or her area of expertise and refers patients to other helpers when needed. All of the above-mentioned helpers would be competent only if they were specifically trained and experienced in doing sexual therapy. Some will work as a team, others will function individually. Both approaches have been found to be effective.

Choosing a Helper

Any time you are going to put your life in someone else's hands you want to be convinced that he or she is the right person for you. You want to be confident that the helper will not lead you in some wrong direction. Get secure by asking questions. Any helper who is threatened by your questions or unwilling to answer them should be suspect. Look for someone else.

What kind of questions can you ask? Ask what qualifies them or what qualifications they have as a sex therapist. Inquire as to their training. Was it a one-day workshop or was it more extensive? Did they have any supervision? What approach were they trained in? Find out also what approach they are currently using. All counselors who provide sexual therapy should be able to outline in brief their own particular approach. Determine what their previous experience has been. All professionals have to get started sometime, but if they are going to start on you, you need to know that and make the choice. Most successful therapists gain experience while being tutored by an already competent sexual therapist. Ask questions about their success rate. Anyone who claims phenomenal success or uses terms like "always," "100 percent," or "the great majority," needs to be questioned further. There are always those situations that do not work out for many different reasons. If a therapist is unwilling to be honest with you about failure, you have reason for reservations.

In addition to asking questions, it is absolutely necessary that you be comfortable with the helper whom you choose to work with. If he or she "gives you the creeps," seems disinterested or boring, or evidences any other personal trait that gets in the way, at least look at other possibilities. There are enough barriers in your sexual relationship; you do not need to have any added by communication problems with your therapist. A sense of ease with him or her is an absolute necessity. A good therapist will always be aware of this issue as the therapy proceeds.

Is it essential to find a Christian therapist? Obviously, if you can, find a person who is fully qualified and shares the same Christian orientation that you do. That will facilitate communication since you already are committed to the same beliefs and understand the same language. However, the truth of creation is not limited to professionals who accept the Christian faith. There are many nonbelievers who do not impose their own value system on the Christian patient, nor do they try to alter your thinking in any way. This is as important in secular helpers as it is in Christian helpers. If you have to choose between an unqualified Christian helper and a qualified secular helper, you will probably receive the greatest benefit from the most qualified person. Merely being a believer does not qualify a person to be effective as a sexual helper.

Sex Therapy and How It Works

Because of the influence of Masters and Johnson and Helen Singer Kaplan, sexual therapy, wherever it is practiced and by whomever it is practiced, is quite similar. The first task is to make a thorough assessment of your sexual dilemma. The counselor will attempt to understand your history, recommend any medical tests or examinations that seem necessary, and get a detailed and precise picture of your current sexual activity. Once the assessment has been made and all agree on the problem, goals will be defined together so that everyone is working in the same direction. As a rule, specific communication and experience assignments will be given. Limitations regarding sexual intercourse will be spelled out. The couple backs up in the sexual relationship to a stage where both are comfortable; then the retraining begins. This is what sexual therapy is about: retraining the couple to function in a way that brings satisfaction to both. The emphasis will often have to be redirected toward the enjoyment of pleasure away from the goal of achieving orgasm.

As the various experiences are undertaken, barriers may develop that block further progress. Sometimes these have to be dealt with either as a couple or individually before the sexual therapy can continue. Thus it becomes obvious that there is no one narrow routine which everyone must pursue. Following the general principles of sexual therapy, each treatment planned for each couple will have its own variations and special emphases. At all times the couple will be encouraged to share their feelings with each other as well as with their helpers in an attempt to avoid any further sexual miscommunication. Your therapist will always want to know your opinions, your feelings and your reactions. To hold back can only hurt your progress.

Be encouraged. Much change can take place in a relatively short period of time. Many have gained sexual fulfillment and happiness after years of frustrations. You can too!

_____35

Questions and Answers

Wherever we travel, whatever kind of group we speak to, people's questions are basically the same. We have selected the most commonly asked questions. Almost inevitably such questions grow out of lives in which people are searching for answers. Some need to relieve pain, others wish to provide greater enhancement.

About the Man

Question: How can a man be taught to begin with words—not just fondling?

Answer: This is probably the one thing that more women ask about men than any other single item. Men seem to find their most natural expression in action, as they have been trained to do from childhood. Women, on the other hand, have learned to express themselves verbally. This disparity continues in love-making. Here both people need to take responsibility. The woman obviously has to communicate to the man that she enjoys reminiscing about the day, talking about the common love that they share, and whispering endearments. Unless the man knows this, he is likely to do what seems most natural for him, that is, to go directly after what he wants. Having heard his wife express her desire for verbal communication, the man can struggle to take responsibility for his response. This becomes more complicated if he feels his wife is making an unreasonable request rather than seeing this as normal desire on her part. It is also important to attend to the location of the fondling. Most women enjoy receiving nongenital and nonbreast caressing as they are warming to the sexual experience. It is mainly direct sexual stimulation that is irritating and jarring at the beginning of the love experience for the woman.

Question: Most of the time I have an ejaculation without a full erection. Is there something wrong with me?

Answer: This pattern of sexual response seems to be a learned response (assuming the man is in good health). It was usually learned during self-stimulation activity: the boy or young man pushed himself to have an ejaculation even if anxiety prevented him from experiencing a full erection. Once learned, it was carried on into the marriage and is now causing some doubt for the man and perhaps providing less vigorous stimulation for the woman. We recommend experimenting with some of the exercises suggested in the chapter on impotence. Be particularly attentive to stimulation before entry, even to the point of orgasm, but stimulate vigorously only when there is a full erection. Even as this pattern has been learned, it can also be unlearned.

Question: Can a man have orgasm without ejaculation?

Answer: Some men report that this is their common experience. It usually takes place when a man has ejaculated in a first orgasm and then is aroused and brought to a climax shortly thereafter. Some men report the ability to be multiorgasmic even as women are, but they represent a very small percentage.

Question: I am often unable to ejaculate after entry, needing to bring myself to orgasm outside my wife's body. Can this be changed?

Answer: This is known as a form of retarded ejaculation. It usually has to do with some early experiences with demanding women, particularly a demanding mother, or with some kind of homosexual preoccupation. If this is your situation, professional advice can often help you understand the problem and provide a way out.

About the Woman

Question: How can I improve my concentration during the sexual act, i.e., forget about everything else?

Answer: Difficulties with concentration usually go hand in hand with passivity. As you become active in the pursuit of your pleasure, it is not likely that you will have difficulty concentrating. Focus on the good sensations in your body, go after more. Focus on the joy and delight of your partner's body and become active in heightening his joy. If there are some persistent things that are on your mind it may be best to clear those out by having a brief conversational time first so that you can leave the concerns of your day aside and be totally involved in your loving.

Question: My husband loves to have me wear something sexy when home and also to strip for him. I don't feel I'm that sexy (being a little overweight bothers me, too), plus, I feel kind of cheap. But we love each other and I want our sex life fulfilled—though it's often great now. What are your thoughts on this?

Answer: As we have said many times throughout the book, anything that enhances the experience of both of you without bringing physical, psychological, or spiritual harm should be used with abandonment. If something is getting in your way, work together to understand what it is. Apparently your weight doesn't hinder him from seeing you as sexy. Obviously your husband loves you. Share your hesitant feelings with him in an attempt to understand what the barrier really is. Keep in mind that teasing is a natural part of love play. As we read the Song of Solomon, we keep having the feeling that the lovers were there and then they were gone; that they were with each other and then searching for one another. This may be one of those places where you push yourself past the barriers. Your husband needs to let you learn to move at your own pace so that you aren't violated in the process. If each of you is reaching out with concern for the other, no one will be hurt.

Question: Regarding submissiveness in the wife, should she submit even though she is mistreated and unhappy with the sexual relationship, or does the Bible teach that she can withhold herself when her husband does not treat her or respond to her as he should? Paul said, "submitting yourselves one to another" and also "defraud not one another." What should she do? Is it her duty to respond?

Answer: As suggested in the question, all the passages that deal with submission of husband and wife include an encouragement to mutual submission, not just submission of wife to husband. I need to give myself totally whether I am the man or the woman, even as Christ gave himself for the church. There can be no greater submission than that. Yet to submit oneself to unloving sexual activity is not a loving act but rather a response to someone else's unlovingness. The Bible never teaches us to perpetuate sin. There is no easy answer. Communication may be a starting place.

Fantasy

Question: I recently read an article in a Christian magazine about the difference between lust and fantasy. The author's ideas were much more liberal than I had ever heard before. Can you tell me biblically the difference between lust and fantasy?

Answer: We can make some inferences from the Scriptures, but the Bible does not talk directly about fantasy. Proverbs 23:7 says, "For as he thinks within himself so is he." The distinction often made between fantasy and lust is that in lust there is usually an intense desire with the hope or possibility of action, whereas fantasy is thought to be something within a person without any intention to act. Fantasies are often so unrealistic that they would be impossible to carry out. Lust usually has to do with real people in real places.

Question: I have always thought it was wrong to fantasize in one's mind about sex *per se* while making love. In other words, a person should think only of what is going on to get turned on. Thinking of the sexual act between people in general should be avoided. Am I right?

Answer: There are many differences of opinion on this issue. Some people's thoughts while love-making only enhance the experience. For others they get in the way. As we mentioned earlier, fantasies take on so many different forms that it is difficult to make a specific statement which applies to all people in all situations. For some, the only way they know to get aroused to the point of orgasm is to engage in some fantasy. Since this brings pleasure to both, it is difficult to say that they should or even could avoid that activity.

A Variety

Question: If premarital play, not necessarily intercourse, has occurred before we became Christians and before marriage to our mate, how can we best forget those experiences and avoid comparing them to our present sex life?

Answer: Comparing usually causes difficulties only when the current partner does not measure up. We need to be careful how we make that evaluation, however, since premarriage and preintercourse experience can never really be compared with what happens after marriage and after we begin full love-making. Sometimes it is most beneficial to be able to share all of these concerns with someone. A competent counselor or pastor may be just such a sounding board. This sharing is not designed to relive the past experiences but rather to get them out in the open. This may free you to move on to a fully satisfying experience with your husband or wife. Keep in mind, too, that God has forgiven you. Only *you* are holding on to the past to keep you from complete joy.

Question: What if you aren't in the mood? Should you go along to please your mate?

Answer: At various times all of us will "not feel like it" but will decide to go ahead and be involved sexually because our partner desires us. There is the possibility that we may become responsive even if we are not initially in the mood. If we never find ourselves in the mood, then there is a serious barrier with which we must deal. Begin by talking with each other about this, and then seek competent help. If lack of interest is only an occasional state, it need not cause concern since it is not likely to have significant impact on you or your spouse. There are many times when we may not be in the mood. If we are open to letting the mood change without pressure or demand for that, often it will come. Occasionally we might even go against our mood.

Question: What is the relationship between sexual fulfillment and length of marriage?

Answer: We have known couples who have been married six months who are experiencing unbelievable fulfillment. We have also known couples who have been married thirty years who have never had a fulfilling sexual experience together. For some couples, surprisingly, complete fulfillment keeps expanding and becoming even more fulfilling. This is one of the ways that good marriages seem to be reinforced. The Lord keeps giving more and more to enjoy as we give ourselves totally to each other.

Question: Please (not to sound smug), but how do I make something better that is already good? Both of us are satisfied and both reach orgasm. What more can be done? (This is a sincere question.)

Answer: What a delightful problem to have! As with any other aspect of life, we can always keep moving toward perfection. In the sexual area we can keep learning to give more and experience more. We are not speaking here of greater frequency but rather greater depth and greater intensity. Expand your experience into new places, new experimentation, new creativity, new books, or new seminars. Look for ways to outgive and outlove one another.

Question: A speaker recently said, "A woman can have six to eleven or more orgasms while the man has one." Could this be true?

Answer: The woman has an infinite capacity for orgasms, but the drive for this should not be the husband's, nor should it grow out of some demand she is putting on herself. Rather, it should come from within herself. Many women are fully satisfied with one orgasm and need nothing more. Others always prefer two or three. Some women prefer repeated orgasmic release during a given experience, but this does not say that they are freer women or better lovers. Any time we establish an outside criterion to evaluate how we are doing, we are not listening to how God made us and responding in terms of ourselves. Once we establish an outside criterion we detract from what is natural.

_____36

Some Final Words

So many concepts have been presented in this book that it may seem impossible to remember them all and even more difficult to put them into practice. All that has been said rises naturally out of who and what we humans are. There are no radical ideas, no concepts that go against what we were born to be. Perhaps this would be the best way to sum up the message of this book: The sexual experience is that ecstatic expression of our total being—physical, emotional, intellectual, and spiritual. When all these dimensions come together with freedom and are shared with the one to whom we are committed, usually sexual fulfillment will follow.

There are a number of *attitudes* which we can bring to our love-making experience and to all of our loving experiences that will positively shape us in relation to one another. We need to see the sexual response as natural and God-given. It is not a result of our perverse natures but rather a part of what we were created to express. Sexual love is a symbol of God's relationship with man. This includes the physical release dimension but is much more than that. Though it is a natural process within us, many barriers have arisen to keep nature from taking its course. Many couples have received the instruction as they prepare for marriage, "Just take your clothes off and let nature take its course." This is fine if you are planning to mate your French poodle but is not very helpful when planning to bring two human lives together. Because of all the input which gets in the way between birth and this point in time, there is no way that nature can take its course. We need education.

Even though we need education and training we cannot think of our sexual love-making as merely requiring a batch of techniques or the learning of some new skills. While skills and techniques are essential ingredients to the fulfilled relationship, we need much more than just knowing the right things to do. Every part of our being is vitally involved.

How we have been trained and how we feel in deep ways will affect our freedom in that loving relationship. We must be able to allow ourselves the right to receive pleasure. God has already given us that right; if we do not experience it, it is because of our own insecurity. When we deeply believe that pleasure is a possibility we will be open to variation and experimentation. We will not be limited by rules about right and wrong, but will rather be guided by our own internal desires and urges. This is one of those dimensions of life that the Bible has left open to our own desire and discretion. We have to be guided from within ourselves.

Recognizing this, we are forced to accept what the apostle Paul teaches regarding our sexual equality. We are not expected to do something for our partner that he or she is not responsible to do for us. Sex is not something we do "to" someone, neither is it something we do "for" someone. Rather, sex is a "with" experience. This is a tough balance to find. It is easy to come to the marital bed with strong expectations for one's self as well as for one's partner, rather than letting the feelings flow freely out of one's body. When we can let those feelings flow, we accept the individual differences between two people and the differences between men and women. These will not be troublesome to us but will rather be used as an additional form of enhancement, delight, and variety. We will not think of our partner in terms of stereotypes or clichés that usually begin, "Well, men always . . ." or "Women always. . . ." We will let the other be a person who is taking responsibility for himself or herself as he or she gives to us.

Our attitudes obviously make a difference, and so do our *feelings*. If we lack the self-worth necessary to be able to receive, we will limit our own pleasure and our partner's joy. For many, receiving is more difficult than giving. They only feel self-worth as they give. It is important to reverse that pattern. It involves the acceptance of our own sexuality, with its maleness and femaleness, as having worth in and of itself, not just in relationship to our partner. Many past experiences of guilt, shame, and discomfort can get in the way of this acceptance.

The level of commitment that we feel for our spouse is central. We must be committed to our partner and must feel his or her commitment in return. Without the feeling of love, sexual response becomes less likely. Many barriers can get in the way of experiencing love and commitment in both directions. Whether these be anger, lack of respect, external tension, or performance anxiety, a couple can move past those barriers as they learn to express and share the love and commitment that they feel.

Even when the feelings of love and commitment are solid, they will make a difference in love-making only as we put them into practice. Once we start *acting* on our feelings, the joy that is a potential becomes a reality. That action can take many forms. It may evidence itself by special preparation that is made, by the spontaneity and flexibility that is shown, or by new ways of sharing ourselves in the actual sexual experience. As we accept our right to pleasure, we tend to be ready to lose control. This grows out of an inner security and follows the internal bodily rhythms. Having grown in our acceptance of ourselves and our partner, we will also feel less need to follow the same hurried routine time after time. As we become more secure, speed will decrease, gentleness will increase, keeping score will disappear, and we will be participants rather than spectators.

The key to all this is *communication*. Sexual decisions must be made in an atmosphere of freedom and openness. There has to be the freedom to express what we want, what we need, what feels good, and what feels bad. Nonverbal communication will also be crucial, whether it is the receiver guiding the hands of the giver, a private signal system, or nonverbal communication that is felt without any prearranged meaning. In this communication, as we accept responsibility for ourselves and for any problems as a couple, we will avoid the pitfalls of blaming ourselves or our partner and hence also avoid the put-downs and teases that may hinder rather than help. In working out problems, negotiation based on each person's having an equal vote will also often be a necessary dimension to the communication.

In this negotiation it is important to keep realizing that the only rights or wrongs between you have to do with what each of you finds pleasant or unpleasant.

As you share yourselves openly you will be received with understanding and warmth, knowing that you are not being judged. You can continue to blossom from that seed of sexual freedom within you to the full sexual beauty that is there ready to be expressed.

> Set me as a seal upon thine heart,
> as a seal upon thine arm:
> for love is strong as death;
> jealousy is cruel as the grave:
> the coals thereof are coals of fire,
> which hath a most vehement flame.
>
> Many waters cannot quench love,
> neither can the floods drown it:
> if man would give all the substance
> of his house for love,
> it would be utterly contemned.
> —Song of Solomon 8:6, 7 (KJV)

Annotated Bibliography

So much has been written about the sexual aspect of our lives that many people find themselves confused as to what direction they should go. We will make a few recommendations in several areas that we have found to be most helpful.

Biblical-Theological Writing

Stephan Sapp, *Sexuality, the Bible, and Science.* Philadelphia: Fortress Press, 1977.
   Sapp follows the development of a view of sexuality as it progresses throughout the Bible and presents an extremely competent and concise theology of sexuality.

Dwight H. Small, *Christian: Celebrate Your Sexuality.* Old Tappan, New Jersey: Fleming H. Revell, 1974.
   Here a Westmont College professor gives us a view of the various ways that a theology of sexuality has developed, and then presents his own views which are both positive and helpful.

Lewis B. Smedes, *Sex for Christians.* Grand Rapids, Michigan: Wm. B. Eerdmans Publishing Co., 1976.
   A professor of ethics at Fuller Theological Seminary, Smedes writes

a most readable and up-to-date book for helping the layman to deal with a variety of topics *around* sexual ethics. We highly recommend this book.

Books for Enhancement

J. Banyolak, *Better Is Your Love Than Wine*. Downers Grove, Illinois: Inter-Varsity Press, 1971.
A brief, earthy, classically written encouragement to the husband and wife by one of Walter Trobisch's students. A great gift idea.

Dennis Guernsey, *Thoroughly Married*. Waco, Texas: Word Books, 1975.
A readable Christian guide to sexual communication in marriage.

Charlie W. and Martha Shedd, *Celebration in the Bedroom*. Waco, Texas: Word Books, 1979.
In their easy style the Shedds answer numerous questions that people have asked of them. As always, their answers are fresh, precise, and reveal much of themselves.

Ed and Gaye Wheat, *Intended for Pleasure: Sex Technique and Sexual Fulfillment in Christian Marriage*. Old Tappan, New Jersey: Fleming H. Revell, 1977.
A basic marital manual with sound medical and Christian advice.

Norman H. Wright, C. L. and J. J. Penner, *In Touch with Each Other: A Couple's Guide to Marital Communication*. Chicago: David C. Cook, 1976.
This is a self-help guide for a couple to use in resolving conflict and finding sexual fulfillment in their marriage.

Alex Comfort, *The Joy of Sex*. New York: Crown, 1972.
We are often asked our opinion of this book. Much of what Comfort says is beneficial information and can be applied to any couple's sexual life. The problem is that his moral or ethical criteria in choosing partners is different from that of a Christian. Anyone who reads the book needs to have his or her own value system clearly established first.

Dick and Paula McDonald, *Loving Free*. New York: Ballantine Books, 1973.
The McDonalds, a Catholic couple, share their pilgrimage from sex-

ual frustration that was about to destroy their marriage to freedom, satisfaction and communication. A very helpful book as you begin to work on your problems.

Books for Problem Resolution

Lonnie G. Barbach, *For Yourself: The Fulfillment of Female Sexuality.* New York: Anchor Books, 1979.
   Barbach, a professor at the University of California at Berkeley, shares her discoveries from working with women's groups aimed at sexual fulfillment. There are very clear steps that women can follow to develop orgasmic fulfillment.

Benjamin Graber and Georgia Kline-Graber, *Women's Orgasm: A Guide to Sexual Satisfaction.* Indianapolis: The Bobbs-Merrill Co., 1975.
   This husband/wife team give precise directions for finding orgasmic fulfillment. Some of the exercises are particularly helpful if a woman has difficulty releasing her inhibitions.

   There are obviously dozens if not hundreds of books that could be recommended. We mention these because they have been found helpful by people with whom we have had contact. Professional sex therapists would obviously refer to another level of written material for their information.
   A number of tape series are available to provide help both in dealing with your family and with each other as husband and wife. We hope to write another book that deals with sex as it relates to families, including sex education, sexual guidance for youth, and issues of birth control. We are also contemplating a series of video tapes designed to communicate more about sexual fulfillment. These will be made available through libraries or churches.

Subject Index